Paris

in the

Fifties

Paris

in the

Fifties

Stanley Karnow

Illustrations by Annette Karnow

THREE RIVERS PRESS

NEW YORK

Published by Three Rivers Press, New York, New York.
Member of the Crown Publishing Group.

Random House, Inc. New York, Toronto, London, Sydney,
Auckland
www.randomhouse.com

THREE RIVERS PRESS is a registered trademark and the Three
Rivers Press colophon is a trademark of Random House, Inc.

Originally published in hardcover and in slightly different form
by Times Books in 1997.

Printed in the United States of America

Book design by Deborah Kerner

Library of Congress Cataloging-in-Publication Data
Karnow, Stanley.
Paris in the fifties / Stanley Karnow.
1. Karnow, Stanley–Homes and haunts–France–Paris.   2. Paris
(France)–Social life and customs–20th century.   3. France–
Politics and government–1945–.   4. National characteristics,
French.   I. Title.
DC715.K38   1997
944'.36082–dc21   97-18521

ISBN 0-8129-3137-8

10   9   8   7

For Dru and Frank White

Ask the traveled inhabitant of any nation, in what country on earth would you rather live? Certainly in my own. . . . Which would be your second choice? France.

—THOMAS JEFFERSON

Preface

$\mathcal{D}$uring the 1950s, when I worked as a *Time* correspondent in Paris, it was standard operating procedure to swamp the editors back in the New York office with voluminous, detailed and often remarkably authoritative reports that they would boil down to a few glossy paragraphs. The process, combined with its anonymity, frequently frustrated me. The result, however, was an enormously successful magazine, and, like the other members of the bureau, I accepted the system. After all, I was enjoying myself in a beautiful city while learning the journalistic trade. But, on the odd chance that they might eventually turn out to be useful, I saved the carbon copies of my original dispatches. A chronicle rather than a memoir, this book contains, in greatly revised form, a selection of those that may evoke the atmosphere of the period and also provide some insights into French life four decades ago. France has evolved dramatically since then; yet to a large extent, as the old saying goes, "*Plus ça change, plus ça reste la même chose*"—which is, for me, one of its most appealing traits.

I am deeply indebted to Lalaine Estella, my research assistant, who diligently assembled, classified and computerized the thousands of pages I had accumulated. Frank White, Dru White and Anne Chamberlin, my *Time* associates in those bygone days, shared their recollections with me. My old and close friend André Wormser read the manuscript and furnished me with valuable comments. I also relied in various ways on R. W. Apple, Jill Brett, Joan Bingham, Christian Chapman, Jean Daniel, Timothy Foote, Burt Glinn, Stanley Hoffmann, Anne Lowenstein, Michael Macrone, Marc Menguy, Claude Moisy, Mark Pratt, Christopher Ogden, Grant Reynolds, James Trager, Henri de Turenne, Catherine Van Moppes and the late Nicholas Wahl. Many of my colleagues, both French and American, indirectly assisted me over the years, and they may recognize their contributions in these chapters. Françoise Champey corrected my French. Sybil Pincus skillfully steered the book through the production process, Naomi Osnos was responsible for its gracious design, and Diana Marsh did a fine job of copyediting. I am grateful to Robert Barnett, my agent, for his services. My thanks as well to Peter Osnos, the former president of Times Books, for his initial encouragement. Every writer needs an editor, and Geoff Shandler patiently offered me his guidance from start to finish.

As usual, I depended for advice on my children—Curtis, Marilyn Englander, Catherine and Michael. Above all, my wife, Annette, deserves my gratitude. Not only did she adorn the book with her illustrations, but her memories of Paris refreshed my own.

S.K.
POTOMAC, MARYLAND
APRIL 1997

Contents

Paris

in the

Fifties

1

Pourquoi Paris

~~~

Thousands of young Americans were flocking to Europe after World War II, and I joined the throng. Late in June 1947, fresh out of college, I went to Paris, planning to stay for the summer. I stayed for ten years.

Pourquoi Paris? Its name alone was magic. The city, the legendary *Ville Lumière*, promised something for everyone—beauty, sophistication, culture, cuisine, sex, escape and that indefinable called ambience. "When good Americans die they go to Paris," ran Oscar Wilde's oft-quoted quip. That was certainly not my purpose in going there, but then, what was it? Perhaps, simply, Paris.

Modern European history and literature had been my major at Harvard, and my courses on France had acquainted me with the ancien régime and the Enlightenment, the Revolution, the Napoleonic era, the Third Republic and, most recently, the valiant Resistance during the German occupation. I had grappled with the works of Molière, Racine, Descartes, Voltaire and *les philosophes*, Hugo, Flaubert, Stendhal, Balzac, Maupassant, Baudelaire, Verlaine, Rimbaud, Zola, Gide, Proust and postwar intellectuals like Jean-Paul Sartre,

Simone de Beauvoir and Albert Camus. Dabbling in art had left me with some notions about Monet, Manet, Degas, Van Gogh, Toulouse-Lautrec, Picasso, Braque, and the Surrealists and Dadaists. I had been enchanted by such French film classics as *La Grande Illusion, La Femme du Boulanger* and *Les Enfants du Paradis,* and knew the songs of Maurice Chevalier and Charles Trenet by heart. Along with the rest of my generation, I had read Hemingway, Fitzgerald and smuggled copies of Henry Miller's salacious novels, and dreamed of retracing their footsteps through Montparnasse, Saint-Germain-des-Prés and the boulevard de Clichy. I was further gulled by the real or exaggerated recollections of GIs and their doughboy fathers of compliant French women—the eternal Mademoiselle from Armentières.

Air travel was then expensive, and most of us crossed the Atlantic by ship, usually third class. My friend and fellow *Harvard Crimson* editor, Anthony Lewis, the future *New York Times* columnist, wangled us passage for fifty dollars each aboard a coal freighter bound for Le Havre. I stuffed some clothes and a supply of Camels into a rucksack and my old army duffel bag, and we sailed from Baltimore. We had been at sea for a week, idly reading and playing chess, when a radiogram advised the captain that a strike had paralyzed Le Havre and ordered the ship to Rotterdam. Both German and Allied bombing had leveled the city. I had served during the war in India and China, agricultural lands that were spared such destruction, and the scene as we docked stunned me. But it was only a prelude to the devastation I would witness elsewhere in Europe.

Tony and I proceeded by train to Paris and made our way to the Lutèce, a Latin Quarter hotel that had been recommended to us. Situated near the Sorbonne, it was cheap, apparently clean—and primitive. My little room opened onto an air shaft and contained a narrow bed, a wobbly table, a tiny armoire and a feeble lightbulb. The toilet next door leaked, the smell of greasy cooking permeated the premises, and from somewhere upstairs came the mournful tones of someone practicing the saxophone. The two French students on the floor greeted me warmly, and, though my French was fractured, we managed to communicate. One of them, Hubert Doucet, was a dapper bon vivant with a silky goatee, whose affluent peasant parents deluged him with weekly parcels of butter, cheese, hams and pâtés, which in those days of acute food shortages made him irresistible to girls. The other, Jean-Yves Gory, attended the École des Langues Orientales. The son of *pieds-noirs,* the label for French residents of Algeria, he would sit up into the wee hours of the morning, assiduously memorizing Chinese ideographs by inscribing them into a notebook with deft strokes of a brush pen. We kept in contact over the years ahead. Eventually he married a Chinese woman, entered the diplomatic corps and rose to the rank of ambassador.

Adjusting to the district, I found a black marketeer who exchanged my dollars for francs at twice the legal rate. Like other student hotels, the Lutèce lacked bathrooms, and my new friends pointed out the public baths, which operated from Thursday afternoon through Sunday morning and charged a nominal fee. Entire families would file in, carrying their own soap and towels; some shared the same tub. For the rest of the week, they depended on eau de cologne. When my Camels ran out, I switched to Gauloises and soon developed a taste for their coarse black tobacco. I became a habitué of the congenial cafés, whose clients could bask on the terrace for hours, nursing a beer or a coffee and observing the passing parade of pedestrians without being disturbed by the waiter. Often I ate in one of the bargain restaurants in the web of streets off the boulevard Saint-Michel, where the otherwise palatable meals were marred by the hard, yellowish bread—the result of a semantic blunder. France had requested aid shipments of wheat from the United States, but the official translator had consulted a British rather than an American dictionary and interpreted the word *blé* as "corn."

With my time limited, I plunged into a feverish tour of the city. I rode the antiquated buses or, undaunted by the stench of stale cigarettes and rancid urine, used the Métro, the world's most efficient subway. Map in hand, I whipped through Notre-Dame, the Sainte-Chapelle, the Tuileries, the Palais-Royal, the Place de la Concorde, the Champs-Élysées, the Arc de Triomphe, and Napoleon's Tomb and ascended Montmartre to Sacré-Coeur, the wedding-cake basilica. Overcoming my vertigo, I took the elevator up the Eiffel Tower. I also ventured out to Versailles to marvel at the Hall of Mirrors, the Trianon and the geometrically patterned gardens.

Presently, realizing that I could not fully appreciate Paris unless I curbed my frenetic pace, I became a *flâneur*—an aimless stroller in a town ideal for aimless strolling. I would meander along the Seine, pausing to browse for old prints and magazines in the quayside *bouquinistes,* outdoor bookstalls, or to watch the barges as they cruised up and down the river, their decks festooned with laundry, their sterns flying French, British, Dutch and other European flags. Perpetual vagabonds, *les clochards,* many of them alcoholics, camped under the bridges; fishermen hugged the banks, seemingly oblivious to whether they ever got a nibble.

Lovely squares dotted the city, such as the Place des Vosges, a square of brick houses designed in the seventeenth century, and the Place de Furstenberg, where Delacroix had his atelier. I was intrigued by capricious street names, like the rue du Chat-Qui-Pêche off the quai Saint-Michel, which dated back to 1540, and a Left Bank impasse that, prior to becoming the site of a seminary in 1646, had been titled the Cul-de-Sac du Ha! Ha!

Unlike my native New York's monotonously numbered thoroughfares, Paris street names were a necrology of famous and forgotten French artists, authors, composers, scientists, politicians, diplomats, marshals, admirals, clergymen and a multitude of saints, male and female. The selection process baffled me. Monarchs, including the guillotined Louis XVI, had not been ignored nor, strangely, had Madame de Montespan and Madame de Maintenon, the titular mistresses of Louis XIV. But the honor was denied Robespierre, the architect of the Terror. Bonaparte the general was awarded a *rue* for defending France

against a European coalition late in the eighteenth century, yet not even an alley hallowed Napoleon the emperor, who had transgressed the republican principles of the Revolution. I was proud to see the numbers of American icons immortalized: Washington, Franklin, Jefferson, Lincoln, Edgar Allan Poe, Edison, Wilson, Pershing, Franklin D. Roosevelt and Georges [*sic*] Gershwin, to cite a few.

The city, I noticed, had still not recovered from the war. Such essentials as milk, bread, butter, cheese and eggs were rationed, and even foreigners like me had to queue up with citizens at the *mairie* of their arrondissement to be issued coupons by functionaries—usually cranky old women, many of them war widows. Neglected for years, public and private buildings needed repainting and other repairs. But the French were *débrouillards,* or manipulators. They got around by bicycle, tricycle, horse carts, rickety trucks and cars, or whatever else moved, including ingenious Rube Goldberg contraptions propelled by kerosene or charcoal engines. Men in shabby suits sported boutonnières, while women achieved a touch of chic by adding a certain je ne sais quoi to their threadbare dresses. Everything from coffee to penicillin was available on the ubiquitous black market—for a price.

One balmy evening I moseyed over to the Right Bank, where the cafés, restaurants, theaters and music halls along the *grands boulevards* were booming. The brothels had recently been shut down, but the municipal authorities had not banned prostitution, and I was astounded by the hordes of hookers, some of them in gaudy gowns, ornate hats and stiletto heels, others in casual summer frocks. They spanned the spectrum from pinups to hags and, I was told, catered to every purse and perversion. There seemed to be nothing furtive, vulgar or desperate about them; they were pursuing a métier like any other, and solicited their prospective johns courteously and cheerfully with the same hackneyed refrains, "*Alors, chéri, tu viens?*" and "*Tu veux faire une conquête?*" This was the permissive Paris of my imagination and, stereotyped though it may have been, I treasured it.

Soon my college roommate, Mitchell Goodman, caught up with me, and we set off into *la France profonde*—the provinces. We had expected to hitchhike—*l'auto-stop*, as the French termed it—but vehicles were scarce. Toting our heavy rucksacks, we trudged the blistering roads in one of the worst heat waves on record. The strenuous trek, however, enabled us to look closely at the countryside, which was slumbering in a time warp. We passed villages clustered around mossy stone churches; peasants in smocks and sabots tilling their fields behind teams of oxen; and barefoot boys herding cows, sheep and goats down dusty lanes. Towns along the route, obliterated during the war, were heaps of rubble. Our initial destination was Chartres, some fifty miles southwest of Paris. As we approached, we could discern on the horizon the misty silhouette of the cathedral emerging from the plains of Beauce, one of France's most fertile regions. It was an inspiring sight that made the ordeal of getting there worthwhile.

Completed in the thirteenth century, the great Gothic cathedral had been overwhelming visitors ever since. The little I could say about it had already been said before—and far better. I was awed by its vaulted ceiling, giant transept and resplendent stained-glass windows, through which rays of sunlight subtly illuminated the interior. The spires and flying buttresses testified to the genius of its architects; the sculpted seraphim and gargoyles on its outer façades to the fabulous craftsmanship of its anonymous artisans. Its magnificence also evoked the phenomenal power of faith and the stupendous wealth of the medieval merchants who had subsidized its construction. Contrary to the widespread assumption that the Catholic Church was moribund, pilgrims from around Europe jammed the cathedral.

I could have lingered there for weeks, but, after a day or two, we zigzagged north to Rouen and the Normandy coast. Concrete bunkers, barbed wire and rusty military equipment, macabre relics of the Allied landings in June 1944, still littered the beaches. We took in Dieppe and Honfleur, then pushed on to Deauville, Trouville and Cabourg, the swanky fin de siècle resorts where Proust had gathered material for À la Recherche du Temps Perdu, his monumental novel.

Hearing that a town in the vicinity was holding a fête champêtre, we drifted over. It was vintage France. Food, drink and lottery stalls had been set up under a canopy of colored lanterns, and couples of all ages in their holiday best were whirling around to a bouncy accordion. I spotted a slender brunette, and we tried the paso doble, which was more of a march than a dance. During the intermission I bought her a syrupy grenadine and myself a tepid beer, and we made a stab at conversation—she in broken English, me in my atrocious French. Finally, clasping my hand, she escorted me to a house and up to a bedroom decorated with a crucifix, where she quickly disrobed. When we had finished, she indicated that un petit cadeau would be agréable, and I peeled off two hundred francs—about a dollar. She gently bussed me on the cheeks and I departed, wondering whether she was a prostitute or just a simple country girl in need of pocket money. My first fling in France, it also left me dubious about the purported boudoir talents of French women. For a while afterward I fretted that I might have contracted a nasty disease.

Mitch and I doubled back to Paris, then swung toward the south. Again we attempted to hitchhike, without much luck, and instead crammed into third-class railway carriages or tramped the scorching roads. After stops at Nîmes, Arles and Aix-en-Provence, we descended the sunbaked, vine-covered slopes of the Midi to the Mediterranean and advanced along the Côte d'Azur from Marseille and Cassis to Saint-Tropez, a languid fishing village yet to be invaded by legions of bikinis and topless bathers. At Cannes and Nice, the playground of the rich, we gawked at the glitzy hotels, palatial villas and sleek yachts anchored in the harbor; looking like hobos in our scruffy GI boots, slovenly khaki trousers and sweaty T-shirts, we also peered into the Monte Carlo casino. Then we headed for Italy.

Despite the favorable exchange rate, we were obsessed with saving money and mooched shamelessly. One night in Genoa we slept on the deck of an American freighter. We wasted too much time in Pisa, only because the commander of an American army unit stationed there coveted company and housed us for nothing. In Florence an American artist we encountered at a trattoria let us sack out on sofas in his flat; in Rome we lodged at a seedy pensione that reeked of olive oil. Nevertheless, we packed in dozens of landmarks, from the Leaning Tower and the Palazzo Vecchio to the Vatican and the Colosseum. Later I would deride tourists who "did" Europe at breakneck speed—but we were doing exactly that.

At Geneva, our next target, we checked into a youth hostel. The war had impoverished most of Europe, but the Swiss had prospered from neutrality, and consumer goods of every kind were abundant. I glutted myself on the food—in particular, the chocolate. As befit its Calvinist heritage, however, Geneva was antiseptic, sedate and numbingly dull, and the idea of staying there repelled me. At the hostel, we met a spirited young Englishwoman called Denise Levertov, and Stephen Peet, a freelance filmmaker. Smitten by her, Mitch announced to me that he was remaining behind. He and Denny were ultimately married. She became one of America's foremost poets, and he abandoned a potential career as an economist to write and consecrate himself to such causes as nuclear disarmament and opposition to the Vietnam War.

I returned to Paris alone, and to the bleak Lutèce. As the summer waned, I contemplated the idea of going home as I had planned. I could not conceive of living abroad for long or, even less, becoming an expatriate, but I had barely scratched the surface of France and felt that I ought to dig deeper. While I wrestled with my predicament, Peet abruptly appeared with a French girl by the name of Claude Sarraute. Though she was not conventionally pretty, her curly chestnut hair, radiant smile, twinkling eyes and particularly her vivacity appealed to me. Soon we were meeting frequently at cafés or secluded restaurants. Her English was fluent; as a child she had been tutored by one of her mother's acquaintances, an obscure and penniless Irish writer called Samuel Beckett, then chiefly known to the Paris literati as James Joyce's former secretary. Later, over drinks with him, I asked Beckett, "If you were marooned on a desert island and could only have one book, which one would it be?" He replied without hesitation, "Boswell's *Life of Samuel Johnson.*"

Now nineteen, Claude was studying law but aspired to become an actress. She was still troubled by her wartime experiences. The Germans had detained her father, and she had single-handedly won his release by pleading with the prison commander. Her mother, originally a Russian Jew, had dodged arrest by the pro-Nazi French militia by concealing herself in a village under a false name. As many French did, Claude admired the Communists for their part in the Resistance and, out of emotion rather than ideology, joined the party. She stirred me with dramatic yarns of the intrepid maquis, most of them—unbeknownst to her—sheer fiction. Following the war, virtually all the French boasted of having participated in the Underground, yet subsequent surveys divulged that, as late as January 1944, fewer than twenty thousand were actually involved. Six months afterward, on the eve of the liberation of Paris, they totaled only some three hundred thousand—a negligible percentage of the population. By comparison, the vast majority supported Marshal Philippe Pétain's regime in Vichy, which collaborated with the Germans by deporting some seventy-five thousand Jews to concentration camps.

Claude and I were simply *copains* until, one rainy day in my hotel room, we ceased to be comrades and she became *ma petite amie*. It was just the impetus I needed to reach a decision: now I would remain in Paris, at least for the foreseeable future. As a veteran, I was entitled under the GI Bill to seventy-five dollars a month—on condition that I enroll in school. It was a decent sum in francs, and I promptly signed up for *La Cours de civilisation française,* a curriculum for foreigners at the Sorbonne. But I was to learn more about France from Claude than from attending classes.

We spoke English, but she set out to refine my abysmal French on the grounds that every educated person ought to be familiar with the language. Supposedly a model of clarity and precision, French had been the lingua franca of elites around the world for centuries. Yet it seemed to me, as I battled to master it, that compared to English it was a swamp of abstractions and ambiguities—and perhaps, like Latin, doomed. Dismayed by that prospect, crusaders were forever organizing conferences and drafting petitions demanding stiff legislation to protect the mother tongue—as though the glory of France hinged on its survival. They also lobbied for the creation of *La Francophonie,* a kind of commonwealth that would promote the preservation of French in France's dwindling overseas empire.

Particularly alarming to these linguistic chauvinists was the barbarous onslaught against the purity of French by "Anglo-Saxon" terms, notably Americanisms, which produced such pernicious franglais as *le briefing, le marketing* and *le packaging*. A big brasserie in Saint-Germain-des-Prés, converted by an entrepreneur into Le Drug-Store, served *les hamburgers* and similar items at its *fast food* counter. The chic drink in the bars off the Champs-Élysées was *un baby Scotch sur les rocks*. Unable to withstand this assault, the Larousse dictionary not only added several Franglais words to its revised edition but used one to define another. Thus, *le racket* was "*une association de malfaiteurs engagés dans le blackmail par le chantage et la terreur.*"

I agonized over grammar, especially tenses—the past, the present, the future, the conditional, the subjunctive, the past imperfect, the more-than-perfect and the tortuous imperfect of the subjunctive. Equally puzzling were verbs—regular, irregular, active, passive, indicative, reflexive. Intractable rules prevented the transformation of nouns into adjectives and adverbs, so that a modifier's position determined its meaning: *un brave homme* was a good man and *un homme brave* a courageous man. Another hurdle was the meager French vocabulary. With only about thirty thousand words, fewer than half as many as in English, one had to do the duty of several and vice versa. Hence, *encore* signified "still," "again" and "yet"; and *faire* recurred hundreds of times, as in *faire la cuisine* for cooking and *faire la cour* for wooing. The French prided themselves on their logic, but genders defied all reason. Why was *le vagin* masculine but one of the many terms for a penis, *la verge*, feminine? Or, just as confusing, why was the province *la Bourgogne* and the wine *le Bourgogne*? I was often misled by *les faux amis*, apparent cognates that really aren't. For example, *amateur* was a connoisseur in French and a neophyte in English. French resonated with extravagant circumlocutions inherited from Versailles, where the king and his courtiers had competed against each other in demonstrations of elegant style. Elaborate phrases freighted banal official notices: a no-smoking sign—IL EST FORMELLEMENT INTERDIT DE FUMER—sounded like an injunction against homicide. As a matter of form, ordinary citizens emulated this highfalutin usage. Even the routine letter attached to a bill from the plumber or the carpenter would terminate with the salutation *"Nous vous prions, mon cher monsieur, d'accepter l'expression de nos sentiments les plus respectueux."*

By persevering, I picked up idioms, colloquialisms and a smattering of argot—a more vivid vernacular than English slang. Gradually my ear also became attuned to the cadence of words, whose syllables all carried the same weight. The French habit of stringing words together with machine-gun rapidity stymied me until, in the Métro one day, I happened to eavesdrop on a couple of prattling women and was able to separate one word from another. I was making progress.

But, as I became more proficient, I found conversations with the French to be frustrating. Reluctant to be pinned down, they had an irksome way of answering questions with *"en principe"*—in theory. So the headwaiter who said that he had a table *en principe* was implying that he reserved the right to give it to a more important guest. Happily, though, regulations also existed *en principe*, which meant that violations were negotiable. I was often exasperated by the propensity among highbrows to convolute the most simple explanation. Again and again they would interrupt their discussions to object: *"Oui, mais c'est beaucoup plus compliqué que ça."* Known as *l'esprit de contradiction*, this was part of their penchant for endless polemics.

Claude was devoted to Paris and, as we wandered around, she explained the city's human geography to me. It was less a cohesive community than a quilt of communities, each with its distinctive characteristics. The nouveaux riches resided in large, bourgeois apartments in the impersonal Sixteenth Arrondissment, the parallel of Manhattan's Upper East Side, while the nobility and old money clung to majestic, often decrepit mansions—*hôtels particuliers*—tucked away in the shaded side streets of the Proustian Faubourg Saint-Germain. Fashionable, well-heeled professionals tended to congregate in nearby Saint-Germain-des-Prés, a district of modish art galleries, antique dealers, interior decorators, publishing houses, bookstores, restaurants, bars and cafés. The smart set also gravitated toward the exuberant atmosphere of the Latin Quarter, or the tranquil Île-Saint-Louis and Île-de-la-Cité, the cradle of the city, whose gentrified flats overlooked the Seine. Claude and I explored the ancient artifacts at the Cluny Museum; the former Jewish ghetto in the Marais; and the Place de la Contrescarpe behind the Pantheon. But not all of Paris was a picture postcard. The Fifteenth Arrondissement, for example, was a dreary district populated by small shopkeepers, office employees, minor functionaries and *rentiers*. In *quartiers populaires* like Belleville and Ménilmontant, on the edge of town, factory workers dwelt in blocks of sleazy tenements with stand-up Turkish toilets.

Cozy cabarets known as *chansonniers* elated Claude, but my French was not yet up to their witty gigs. We tracked down quaint bistros, like one in the serpentine rue Mouffetard, whose *patronne*, reputedly a retired prostitute, chanted ribald ditties. Late at night we might go over to Les Halles, the bustling central market, for *soupe à l'oignon, escargots* and *boudin*. Now and again we would drop into Le Bal Nègre, in the rue Blomet, where young Africans and white women gyrated to pulsating rhythms—a sight that initially startled me. One weekend we cycled through the Loire Valley, sampling its crisp white Vouvray and scouring its Renaissance châteaux—Amboise, Blois, Azay-le-Rideau, Chambord and the exquisite Chenonceau.

We were addicted to movies and would see three, even four, a week. Not only did they help to improve my French, but many of them were perceptive social commentaries that provided me with insights into the complexities of France. Particularly absorbing were those produced during the 1930s, when the French, still reeling from their frightful losses in World War I and shattered by the Depression, had grown profoundly pessimistic and cynical. No director captured their mood as brilliantly as did Jean Renoir in *La Grande Illusion* and *La Règle du Jeu*. Among the exponents of the gloomy genre labeled "poetic fatalism" was Marcel Carné, who made *Hôtel du Nord, Quai des Brumes, Le Jour Se Lève* and his crowning achievement, *Les Enfants du Paradis.* I was also riveted by Marcel Pagnol's bittersweet trilogy of Provençal life, *César, Marius* and *Fanny,* and by René Clair's satires, *À Nous la Liberté, Quartorze Juillet, Le Million* and *Sous les Toits de Paris.*

Crucial to the industry's success were such screenwriters as Jean Cocteau, Jacques Prévert, Charles Spaak and Henri Jeanson, men steeped in the theatrical tradition. The best films owed their luster as well to an array of dazzling actors, like Raimu, the poignant Marseille café proprietor in the Pagnol movies; Jean Gabin, the forlorn fugitive in *Pépé le Moko;* and Jean-Louis Barrault, the melancholy mime in *Les Enfants du Paradis.* Others included Fernandel, the toothy bumpkin; the feline Michèle Morgan; and Gérard Philipe, the heartthrob who soared to fame in 1947 in *Le Diable au Corps,* the tragedy of an awkward adolescent in love with his married schoolteacher. One of the most versatile, Michel Simon, a burly, gravel-voiced former circus clown, excelled at portraying droll eccentrics and tormented souls. I saw *Hôtel du Nord* so often that I could imitate Arletty's saucy retorts to Louis Jouvet, her sardonic costar. Jailed after the war for having had a liaison with a Luftwaffe officer, Arletty was barred from the screen until 1949.

The Paris intelligentsia revered films with a solemnity that was almost religious. Latin Quarter theaters featured lengthy audience debates following their *séances,* and the weekly literary journals ran lengthy articles analyzing *le cinéma* in tedious detail. Artsy critics had a flair for finding esoteric traits in movies; one of them, for instance, described *Hellzapoppin,* a slapstick Hollywood production, as *"un bel exemple du retro-surréalisme."* Forbidden by the Germans during the war, American pictures were then just returning, to the delight of the French. They worshiped Laurel and Hardy, Harold Lloyd, Buster Keaton, the Marx Brothers and, above all, "Charlot," their sobriquet for Charlie Chaplin. Hugely popular in the provinces, Westerns were invariably dubbed into French: a cowboy strides into a saloon, slams his fist on the bar and barks, "Gimme a shot of red-eye"—and, lips flapping, his voice comes out, *"Un Dubonnet, s'il vous plaît."*

By now Claude had added a new and serious dimension to our relationship by introducing me to her family. Raymond, her father, was a tall, bespectacled, graying lawyer in his late forties. Roughly the same age, her mother, Nathalie—a lean, severe-looking woman with a hawk nose, piercing black eyes and combed-back ebony hair—had studied at Oxford and spoke flawless English. They had two younger daughters—Anne, a quiet teenager, and an ebullient twelve-year-old, Dominique. Their spacious apartment in the Sixteenth Arrondissement was typically *haut bourgeois*, but little else about them seemed to fit that label. Impassioned by art, Raymond preferred prowling around museums and galleries to practicing law, while Nathalie, who had published a novel before the war, was immersed in another. They welcomed me cordially and—dispensing with Gallic decorum, which would have required me to address them as *monsieur* and *madame*—Nathalie encouraged me to call her Natasha, her Russian diminutive, and Raymond by his first name. They also urged me to use the intimate *tu* form with them, a further break with formality. Urbane and cultivated, they differed drastically from my lace-curtain parents back in Brooklyn, and I was instantly attracted to them.

To gratify my journalistic impulses, I started to send pieces to a Connecticut weekly, whose proprietor I had met through a friend. He gave me a boldface byline in lieu of payment. I wrote the usual stuff about France and, in November 1947, embarked on a journey to Prague. The city, one of the oldest in Europe, retained a medieval flavor, notably in the Jewish cemetery, with its tiered tombs. Czechoslovakia straddled the frontier between the Western democracies and the Soviet Union; and, with the Cold War then intensifying, I sought to determine whether the country could maintain that precarious position. Though a coalition of Socialists and Communists ruled the country, the Communists controlled the security police and much of the army, and they were obedient to Moscow. So the Russians had only to give the order for them to seize power. My sole sources were a few Czech students at Charles University, and they sounded optimistic yet uncertain. As one of them said, "We can cope with our problems if we're left alone, but will we be left alone?"

My erstwhile Harvard professor of American literature, F. O. Matthiessen, who had a special affinity for the Czechs, was lecturing at Charles, and I dropped in to hear him. He recognized me and, presuming that a former student had come all that way for his sake, was visibly affected. Like his friend Jan Masaryk, the foreign minister, he was convinced that Czechoslovakia could steer a middle course and later, over drinks, emphasized that belief to me. They were both woefully wrong. In February 1948 the Communists staged a coup and murdered Masaryk by shoving him out of a window. Dejected, Matty leaped to his own death in 1950 from the window of a Boston hotel. He was, I always thought, one of the earliest casualties of the Cold War.

I returned to Paris and induced Claude to move in with me. After scouting around, we singled out the Grand Hôtel des Principautés Unies, which despite its preposterously grandiloquent title could have been the set of *La Bohème*. Our garret had a mansard window, a slate floor, a sloping ceiling, a defunct fireplace and no bath. But we were charmed by its location on the rue Servandoni, a cobblestoned street named for the architect of the nearby Église Saint-Sulpice, a ponderous granite church noted for Olivier Messiaen's organ recitals. It was also convenient to the Jardin du Luxembourg and to Saint-Germain-des-Prés, one of our haunts. I was mystified by the wizened crone in the room beneath us. Swathed in black, she would creep up and down the stairwell as she went about her errands. Snooping was considered to be a grave breach of privacy in discreet Paris, but, unable to restrain my curiosity, I pressed our landlady, Madame Gargne, to tell me about her—and, with some reluctance, she related the following story.

When I was young, I went to Saint Petersburg to work as a governess for an aristocratic family. Then came the Bolshevik Revolution, and suddenly they vanished. Were they executed? Who knows? I fled to France, married and my husband purchased this hotel. One day, years later, a old Russian woman appeared from nowhere. Of all things, she turned out to be the mother of the princesses who had been my pupils. How she endured her plight is a long story, but she was destitute. *Eh bien*, what could I do? I gave her a room—free, it goes without saying—and a small allowance. She's been here ever since, and I suppose she'll die here.

Claude spent much of her time with a troupe of novice actors and I with my American chums, most of whom were riding the GI Bill and studying—or pretending to study—such subjects as art, literature, ballet, even haute cuisine. Some of them were having affairs with French women, others with American girls who had come to Paris to shed their inhibitions. At night we hung out in cafés, arguing about everything from politics to baseball. Many of us had ambitious plans, but life at the time was too leisurely and pleasant to fuss about them. Conspicuously absent from the group was a veteran and Harvard graduate, Norman Mailer. He and his wife, Bea, had a modest apartment in Montparnasse and were seldom seen on the café circuit. Disciplined and industrious, Mailer was completing his first novel, *The Naked and the Dead,* which was to become a blockbuster best-seller and make him the most acclaimed writer of his generation. I got to know him better shortly afterward in New York.

Late in the spring of 1948, I concluded that, however much I relished lotus-eating in Paris, the time had come to return to the real world of America for good. I was confident that my year abroad had made me a suitable candidate for a newspaper job. To allay

Claude's doubts, I blithely assured her that a bilingual actress would take Broadway by storm, and she consented to accompany me.

We arrived in New York and accepted my parents' offer of a room in their cramped apartment—a grievous error. As a child, my mother had herself been an immigrant from a Galician *shtetl*, but now she contemptuously referred to newcomers as "greenhorns." She dismissed Claude as an unwanted alien—even asserting in Claude's presence that I could have made a better match with the daughter of a wealthy businessman. My father, mainly chagrined by my lack of drive, chided me: "A Harvard man, and you're spinning your wheels." The constant nagging reduced Claude to tears, and, recalling her family's kindness toward me, I was appalled and ashamed. I sublet a cold-water flat in Greenwich Village for seventeen dollars a month, and we moved in.

After registering for unemployment insurance, I pounded the pavements in search of a job—in vain. Claude, for her part, was selling ladies' undergarments in a schlocky Union Square department store—where, to her amusement, the other clerks called her "Frenchie." The heat was ferocious, and our grungy flat lacked an air conditioner or even a shower. Though I was despondent, Claude, peculiarly, appeared to be enjoying herself and would regale me in the evenings with hilarious tales of yentas frantically clawing each other over corsets, bras and girdles. I wanted to show her New England but, childishly puritanical, worried that the hotels would rebuff us unless we were married. A friend mobilized a judge, who perfunctorily performed the ceremony at City Hall. We rejoiced in being man and wife; in reality we were a pair of rudderless kids.

But we submerged our difficulties in New York's simple pleasures. We climbed the Statue of Liberty, ambled around Coney Island, crossed the Brooklyn Bridge on foot, ate clams in Hoboken, and sat around the White Horse Tavern, where the mellifluous Dylan Thomas held forth. Now the toast of the town, Norman Mailer invited us to one of his bashes, and *le tout Manhattan* was there—

writers, publishers, editors, critics, actors, models, trendy stockbrokers and assorted groupies. Among them, oddly, was a German on a fellowship at Columbia. He was drunk and pawed Claude, sputtering, "You remind me of a French girl I knew during the Occupation." Despite the din, Mailer overheard the remark and lunged at him, and the party degenerated into a brawl. Years later I ran into the German and, amazingly, he recognized me. "What I did that night was absolutely unforgivable, and I've never forgotten it," he said. "Please give my apologies to your wife."

At the time former Vice President Henry A. Wallace was campaigning for president on the Progressive Party ticket. He was warning that the rising tensions between the United States and the Soviet Union imperiled peace, and, though I subscribed to his concern, I rejected his belief in Stalin's innocence, a stance that either reflected his credulity or had been foisted on him by the Communists in his entourage. Still, I intended to vote for him against Harry Truman. One evening Claude and I tagged along with Mailer and his wife to a Wallace rally in Yankee Stadium, where a spotlight was focusing on celebrities in the crowd. Already exhibiting the machismo that was to become his signature, Mailer said, "When it reaches me, I'm going to declare that tomorrow I'm joining the Communist Party." But, when it did hit him, he acknowledged the applause by merely standing up, nodding and, like a prizefighter, clenching his hands over his head.

In September, disappointed by our failure, Claude and I decided to retreat to Paris, where poverty was no disgrace. I had three more years left under the GI Bill, but I itched for a journalistic outlet. A "progressive newsweekly," the *National Guardian,* was being launched to champion Wallace, and Mailer put me in touch with the editor, Cedric Belfrage. A suave Englishman, who among his past activities had been a junior Hollywood screenwriter, Belfrage suggested that I freelance for the paper. I realized that it was a fringe publication, but I could call myself a foreign correspondent and obtain press credentials—and grabbed the offer.

Returning to Paris felt like being home. I retrieved our old room at the Principautés Unies, which had acquired several new residents. One of them, Claude Luter, a young French clarinetist, spent hours glued to Sidney Bechet and Benny Goodman records, imitating their riffs; subsequently, he formed a combo that became all the rage in the cellar *boîtes* then proliferating around Saint-Germain-des-Prés. Another, a gangly former *Harvard Crimson* editor, Otto Friedrich, was amassing notes for some sort of Paris journal. Hemingway's mentor, Gertrude Stein, had died two years before, and her companion, Alice B. Toklas, adopted Friedrich. He was also close to a fellow American writer, James Baldwin. They were fixtures at the Reine Blanche and the Pergola, nearby cafés, and from time to time I joined them, along with David Hersey, another Harvard friend, who ended up in Hollywood as a second-rate successor to Sydney Greenstreet. Baldwin would reminisce acrimoniously on growing up black in Jim Crow America, a theme of his future novels. Unable to fathom the depths of his anger, I once asked him, "Don't you think that conditions will inevitably improve?" He looked at me with his liquid, bulging eyes and answered, "Maybe, but I'm living now."

Yet another neighbor at the hotel was John Beckett, an Irishman. Sam's nephew, he had shaggy black hair and bore an uncanny resemblance to Beethoven; appropriately, he was studying composition. One day he introduced me to a pal of his, Brendan Behan, who had just flown in from Dublin. A muscular, florid-faced figure, Behan insisted on our going out for beers. At the first café he stupefied the clients by buying them all drinks. Soon he was staggering from one café to another, boisterously yelling, singing revolutionary hymns and embracing everybody in sight. Finally John and I dragged him back to the hotel, where he slept off his binge on the floor of John's room. Early the next morning he resumed his boozing, and I accompanied him. As we toured the cafés, he consumed immense quantities of beer, wine and cognac, and nattered away about himself in a brogue as thick as oatmeal. Whether he was telling the truth scarcely mattered. I was mesmerized by his eloquence and listened to him spellbound.

He had volunteered for the Irish Republican Army and in 1939, at sixteen, was arrested by the Liverpool police for carrying explosives. At his trial he confessed that he had come to England to "remove the baneful influence of British imperialism" from Ireland, and he was sentenced to three years in Borstal. He jokingly glossed over the rigors of jail—the screws, puffs and hard labor—saying that he had used the stretch to devour everything from Gibbon and Yeats to Galsworthy and Bernard Shaw. "Borstal was my university, not your fucking Trinity, Oxford or Harvard," he said. He later tried to enlist in the Israeli underground fighting the British in Palestine but was turned down. "They only wanted Jews," he told me, "and I wasn't about to have the tip of me pecker lopped off." Though his father had been excommunicated, along with thousands of other Republicans, he had not forsaken the Church. To show me that he still knew his Latin prayers, he intoned *Lachryma Christi*, the Tears of Christ.

Now he was earning a mint painting lighthouses, a job that isolated him for weeks on some remote island. He also made money writing poems and essays in Gaelic for the Irish press under the byline Breandán Ó Beacháin. "They don't give a shit what you say," he explained, "just as long as it's in Gaelic." Prohibited from stopping in England, he would periodically fly over to Paris, shoot his wad on a bender and return to the lighthouses. Never could I have imagined then that he would become one of Ireland's leading writers—nor, perhaps, did he.

This time I matriculated at the prestigious École des Sciences Politiques, again cut classes and concentrated on my *Guardian* dispatches. I naively allowed my own left-wing slant to be tilted even further by the attitudes of France's enormously influential intellectuals, the majority of whom were either Communists or fellow travelers. Later I became more realistic—though at the time, swayed by this climate, I disparaged the Marshall Plan, one of the most generous programs in American history, as a disguised maneuver to dominate Europe. I also minimized the Soviet threat of aggression and criticized the rearmament of West Germany. But the leftists, whatever their motives, were not always misguided; taking my cue from their reports, I wrote about France's futile conflict to regain its colony in Indochina and its ruthless suppression of an independence movement in Madagascar, a little-known episode that claimed some eighty thousand lives.

The *Guardian* could not afford to pay my expenses, and, traveling on a shoestring, I pursued stories outside Paris. Roaming around France's industrial north, I spent a week in grimy towns like Lille and Roubaix, where workers and their families lived in tumbledown houses without heat or indoor plumbing. I thumbed my way through Spain and did a series on the Franco regime, the archaic Catholic Church, the effects of the ghastly Civil War and, copying Hemingway, death in the afternoon in Madrid. Soon I was contributing to *L'Observateur,* a liberal French weekly founded by Claude Bourdet, a tweedy intellectual, and to the *New Statesman,* a British magazine, whose editor, Kingsley Martin, a donnish English Labourite, had probably never met a laborer.

Soon I became a magnet for visiting American lefties, many of them doctrinaire dimwits. One of the exceptions was I. F. Stone, who toed nobody's line but his own. I had read his columns in *PM,* the *New York Post* and other papers for years, and admired his irreverence. Pudgy, myopic and hard of hearing, he had come to Paris to write a book, and was leasing former premier Léon Blum's house in Jouy-en-Josas, a nearby village. An old reporter accustomed to the clatter of the city room, Izzy could not tolerate the silence of the countryside and persuaded *The New York Times*'s bureau chief, a friend, to lend him a desk next to the teletype machine. He celebrated his son Jeremy's fifteenth birthday by taking him to see the nudes at the Folies-Bergère. A relentless gourmet, he enjoyed nothing more than touring his favorite restaurants, and now and again I would go along. When came the revolution, I cautioned him, he would be summarily shot for bourgeois deviationism. "*Carpe diem,*" he retorted as he polished off a *foie gras de canard glacé,* a *poularde à la bonne femme* and a bottle of chilled Meursault.

By contrast, there was Ella Winter, the widow of Lincoln Steffens, the renowned turn-of-the-century muckraker and one of my heroes. She had married screenwriter Donald Ogden Stewart, whose breezy scenarios had won him an Oscar. Blacklisted by Red-baiters, he had settled with Ella in London. At dawn one day she telephoned to say that she had to see me urgently, and I hastened over to her upscale hotel in Saint-Germain-des-Prés. Ushering me into the suite, she gestured ominously at a lamp to suggest that it was bugged; then, whispering hoarsely, began to outline some birdbrained scheme to promote Henry Wallace to the French. We were huddled together on a couch when Stewart, a bald, lanky man, shuffled in from the bedroom, still in his pajamas. After staring at us for a moment, he leaned down and whispered, "Anybody know what's happened to the toothpaste?"

2

En Famille

～⌒

oward the fall of 1949, Claude and I accepted her parents' invitation to move in with them. After a year in a garret, I could not resist the temptation of a large apartment with central heating and a bathroom, though I had misgivings about forsaking the lively Left Bank and my buddies at the Principautés Unies for the *triste* Sixteenth. I was also unsure whether I could cope with Natasha's moods—the erratic Slav temperament. She could be uptight and relaxed, petulant and amiable, dour and jolly. Even so, I adored her—or perhaps it was the intellectual electricity of her company. Her dinners were monastic: a dry omelet or chop, pallid vegetables, soggy salad, tired cheese, fruit, yogurt and *vin ordinaire*. But the food was secondary to the ambience. Subtle, sensitive, eclectic and stimulating, she orchestrated the conversation, which might range from discussions of Kafka or Jean Genet to the new Anouilh play, a recent Swedish film or Piaf's current revue at the Olympia. She reveled in gossip: Picasso's latest mistress, Jean-Paul's quarrels with Simone. When the talk got too complicated for my rudimentary French, I would sit there mutely, nodding, smiling and pretending to fathom it all. For Natasha, virtually everything had to contain a literary allusion; construing my silence to be humility, she dubbed me Alyosha, the saintly Karamazov brother. It was a tender sobriquet and, I suspected, she regarded me as the son she yearned to have had.

She balked at disclosing much about her personal life, contending that all she wished to divulge could be gleaned from her novels. Periodically, however, she would reveal a few details to me, and Claude also provided me with scraps. The daughter of Ilya Tcherniak, a chemical engineer, she was born in 1900 in Ivanovo, a city about one hundred and forty-five miles from Moscow. The region lay "beyond the pale"—out of bounds to Jews—but Tcherniak was granted an exemption because he had invented a new process for coloring textiles, and a large factory there coveted his skills. Natasha's mother, Pauline Chatunovski, wrote mawkish novels and short stories. One uncle was a noted mathematician, another a terrorist who escaped to Sweden after attacking a train and later wandered around Europe as a fugitive.

Natasha's early years sounded traumatic. She was three when her parents divorced. Her mother took her to Paris, where they briefly lived with her mother's lover before returning to Russia. In 1909, disgusted with the oppressive czarist regime, her father also immigrated to Paris. He founded a small dye plant, prospered and married a Russian woman who bore him two children. Natasha shuttled between her mother and father until she finally settled with him. Though she was a burden on his new family, he encouraged her education. She excelled in Latin and French at her lycée, graduated with honors, won a degree in English at the Sorbonne and another in history at Oxford, spent six months in Berlin and, back in Paris, studied and subsequently practiced law. In 1925 she married Raymond and started to write. If she had ever held a grudge against her father for her insecure childhood, she sublimated it. He was now in his seventies and infirm, and she doted on him, visiting him regularly and schlepping along Claude, her sisters and me to genuflect to *diedushka*—"grandpapa."

His stuffy apartment could have been in Moscow. A samovar steamed away on a sideboard piled high with Russian pastries, and assorted Russians always seemed to be hanging around. His wife hovering over him, the wrinkled patriarch sat slouched in an armchair, wearing a beret, a muffler, a sweater and carpet slippers, sipping tea from a glass and, defying his doctor's orders, inhaling Gauloises. He would reminisce in his heavy Russian intonation about his youth in Paris prior to World War I, when he played chess with Lenin and other banished Russian revolutionaries in the garden of La Closerie des Lilas on the boulevard Montparnasse—or so he claimed. From time to time he would advise me on my career, repeating, "*Apprenez votre métier. Avant tout c'est le métier qui compte.*"

After France surrendered to the Germans, he avoided the fate of thousands of Jews by fleeing to Switzerland. Rather than accompany him, as she could have done, Natasha chose to remain behind with her own family. She refused to register as a Jew or wear the requisite yellow Star of David, and concealed herself in a village in the vicinity of Paris, where, under the alias Nicole Sauvage, she posed as the governess of her younger daughters. In 1948, a year before her father died, she obliquely described her complex sentiments toward him in her novel *Portrait d'un Inconnu,* for which Sartre wrote the preface. A succès d'estime, it validated her as a promising avant-garde author and gained her entry into the outer rim of the inner literary circle.

An experimental movement known as *Le Roman Nouveau* was then beginning to gather momentum. Led by Michel Butor and Alain Robbe-Grillet, two young writers, its intent was to shatter the mold of classical fiction and examine, as if through a microscope, the impact of contemporary existence on human psychology. Natasha had long been an exponent of the genre. Her novels—"anti-novels," Sartre labeled them—substituted explorations of the subconscious for action. "Not once," she explained in an interview, "does a character of mine close a window, wash her hands, put on an overcoat." Instead, the people in her books involuntarily oscillate in

their orbits like tropisms, sometimes missing one another, sometimes colliding fatally. Influenced by Proust, Joyce and Virginia Woolf, she had been toying with the notion for years; her first novel, which she started in 1932 and published in 1939, was titled *Tropismes*. Though Simone de Beauvoir had no qualms about Sartre's affairs with mindless women—and even procured them for him—she resented his admiration for Natasha, whose intelligence rivaled hers. She impugned Nastasha's style as "nihilism," asserting that "nothing was there, no concrete reality." Such backbiting typified the waspish intellectual community, but Natasha, confident that she was on the right track, plodded on.

Like many French authors, she wrote in cafés, usually in some out-of-the-way bistro whose proprietor respected the privacy of his clients. Plunking herself down at a rear table, she would order a coffee and, oblivious of the noise, work for hours, chain-smoking and laboring over every word as she groped for the exact nuance. She permitted only Raymond to read and comment on her manuscripts. Had she solicited my views, I would have been flustered. Her novels mystified me, and to tell her so candidly, I feared, would have alienated us. As it was, she never asked me for my opinion; perhaps she deemed me incapable of rendering a judgment. But if my failure to appreciate her books disappointed her, it did not affect our relationship.

She treated me as she did her children, proudly showing my articles in the Paris journals to her friends, attempting to improve my crude manners and expressing her dismay at my sloppy clothes. Her maternal concern for my welfare could be annoying, but I felt gratified that she considered me to be an integral part of the family. I was puzzled, though, by her petty snobbishness. Her loftiness notwithstanding, she was impressed by aristocrats and particularly voguish highbrows. She would have been delighted, I imagined, if one of her daughters married a famous writer or painter.

The undertow of anti-Semitism pervading France could be a hurdle for social climbers, but Natasha made no secret of her Jewishness. When someone depicted her as half Jewish, she corrected him: "Pardon me, *all* Jewish." Still, Jewish class distinctions mattered to her. Occasionally she would tease me as *"un petit Juif de Brooklyn"*—a ghetto rather than an upper-crust Jew like herself. Then she discovered that I played tennis, a posh sport in France, and I soared in her esteem.

I was intrigued by Raymond, whose remarkable erudition counterpointed Natasha's creativity. Encyclopedic on the subject of art, he could identify nearly every painting and sculpture in the Louvre and had also combed the Tate, the Prado, the Pitti and scores of other European museums and galleries. He was versed in philosophy, math, science, the French classics, Shakespeare, Dante, Goethe, Tolstoy, Mark Twain. His only flaw—if it could be called a flaw—was his weakness for women. When the Kinsey Report estimated that fifty percent of American men indulged in extramarital relations, he indirectly confessed his own infidelity to me, laughing, "Only half? Here the figure would more be like ninety percent." At first his admission shocked my prudish American sensibilities, but it reflected one of the realities of France: adultery, unless it led to divorce and violated the sanctity of the family, was a harmless diversion that merely added a dash of spice to the humdrum diet of daily existence. The staple fare of popular boulevard comedies—the cuckolded husband, his duplicitous wife and her nimble paramour in hilarious combinations and permutations—was contrived though true. The *crime passionnel* was routine, yet polls indicated that most French women preferred a disloyal spouse to a disrupted home. So while Natasha may have been aware of Raymond's dalliances, they were intensely faithful to each other—and their marriage flourished.

In 1949 Natasha purchased and renovated a dilapidated farmhouse in Chérence, a minuscule village on the fringe of Normandy, approximately fifty miles northwest of Paris. It was vintage France: the crumbling stone church, the café and the *monument aux morts* testifying to humiliating defeats and pyrrhic victories. With my GI Bill dollars I could obtain unrestricted quantities of normally rationed gas and, squeezing into Raymond's prewar jalopy, the family would drive there on weekends. The iridescent light that had inspired Monet and other Impressionists bathed the landscape of wheat, beet and barley fields, pear, peach and apple orchards. It was fine walking country. I would trek across the meadows, past grazing cows and sheep, to a nearby village, pausing at its café for a bracing glass of wine or cider. Or I would hike two or three miles to the chalk cliffs above the Seine to watch the barges snaking their way from Paris to the sea. Soon Natasha's friend and later translator, Maria Jolas, came to the village with her husband, Eugene, in quest of a house, and their experience taught me something about French attitudes toward foreigners.

A Kentuckian by origin, Maria had an ample girth, a sweet disposition, a large fortune and a generous nature. She had arrived in France during World War I as a Red Cross volunteer, stayed on and married Gene Jolas, an American born in Alsace. Paris of the twenties comprised the most remarkable American expatriate literary colony ever assembled, and they belonged to it. They hobnobbed with Hemingway, Scott and Zelda Fitzgerald, Gertrude Stein and Alice B. Toklas, John Dos Passos, Kay Boyle, e. e. cummings, Djuna Barnes, Glenway Wescott, Archibald MacLeish and transients like Ezra Pound and T. S. Eliot. Their rendezvous was Sylvia Beach's lending library and bookshop, Shakespeare and Company, on the Left Bank. In 1927, with Maria's backing, Gene Jolas joined Elliot Paul, an American writer, to launch *transition*, a little magazine that published, among its other innovations, an excerpt from Joyce's "work in progress"–the embryo of *Finnegans Wake*, which was to be more read about than read.

Though Maria treasured those brilliant years in Paris, she and Gene now hoped to sink roots in some idyllic corner of rural France. Chérence was perfect, but its inhabitants–peasants, artisans and a few shopkeepers–had an aversion to outsiders. Presumably Natasha had slipped past because Raymond was French; to admit the Jolases portended a foreign invasion of epic dimensions. Maria vaulted the obstacle in her customary fashion–by shelling out money.

She never complained when the tradesmen overcharged her, while Gene, a gregarious guy, became a habitué of the café, where he played *belote* with the locals and stood them all to drinks. Finally, their dream fulfilled, they settled into the village. Several years later, though, the episode had a poignant sequel. Gene died and Maria endeavored to have him buried in the cemetery, but the citizens shuddered at the thought of *un étranger* contaminating their graveyard. After protracted haggling she paid them a healthy sum, they acquiesced–and the Jolases, *grands amis de la France*, were approved.

After eight months of living with her parents, Claude and I felt ourselves reverting to adolescence. Searching for an alternative, we encountered Robert-Jean Longuet, who had two rooms for rent in his Montparnasse apartment. He seemed to be congenial; we moved in and cemented a new friendship.

Situated on the street level of an eighteenth-century building, the flat had floor-to-ceiling windows opening onto a walled cameo garden overrun with ivy, mint, wild strawberries and unpruned rosebushes. The structure had initially been the residence of Jean-Dominique Cassini and his son Jacques, astronomers at the nearby observatory. It later housed Balzac, who had installed a subterranean passageway to enable his mistresses to sneak in surreptitiously and through which he could evade his legions of creditors. The place looked as though it had not been cleaned since then. Filthy pots, pans and other utensils littered the kitchen. Cobwebs and layers of dust blanketed the other rooms, which were a clutter of broken furniture, tattered rugs, faded curtains, shelves filled with frayed volumes and objets d'art too shoddy for even the sleaziest flea market. This musty atmosphere ideally fit Longuet's fixation on the ghost of his legendary great-grandfather, Karl Marx.

Longuet rambled on about his ancestry ceaselessly. The French branch of the family reached back to the marriage of Marx's eldest daughter, Jenny, to one of his disciples, Charles Longuet, a hero of the aborted Paris Commune of 1871. Their son Jean, a prominent Socialist, was awarded a portfolio in Léon Blum's Popular Front cabinet in 1936. A lawyer and sometime journalist, Robert acted as his father's secretary until the Occupation, when he ducked the Germans and got to America. He lectured on French politics at Rutgers, wrote for Gaullist publications, broadcast Free French propaganda to France from Washington for the Office of War Information—and, if his memories could be believed, bowled over countless numbers of Francophile women. Those exciting years were the pinnacle of his life, and he never forgot them.

As slight as a bird, Robert had wavy salt-and-pepper hair and wore suede shoes, button-down shirts, foulard ties and Brooks Brothers suits brought back from New York. He drank Scotch and smoked costly Balkan Sobranies. How he managed befuddled me. His total income, as far as I could discern, was my modest rent. When I initially met him, his father had long since been dead, and he had nothing to do and few prospects. He would sit at a desk behind mountains of documents, optimistically spinning out plans for ambitious ventures that nobody wanted. Communist officials begged him for endorsements, but he rejected them. His only connection with Marxism was his pedigree. One day his elderly mother came by to collect his laundry and, over tea, whimpered to me, "*Ah, le pauvre Robert.* It's sad for a boy to be without a father, *n'est-ce pas?*" By then Robert was in his fifties. Now and again an American lady would pull up in a limousine and sweep him away for a week or two.

Dissidents from nearly everywhere, lured by the Longuet name, floated into and out of the apartment. Exiled Spanish Republicans would cook paella, play their guitars, and sing and dance the flamenco. Longuet *père* had been one of the early foes of colonialism, and nationalists from France's possessions—Algerians, Moroccans, Tunisians, Vietnamese, Cambodians—would appear for guidance on how to organize meetings or draft pamphlets. Nostalgic for his days as his father's aide, Robert eagerly helped them. I kept in touch with many of them, and later, when I covered their struggles for independence, they proved to be indispensable sources. The most valuable tool for a reporter, I had learned, is an address book.

By now I had saved up enough to acquire a car, my first. It was a tiny Renault with a four-horsepower rear engine and a sliding roof, and cost me nine hundred dollars, new. Within a week I could navigate through the Paris traffic, which resembled the "dodgem" rink at a carnival. Owning a car was exhilarating. Never again would I have to hitchhike or cram into a sweaty third-class train compartment. Free to take off at our leisure, Claude and I spent our weekends at the beach in Normandy or Brittany. We motored down to the Alps and around Provence, and crossed northern Italy to Lake Como, Lake Maggiore and Venice. Among our other trips, we drove to the Pyrénées and, along the route, Claude showed me the ancient fortified town of Carcassonne, the origin of her paternal family. Best of all, we could get out of Paris in the evening for dinner at country inns.

Many years later, when I was a correspondent in Asia, a contact in the Central Intelligence Agency told me a bizarre story. He had requested authorization to deal with me and had been warned to exercise caution; an item in my file in Washington alleged that, during one of my journeys, I had been spotted at a bullfight at Arles with Picasso, a Communist. I was astounded. Not only had I never attended a bullfight with Picasso, I had never even met him. Eventually it dawned on me what had happened. Picasso and I had indeed been in the stadium together, but he was in a box in the deluxe section and I, at least three hundred yards away, in the bleachers. I subsequently returned to Montparnasse, swaggered into the Sélect café and bragged to my cronies, "Hey, guess what, I just went to a bullfight with Picasso." One of them must have been a freelance spook who picked up extra cash by snitching on his fellow Americans.

The longer I remained in France, the more its intricacies daunted me. But I derived some consolation from observing that the French themselves—philosophers, psychologists, sociologists, clergymen, novelists, poets, journalists and just ordinary folk—seemed to be just as bewildered as they constantly sought to define their society.

Though emblematically *une et indivisible,* France was riddled with baffling and often incomprehensible contradictions. The French were simultaneously sophisticated and parochial, methodical and anarchistic, individualistic and conformist, flexible and stubborn, liberal and antediluvian, prudent and rash, puritanical and wanton, logical and wildly irrational. While espousing the principles of the Revolution—*liberté, égalité, et fraternité*—they recoiled from performing the most elementary civic duties. They combined tolerance with bigotry, kindness with malice, elegant taste with appalling vulgarity. Politeness ranked high on their list of virtues, yet they could be uncommonly rude, not only to foreigners but to each other. Beneath their exterior of lighthearted gaiety, the "ooh-la-la" stereotype that attracted tourists, they were frequently morose—a trait dramatized in films about tragic love triangles and the desolation of provincial life.

Their cavalier *"je m'en foutisme"* also veiled their perpetual paranoia. To hear them tell it, they were forever under siege—by everyone from their mother-in-law and the tax collector to the neighbor's snarling dog. Their standard reply to the greeting *"Comment ça va?"* was a shrug and a grunted *"Je me défends."*

Yet another incongruity was the contrast between their contempt for government and their veneration for the state, a perplexing notion for an American accustomed to authority vested in a constitution that could be amended. But, to the French, *l'état* was the durable, indestructible entity that assured France's immortal continuity. This concept, which preceded the idea of nationhood, developed from the efforts of successive monarchs to centralize their sovereignty and operated through a permanent civil service that regulated the country's essential institutions—judicial, economic, fiscal and educational. The apparatus was refined during the eighteenth century by Louis XIV, the divine incarnation of *l'état*, and his minister, Jean-Baptiste Colbert, one of the architects of modern France. It evolved over the years into an elite corps rigorously trained at the three *grandes écoles:* the Polytechnique, the École Nationale d'Administration, and the École Normale Supérieure. Locked into generations of tradition, functionaries were still confined after World War II to antiquated offices without typewriters or adding machines, consulting dossiers tied with ribbons. They were responsible only to their hereditary hierarchies and stood aloof from the wrangles of ephemeral politicians. Like Chinese mandarins, they owed their positions to stiff examinations; appointed for life, they could hire or dismiss officials, and even revise parliamentary decisions merely on the grounds of *"raison d'état."* In short, they were supreme—or, as the cliché put it, France "was administered rather than governed."

Whatever their differences, the French fundamentally shared the ambiguous yet pregnant vision of Jules Michelet, the distinguished nineteenth-century historian, that France was *"une personne."* This picture of the country as human habitually consumed postprandial orators, for whom France was *douce, meurtrie, douloureuse, généreuse* and, above all, *glorieuse*. Schoolchildren chanted hymns to *"la France bien-aimée,"* priests invoked *"l'âme de la France,"* soldiers flung themselves into battle for *la belle France*. Peculiarly, too, France was feminine—*"La Mère Patrie,"* its incarnation the exquisite Marianne, its foremost saint the martyred Jeanne d'Arc. For the Duc de Sully, one of Henri IV's courtiers, France was a mother whose breasts nourished its peasants and shepherds; for de Gaulle a fairy-tale princess; for others a queen or a madonna. During the Middle Ages, when the future nation was still limited to the area surrounding two small islands in the Seine, a woman poet made its name synonymous with her own: *"Marie ai nom, si suis France."*

Again like the Chinese, the French were imbued with an overweening sense of their superiority. They were the navel of the earth— an ethnocentric conceit that they spoofed as *nombrilisme*. Flaubert extolled them as *"le premier peuple de l'univers,"* and Hugo wrote, *"France, France, sans toi le monde serait seul."* Inculcated from infancy with such chauvinism, the French were convinced that every aspect of France, from its culture to the contours of its landscape, was unique; if they went abroad, which they seldom did, it was only to find other countries barbaric. Some Parisian friends of mine returned from a vacation in London ahead of schedule, carping that English food was inedible. France, the French maintained, was the paradigm on which other peoples ought to model themselves. In addition to seeking markets and raw materials, French imperialists were dedicated to *la mission civilisatrice,* a commitment to convert Africans and Asians into facsimile Frenchmen. The caricature of this crusade was the Senegalese or Laotian kid reciting by rote: *"Nos ancêtres les Gaulois . . ."* So tenaciously did the French cling to the illusion of their preeminence that to challenge it was to incur their wrath and be denounced as *anti-français*. In a perceptive essay published in 1932, the German writer Friedrich Sieburg crystallized that notion in a rhetorical question: "Is God a Frenchman?"

$\mathcal{N}$o holiday stirred French emotions more than did Bastille Day—*Le Quatorze juillet.* Throughout the country flags bedecked streets, squares and public buildings. In Paris crack infantry battalions and cavalrymen in plumed helmets paraded down the Champs-Élysées to the cadence of martial music. Many of them in wheelchairs or on crutches, their chests draped with medals, veterans solemnly rekindled the flame and laid wreaths at the Tomb of the Unknown Soldier under the Arc de Triomphe. Politicians in tricolor sashes, their voices quivering, delivered pompous speeches exalting the Revolution, and the crowds sang the "*Marseillaise*" before going on to dance until dawn.

But, though it introduced the beginnings of democracy to France, the Revolution was never entirely consummated. The bourgeois classes, while pledging allegiance to its egalitarian tenets, arrogated to themselves the power and privileges of the neanderthal ancien régime nobility they had supplanted. From the early nineteenth century onward, with the complicity of an entrenched bureaucracy determined for its own sake to preserve the status quo, they supported any government that furthered their narrow interests. Their unbridled greed and venality provoked a series of financial swindles, stock market crashes, and huge scandals involving senior officials. They conspired to discourage competition, artificially curbed production as a device to keep prices high and, to protect their domestic markets, overvalued the currency, imposed quotas and erected tariff barriers against imports. Calculated to promote stability, these and other such policies propelled France into stagnation and decay.

By the early 1950s, the economy had made practically no headway in four decades. Meanwhile, the population had been steadily dwindling, the result of the carnage of World War I and a consequent decline in marriages, exacerbated by inheritance laws that deterred families from having large numbers of children. The population would have fallen even more had not France, suffering from a severe labor shortage, brought in multitudes of immigrants from Poland, Italy and elsewhere to work in its mines and factories. In 1935, for the first time in history, deaths exceeded births, and the lopsided demographic pyramid augured danger for the nation's destiny. Politicians, military strategists and foreign diplomats all recognized as World War II approached that the French were too exhausted to confront a German onslaught, but, driven by hubris, they plunged into the abyss.

The years of sclerosis had left a widening gap between rich and poor that triggered strikes, boycotts and bloody riots as the dispossessed struggled for social justice. The chronic strife polarized France into the forces of order and the forces of change, reactionary and radical, royalist and republican. During my first days in Paris, the ideological pendulum was still swinging from one extreme to the other. The war had recently ended, and the French were squabbling over whether the Resistance had been justified in summarily executing Vichyites and other pro-German collaborators. An estimated ten thousand were shot, chiefly on the eve of the Allied landings, when rival cliques began to jockey for the roles they would play following the Liberation. The vast majority of those killed undoubtedly deserved to be punished, though many of them were the victims of personal vendettas. Under the pretext of purging traitors, the Communists went on a rampage, exterminating anyone they believed capable of frustrating their future political aspirations. After the fierce factional splits that had fragmented the Underground, it was understandable that the orgy of vengeance would spark controversy. But it amazed me that the French should have, with the same fervor, continued to debate issues as obsolete as the Dreyfus case and state subsidies to Catholic schools. Deploring their divisions, de Gaulle remarked, "How can you govern a country with three hundred varieties of cheese?"

But if France seemed to be languishing in a precapitalist warp, its quaint charm was precisely the aura that enchanted me. The French cherished smallness, which reminded them of the simple, human proportions of rural life. They endowed stores, cafés and restaurants with such names as La Petite Confiserie, Le Petit Zinc and Le Petit Riche; the favorite newspaper of the petite bourgeoisie was *Le Petit Parisien*. Suspicious of large enterprises, they preferred mom-and-pop shops. Equating debt with crime, they would rather starve than borrow. They distrusted banks, dealt only in cash and, like the proverbial peasant, stashed their savings under the mattress. One day my otherwise urbane father-in-law showed me the gold bars he had hidden in a closet.

*I*n 1950 I stopped writing for the *Guardian*, which under sectarian left-wing editors had deteriorated into a clone of *The Daily Worker*. I also quit school and began to look for work in the Paris office of a mainstream American news organization. All I could land was a job as a public relations man with the Joint Distribution Committee, a Jewish refugee agency. I was not enthusiastic, but it would do until something better came along. The salary was thirty dollars a week, more than the GI Bill—except that I would have to work.

Among my tasks, I had to entertain affluent Jewish American donors and their wives, most of whom where passing through Paris on their way to Israel. The Joint, which relied on their munificence, accorded them VIP attention. I booked them into luxury hotels near the Champs-Élysées, like the Plaza Athénée, the George V and the Royal Monceau, where multimillionaires and movie stars stayed. During the day I showed them the town, took them shopping and, to cadge a super dinner for myself at their expense, escorted them to such three-star restaurants as Maxim's, Ledoyen and La Tour d'Argent. Regrettably for me, their tastes tended to be modest. They would shun the *spécialités de la maison* and instead order a prosaic *filet de sole* or a *côte de veau* and, if any, one glass of wine. Under the circumstances, I could not decently savor a marvelous *pièce de résistance* and had to choose something just as banal.

My other assignment was to churn out press releases on the Joint's kindergartens, youth centers, nursing homes and clinics. Now and again I also traveled to Germany to write about projects to assist Jewish survivors of the Holocaust. Euphemistically designated "displaced persons," they were consigned to squalid camps while waiting to depart, mainly for America or Israel, and I described their plight— which could have been my own had not my grandparents immigrated to the United States. The Joint circulated my articles to the newspapers on the theory that publicity helped to raise funds, yet few were ever published. I began to feel as though I were throwing bottled messages into the sea—until I got an unexpected reaction to one of them.

It concentrated on a relief program for Moroccan Jews, aboriginal Berbers converted to Judaism well before Islam swept into North Africa. They lived in primitive mountain villages, where they were harassed by Muslims. Stitched together from material shipped to me by the Joint's man in Casablanca, my story seemed to me to have the ingredients of an exotic magazine piece, and I took it to the *Time* bureau. Instead of being fobbed off on a drone, I was received by the chief himself, John Stanton, a portly leprechaun with a ruddy face— and, I later discovered, an incalculable capacity for booze. I made my pitch, but he was more interested in me than in either Jews or the Joint and grilled me: where did I come from, where I had gone to school, how long I had been in Paris, whether I spoke French, what was I doing, what did I hope to do in the future. After a half hour he explained that he needed an all-purpose interpreter, researcher and legman, and asked if the job appealed to me. As a "local employee" I would be paid fifty dollars a week, with none of the benefits extended to staffers recruited in New York, like a pension, a rent allowance, home leave and medical insurance. The offer overwhelmed me. This was my opportunity to become, ultimately, a genuine foreign correspondent. Of course I would take it.

At that stage, having been there for three years, I had no doubt that, given the chance, I could demonstrate that I was more than qualified to cover France. My gospel would be Harold Ross's dictum to Janet Flanner when, in 1925, he sent her to report on the French for *The New Yorker:* "Don't tell me what *you* think, tell me what *they* think."

3

Grope Journalism

The *Time* bureau occupied the two floors above a bank in a magnificent eighteenth-century building on the Place de la Concorde, one of the splendors of Paris, if not the world. The office's spacious windows framed a spectacular vista: the pink Obelisk of Luxor surrounded by ornate fountains, terraces, pavilions, and statues symbolizing France's major provincial capitals; and, on the other side of the Seine, the classical façade of the Palais Bourbon, originally the residence of one of Louis XIV's illegitimate daughters, now the seat of the French legislature. Around the corner, at the end of the rue Royale, stood the Madeleine, the church commissioned by Napoleon, patterned after a Roman temple to reflect his imperial ambitions.

Depending on the climate or my mood, I went to work by various routes. If I was hurried, I would crowd into the Métro. Sometimes I gripped the rail of the rear open platform of a creaky bus, smoking and absorbing the scenery as we wound through our circuitous itinerary. On balmy mornings I might stroll along the quais, cross one of the bridges, pass the Louvre, then amble under

3

43

the acacia and chestnut trees lining the Jardin des Tuileries, never ceasing to gaze at the panorama stretching beyond the Champs-Élysées to the Arc de Triomphe.

Despite my menial status—Stanton called me his "thin brown native boy"—I was elated to be employed at *Time,* one of America's top publications. But soon I realized that its subtitle, "the weekly newsmagazine," was a misnomer. Apart from piling up enormous profits, its principal purpose for its founder and editor in chief, Henry Luce, was to propagate his personal opinions, without the slightest regard for objectivity, much less balance. A die-hard Republican, he expected *Time* and its siblings, *Life* and *Fortune,* to mirror the party line. In 1952 he granted leaves of absence to a number of his senior associates to help Dwight D. Eisenhower promote his campaign for the presidency and, following Ike's election, encouraged them to serve as White House aides. Luce defied easy definition, however. Though he was a visceral anti-Communist, he refused to bless the GOP's opportunistic endorsement of Joe McCarthy and, from an early date, ordered his editors to disparage the demagogic senator. As an internationalist, he also rejected the isolationism of many Republicans.

If one trait encapsulated him, it was his Presbyterian ardor. The son of China missionaries, he fervently believed in America's superiority in the global struggle between good and evil, and disdained countries that failed to meet his lofty standards. The French fit that mold. No matter how chic and creative they might be, to him they were morally permissive and thus unreliable allies. Luce never imposed that view on the bureau, but it filtered down to us, and we tended to treat the French with contempt, condescension, derision or, at best, amusement. After a while, I began to feel, a *Time* subscriber might conclude that, by and large, France was a degenerate nation of gourmets, adulterers, leftist intellectuals and volatile politicians who could not prevent their government from collapsing every few months.

Luce's prejudices seldom intruded into the "back of the book" departments—Medicine, Education, Science, Theater, Art and Books—which were admired even by readers revolted by *Time*'s political slant. A primary goal of the magazine was to entertain—and it did. No longer ran the sentences backward until reeled the mind, as they had in its infancy: "Pleased as punch was Babe Ruth after hitting his record-breaking homer." Nor were characters still depicted as "beady-eyed," "pig-faced" or "snaggletoothed." But much of the jazzy Timestyle minted by Timeditors remained intact. Labeled "tycoons," big bankers and corporation directors invariably "strode" rather than walked into boardrooms. Hollywood executives were "moguls," whose movies attracted "cinemaddicts." A dead hero was the "late great," a mistress a "great & good friend." On the theory that exaggeration sells, a concept dear to tabloids, credibility was sacrificed to readability. Once, when I haggled over a fine point, I was told, "Don't let the facts interfere with a good story."

But whatever the magazine's idiosyncrasies, the company had transformed the traditional craft of journalism into an industry that functioned with assembly-line precision. The collegial procedure, advertised as "group journalism," was supposed to provide *Time*'s audience with the best available expertise, compressed into simple, digestible bites devoid of troublesome nuances and complexities.

A worldwide network of anonymous correspondents would cable long and frequently authoritative dispatches to the headquarters at Rockefeller Center in New York, where they were completely revamped—and inevitably distorted—by skilled wordsmiths into a few silky-smooth, swift-paced, adjective-riddled paragraphs. Assiduous women researchers then placed a red dot over every word to indicate that it had been checked and double-checked for accuracy, yet the final product was filled with errors. Many editors spoofed the system as "grope journalism." Frustrated, some of the brightest—Archibald MacLeish, Louis Kronenberger, James Agee, Theodore White, John Hersey, John McPhee—resigned and became prominent authors. Most of the others stayed. The pay and perks were generous, the hours short, the camaraderie congenial. A warm, benevolent paternalism also suffused the company. Staffers could anticipate Luce's condolences on a relative's death or, on the birth of a baby, a silver Tiffany porringer engraved with the inscription "To Cathy from Harry Luce and all her father's friends at Time Inc." For its myriad employees and their spouses, the organization was an extended family; years after their retirement they would congregate at annual reunions, at which they drank to excess and tearfully exchanged memories.

Addressed as Harry by everyone, Luce rejoiced in debate, for which even his most implacable critics respected him. After Eisenhower appointed his wife, Clare, ambassador to Rome, he often visited Paris—and the ritual was always the same. The members of the bureau would assemble in a private room at an overpriced restaurant and, my lowly position notwithstanding, I was included. Luce, who dismissed food as "just fuel," rushed through the meal, then guided us into a bull session. The complex subtleties of a question bored him. Instead, like his magazines, he had a knack for shrinking a broad canvas down to a quick sketch. Nothing symbolized Europe's postwar recovery more vividly than did the motor scooter, he once proclaimed—thereby touching off a slew of stories on motor scooters. He was the precursor of television news.

During those days, however, none of this ruffled me. I was in radiant Paris, gaining experience and having a ball while my chums back home were striving to launch their journalistic careers in Hartford, Dayton or Sacramento.

Unlike the grind that confronted newspaper or wire agency reporters, our rhythm was cyclical. On Tuesday morning the staff of five or six correspondents and assorted assistants sank into sofas in the bureau chief's large office to bat around possible stories.

The heavy hitters usually offered cosmic ideas—"deep dish," we termed them—such as developments in the effort to integrate the

European economy, or the problems of the Atlantic Alliance as a result of France's resistance to West Germany's rearmament. Unless we could dig up a fresh angle, the perils of the fragile French cabinet were stale. Groans and moans invariably greeted important but lusterless proposals, like the growing pollution in Burgundy's canals or the prospering lace trade in Brittany. By contrast, a juicy murder, particularly one involving sex, was surefire. Our territory ranged from Holland, Belgium and Luxembourg through Switzerland, Spain, Portugal and North Africa; and stringers in those places intermittently weighed in—though we never heard from our man in Gibraltar. We would send the suggestions to New York for approval, and the editors would cable back their preferences the next day.

The deadline for copy was Friday. Some correspondents strained to turn out a finished piece; others, knowing that it would all be homogenized, just shoveled in whatever they had accumulated. Furiously competing for space, the writers in New York dunned us for cutesy if irrelevant factoids that would enliven a story. One of my tasks was to field their queries, and I often concocted the answers. Asked if Charles de Gaulle wore false teeth, for example, I responded, "Sources here say only molars." Anne Chamberlin, my spunky analogue at *Life*, was more diligent. Requested to confirm a rumor that the famous artists' model Kiki de Montparnasse had no pubic hair, she polled several of Kiki's former lovers and replied: "Some but not much."

The immense sums at their disposal enabled the editors to schedule more stories than could ever be published, which gave them the advantage of choice; but it was probably the most costly operation in journalistic history. We would file thousands of words—and see only a minuscule fraction of them in print. The "usage cable" we received every Monday contained the score. For the week ending April 23, 1952, for instance, fewer than three hundred lines were distilled from eighteen dispatches. To boost their morale, the authors of discards were complimented in phrases like "wonderful but killed due makeup problem" or "excellent but outspaced." The euphemism "held for revival" meant burial in an archive in New Jersey.

Paris spawned a vast smorgasbord of publications, and I pored over as many as I could for story ideas. The morning dailies spanned the ideological spectrum from the Communist Party organ *L'Humanité* and the fellow-traveling *Libération* to the right-wing *L'Aurore* and *Le Figaro,* the bible of the conservative bourgeoisie. I perused *La Croix,* the voice of the Catholic Church; the faintly Trotskyist *Franc-Tireur;* and *Combat,* the canon of the liberal intelligentsia. The big-circulation rivals, *France-Soir* and *Paris-Presse,* draped the kiosks in the afternoon alongside *Le Monde,* dishwater dull but France's most influential paper. I flipped through *Les Échos* for financial news, *L'Équipe* for sports. My weekly diet included *L'Express,* a clone of *Time;* the progressive *Observateur;* and, above all, the irreverent *Canard Enchaîné,* a repository of political gossip and scandal. For high-brow trends, there were *Les Nouvelles Littéraires* and *Les Lettres Françaises,* its Communist competitor. I also scoured the iconoclastic *Crapouillot,* which devoted entire issues to a single theme, usually the seamy side of French society.

For inside stuff on French politics, I relied on the bureau's indispensable *tuyauteurs,* or tipsters, Robert Boulay and Jean-Louis Guillaud. Other sources for me were my confrères in the Paris press corps—among them Jean Daniel of *L'Observateur,* Henri de Turenne of *France-Soir,* and Henri Pierre, Eugène Mannoni and Raymond Barillon of *Le Monde.* Unlike American journalists, who were trained to tell it straight, they prized the adage *"Le style, c'est tout,"* which esteemed literary rather than reportorial ability. Hubert Beuve-Méry, the editor of *Le Monde,* appreciated nothing more than *"une belle plume."* He relegated hard news to squibs while filling the paper with eloquent if interminable series on Yemen or the Yucatán, or didactic essays on Proust or Tolstoy—all better suited for reading over cognac and coffee than in the crammed Métro. One of the few commentators worth reading was the erudite Raymond Aron, who wrote for *Le*

Figaro; the others, undaunted by a dearth of information, would speculate pompously on the Bulgarian economy, Argentine agriculture or the topic that intrigued them endlessly: racial tensions in America.

I adored crime news, the best of which appeared in *Le Petit Parisien,* a paper treasured by concierges and petty shopkeepers. Its reporters vented their imagination in grisly fantasies that Poe or Maupassant might have envied. I could envision them in pipe and slippers as they wove the strands of a homicide, rape or kidnapping into narratives that rambled on for pages. They observed certain formulas: females in their stories were always either *"jolie"* or *"ravissante,"* never plain or ugly. They had no qualms about labeling a suspect *"l'odieux assassin,"* invading the privacy of his family, or maligning inept detectives and magistrates. It was no accident that one of my idols, Georges Simenon, the author of the marvelous Maigret novels, had started out as a young crime reporter in Paris.

At about noon every day, we repaired for martinis to the Crillon Bar, situated in the elegant Hôtel Crillon next to the bureau. The bar was the favorite oasis of American and English correspondents; Sam White of the *London Standard* did all his reporting from a telephone in his exclusive niche in the corner. Louis, *le barman,* was right out of Central Casting, with his patent-leather hair, unctuous smile and flaccid handshake. From there we would go on to La Truite or Madame Albert, where we knocked off a bottle of wine each over a four-course lunch. Only our *Time* colleague Fred Klein deviated from this routine. A cranky, reclusive Swiss, he religiously ate alone at Le Rompanneau, his newspaper propped against his carafe of wine. Once, when the maître d'hôtel casually remarked on the weather, Klein stalked out and never returned.

After lunch we would stagger back to the office to gather for our daily diversion—gin rummy. A compulsive gambler, Klein arranged the game. The regulars, in addition to myself, included Dmitri Kessel, the *Life* photographer; the head of the *Life* team, Milton Orshefsky; and Art Buchwald, the Paris *Herald Tribune* columnist. Some-

times visitors from New York joined us, like Gjon Mili, a freelance photographer, and Emmet Hughes, a *Fortune* editor who was to become Eisenhower's speechwriter. Catastrophe struck in 1952, when Eric Gibbs, a priggish former British Army colonel, took over as bureau chief and forbade gin as frivolous. Our afternoons dragged on morosely until one day in May 1954, when we learned that he had died of a massive heart attack while on a story in Geneva. Klein immediately organized a game—and, as he shuffled the deck, exclaimed, "Thank the Lord for our bereavement!"

Frank White succeeded Gibbs, happily resumed gin and also introduced poker. With the assent of his hospitable wife, Dru, he would invite us home to continue a game that had begun in the afternoon. He and I played in trains and airplanes—and once, while covering a riot in Morocco, even in the back of a taxi, juggling the cards on an attaché case as tanks and armored cars sped past us.

Aside from going out for a drink, Stanton never stirred from his desk. Instead, I supplied him with the details for his dispatches. His hulk bent over his typewriter, a cigarette dangling from his lips, he would pound out a page, tear it up and begin again. On one occasion, stymied by a story on the French economy, he barked at me, "What this piece needs is statistics. Get some goddamn statistics." I rifled through our library, but the only statistics I could find were in *L'Humanité*. "They're phony," I warned.

Snatching them from my hand, he growled, "They're statistics, ain't they?"

One day in August 1951 he ordered me to accompany him on a story. With Lucien the grouchy office chauffeur at the wheel, we headed south. It was the kind of excursion I cherished. We stopped for the night at a snug country inn, polished off a sumptuous dinner and, next morning, reached our destination—Pont Saint-Esprit, a quaint town nestled among tiers of vineyards on a hillside overlooking the Rhône near Avignon.

A week earlier the local doctors had been deluged with calls from townsfolk complaining of nausea and cramps. They diagnosed it as a mild epidemic of food poisoning until some citizens suddenly went into convulsions. Two men dashed through the narrow streets, shouting that they were being pursued by enemies; a peasant, claiming that monsters were after him, began discharging his shotgun wildly. Charles Graugéon, an eleven-year-old, tried to strangle his mother; Madame Marthe Toulouse jumped into the river, screaming that snakes were burning in her belly. Even cats and dogs had spasms. At hospitals, frenzied patients thrashed around on their beds, yelling that their bodies were sprouting flowers or that their heads had turned to molten lead. The week's casualty list totaled four dead, thirty-one insane and two hundred critically ill. The bistros simmered with guesses—among them the notion that terrorists were responsible. I remembered Aldous Huxley's novel *The Devils of Loudun,* in which a sort of medieval madness punishes a town for its sins. Huxley had based his plot on Saint Anthony's Fire, a lunacy that swept across Europe during the Middle Ages. I tested that thesis on Stanton, but he would have none of it.

Neither would the police, who attributed the outbreak to bread from Roch Brian's bakery, the best in town. After analyzing a baguette, a Marseille toxicologist, Professor Henri Olliver, discovered ergot, a fungus that grows on rye in damp weather, and which can atrophy the nervous system. Gendarmes traced Brian's tainted flour to Maurice Maillet, a miller in the Vienne *département,* about three hundred miles away. Detained, Maillet admitted that he had bought the rye from an unscrupulous baker, who had purchased it from a dishonest peasant and illegally blended it with wheat. He explained that he had shipped the flour to Pont Saint-Esprit "because I don't know anyone there." He and the baker were indicted for "involuntary homicide," fraud and tax evasion; so greed, not demons, had been at the root of it all.

We were interrupted on our journey back to Paris by a frantic call from the bureau. The British diplomats Guy Burgess and Donald Maclean had vanished and were said to be defecting to Moscow. One rumor had it that, for the moment, they were hiding in a château not far from our route. Could we check it out? Stanton was visibly irritated. He was looking forward to dinner at a three-star restaurant ahead, and the detour would delay us.

Locating the place on the map, we instructed Lucien to proceed there. As we neared the château, Stanton told me to go in. "Absolutely not," I objected. "You're the bureau chief." He glared at me. "Come on, don't you want to be a real journalist? You can make a name for yourself, win a trophy or something." We circled around, arguing. Finally, Lucien drove up to the heavy oak door. Stanton rang the bell and stood there awkwardly until a small man peeked out. *"Je m'excuse de vous déranger, monsieur,"* Stanton stuttered in tonal French, *"mais Burgess et Maclean, vous savez les diplomates anglais, est-ce qu'ils sont ici, par hazard?"* The man, whoever he was, answered politely in flawless English, "No, I'm afraid you're terribly mistaken." Relieved, Stanton responded, "Oh well, I just happened to be in the neighborhood, and I thought I'd ask."

Somehow Stanton and I had cemented a bond on our voyage. He released me to file my own stories—as long as I fulfilled my other duties. I sought subjects that, though trivial, nevertheless shed light on the singularities of French life. My first effort was fluff, yet it revealed the attempts by French business groups, jealous of American public relations techniques, to emulate Madison Avenue.

In October 1951 an association of Paris shoe designers and manufacturers contrived a stunt to ballyhoo their wares at the Lutétia, a mammoth Art Deco hotel on the Left Bank that catered to conventions. Out of curiosity, I took the Métro there to have a look. Flashbulbs and champagne corks were popping in the grand ballroom, with its baroque ceiling and crystal chandeliers. Lovely mannequins were slinking around, and on the dais sat twenty pretty, giggling girls, all of them under the age of eighteen, contenders for the title of "Miss Cinderella"—the one with the smallest feet. They each extended a shapely leg as the judges tried to squeeze on a gold felt slipper; to their distress, none fit. The master of ceremonies thereupon announced that the contest was open to any woman in the hall. Several came up; all failed to meet the test. Then a withered old lady in black climbed onto the stage, and the audience, figuring her for a clown, roared with laughter.

At eighty-three, Madame Albane de Siva was a widow who lived in a squalid Montmartre tenement, where she scraped by as an astrologer. Proud of her tiny feet, she demanded to participate but, like wicked stepmothers, the judges shunted her aside. Finally, as a gag, a Prince Charming among them knelt before her and, with a flourish, tried the slippers. They both slid on easily. "They fit, they fit," cried Madame de Siva, prancing around the platform. Dumbfounded, the judges wrested the shoes from her feet, muttering, "It won't do, it won't do." They hustled her, barefoot and kicking, off the stage, hastily went into a huddle and picked the winner, Huguette Granet, a thirty-year-old stenographer. "It's a disgrace, I'll call the police," Madame de Siva protested as a bouncer courteously escorted her to her pumpkin. Crushed by the bungle, the event's organizers later confided to me, "*Quel désastre!* If we were Americans, we would have rigged it all in advance."

Shortly afterward I encountered an even more embarrassing episode. The two thousandth anniversary of the founding of Paris was being commemorated with a concert at the ancient cathedral of Saint-Denis, the site of France's royal tombs. Among the distinguished guests were members of the French cabinet, the archbishop of Paris and the diplomatic corps, including the papal nuncio in his purple robes. The program featured the coronation mass for the French kings, or *Missa Sacri Regum Francorum,* a combination of voices, strings and trumpets by Étienne Moulinié, an obscure seventeenth-century composer. Long forgotten, the work had been unearthed not long before by Father Émile Martin, director of the superb choir at the Église Saint-Eustache, which was renowned for its organ recitals and other musical activities.

The critics were ecstatic. Marcel Schneider of *Combat,* who remembered having heard the mass before, now judged its "veneration and piety" for France's divine rulers "even more imposing." The other experts echoed his rave. "Never has prayer attained such fervor," wrote René Dumesnil in *Mercure de France;* seconded Bernard Gavoty of *Le Figaro:* "Sincere, admirable, even passionate."

The accolades resonated for months until Félix Raugel, a noted musicologist, blew the whistle. One evening, over intermission drinks at the Opéra buffet, he astonished and dismayed his colleagues by disclosing that the soi-disant mass was counterfeit. Their reputations on the line, they indignantly demanded proof, which he furnished. Moulinié never wrote a mass for a king or anybody else. He was court composer to the spineless Gaston d'Orléans, the brother and enemy of Louis XIII, and would certainly have been banned from the regal entourage. Except for the enthronement of Charles X in 1824, the daily mass, rather than any special work, was sung at coronations. Among the other anomalies in the purported

Moulinié piece, trumpets came into vogue as musical instruments only in the eighteenth century; until then they were chiefly used to awaken sleepers during ceremonies that would last for hours.

I met with Raugel at a café near the Opéra. A florid figure with a bristling gray mustache, he told me that he had smelled a hoax from the outset. To be sure, he had explored the cathedral at Reims, where French kings were crowned, rummaged through the archives at the Bibliothèque Nationale and concluded that the mass was a sham. "What Martin did was unforgivable," Raugel said. "With foreign dignitaries at the concert, the very honor of France was at stake. That priest has *une tête de gangster.*" Did the music have any value? "Perhaps," he replied with a shrug. "But an average conservatory student can write a Bach fugue, a Mozart sonata or a Beethoven symphony."

The critics implored Martin to confess but he waffled, explaining that he had synthesized works by Moulinié and his contemporaries and, to avoid confusion, ascribed the result to Moulinié. The original manuscripts, he added, belonged to a private collector, who refused to make them public.

The cuckolded critics howled. "The question is not the caliber of the music," said *Combat*'s Schneider. "Martin has abused our patriotism, our fidelity to France's grandeur." Charging blasphemy, Antoine Golea of the *Témoignage Chrétien* insisted that the "mass" be outlawed: "This is not a purely aesthetic issue; it touches a spiritual truth." Writing in *Carrefour,* a conservative weekly, Claude Rostand suggested that Martin be defrocked: "He is unworthy of his robes."

Amid the brouhaha I took a taxi over to see Martin at Saint-Eustache, whose Renaissance spires loomed above Les Halles, the bustling central market. An affable, chubby curé in his late thirties, he wore a cassock and was chewing a cigar. He invited me into his cubicle and said with an impish grin, "Of course I fabricated the mass—though not deliberately. I was engaged in music research and stumbled onto

Moulinié and, since we had the same initials, stuck his name on a work of my own. The critics acclaimed it, and what could I do? I was a prisoner of success."

Another mortifying story involved Louis Metra, for twenty years the chief of the Vice and Narcotics Brigade. Stocky and taciturn, he was tagged *Loulou le Beau Chasseur* by the Paris underworld—a begrudging tribute to his proficiency in cracking down on prostitution and drug rings. During the 1930s his sterling connections in the Montmartre *milieu* enabled him to round up the notorious Mancuso brothers, who held the French franchise for Lucky Luciano, the powerful international dope merchant. He was also adept at extricating wayward politicians, aristocrats and businessmen from delicate predicaments. Once he recovered a precious jewel, impulsively presented by a foreign prince to a homosexual blackmailer, and in two hours had the bauble back in its rightful owner's safe—with no one the wiser.

While tracking the peddlers, however, Metra developed a sympathy for romantic addicts—artists seeking stimulation, millionaires out for thrills, former colonial officials who had acquired the habit overseas. Elite Parisians all knew that luminaries like Jean Cocteau and General Raoul Salan, the French military governor of Indochina, were hooked on opium. "When I watch an opium smoker performing his rite," Metra once ruminated, "I am reminded of a priest exalting a divinity, the bluish smoke curling like incense around some ethereal goddess."

In 1948 Metra turned in his badge, saying, "Now I can finally go fishing." But he was restless and, as retired cops often do, became a private detective. Years later, agents of the Sûreté, the national police, began to follow known junkies in hopes of being led to the dealers. They spotted many beating a path to Metra's office in Montmartre—among them a pair of middle-aged, well-dressed women, who arrived empty-handed and left with a large parcel. Tailing the ladies home, the inspectors surprised them in possession of a batch of opium, presumably procured from Metra. Though that in itself was not enough for an arrest, they cautiously tracked him. As a veteran, they knew, he was familiar with their tactics, and they replaced their usual black Citroën *traction-avant* with a sporty Buick convertible—not quite the car for maneuvering in congested traffic. They also had to nab him red-handed, or the Paris force, which detested the Sûreté for intruding into its terrain, would raise a ruckus.

At nine o'clock one morning, Metra parked his rickety little Renault in front of a posh apartment building on the boulevard Suchet, facing the Bois de Boulogne. A couple of Sûreté men stopped him clutching a package under his arm, and he surrendered quietly. Inside the apartment, Philippe de la Cour de Balleroy, a sixty-year-old Norman marquis, lay on a couch in the dimly lit salon, stoned on opium. He testified later that he smoked to ease the pain of an injury suffered during World War I, and fingered Metra as his supplier.

I got only a glimpse of Metra at his arraignment. From his dazed expression, I assumed that, like crooks who regard themselves as inviolable, he had never expected to be caught. I interviewed a few of his comrades, and they were mystified. "Perhaps he started by doing favors for his old *copains* and couldn't resist the money," one conjectured. "Our métier has its pitfalls. You chase criminals, always risking the possibility that you might become one of them. After all, we're two sides of the same coin."

As I noticed soon after my arrival, an inescapable aspect of Paris was its multitude of prostitutes. The vice squad estimated their number at seventeen thousand, which was probably low. They came in every size and shape, and, entrepreneurs that they were, charged what the market would bear. The dazzling beauties in the bars near the Champs-Élysées commanded high fees, while the blowzy *putains* in the Place de la Bastille could be had for a pittance. Prior to World War II, the majority of professionals had been ensconced in roughly three hundred licensed brothels, euphemistically labeled *maisons de tolérance*. They ranged from cheap, dingy joints for workers to plush establishments that accommodated prestigious politicians, wealthy businessmen, playboy aristocrats and visiting royalty. Among the most luxurious of them was Le Sphinx, also known in English as Le One-Two-Two, for its address on the rue de Provence, in the Ninth Arrondissement. Owned by a rich manufacturer, it was adorned with expensive furniture, antiques and paintings. A gentleman would select one of the scantily clad women flitting around the salon, chat with her over a drink, then retreat to an opulent chamber upstairs. Even more extravagant was La Maison des Nations, whose rooms evoked different countries. Decorated with pictures of Rome and Florence, the Italian room was equipped with a speaker that piped in arias. The Japanese room had a tatami on the floor and a wood-block print of Mount Fuji on the wall. Railroad buffs could fornicate in a facsimile wagon-lit as a train whistle sounded and scenes of the countryside rolled past the window. Gorgeous African, Asian, Scandinavian, Slavic and other foreign girls gave the place a cosmopolitan aura. For voyeurs there were blue movies and live sex shows—and, for sadomasochists, whips and chains.

I had long been amassing material on prostitution, in part because it appealed to my rakish reveries, and also because it had the ingredients of a good story. The golden age of whoredom was the turn of the century, when voluptuous courtesans like Émilienne d'Alençon, Liane de Pougy and La Belle Otéro serviced kings and noblemen, and La Chambre Seize at the Café Anglais could be reserved for orgies. One bordello proprietor had a special bed constructed for the obese Prince of Wales, a notable philanderer and later Edward VII. This background proved useful when I did a piece on the controversial Marthe Richard.

A reformist member of the municipal council, Richard began shortly after the Liberation to agitate against whorehouses, decrying them as "putrid sewers that tarnish our national image." Finally, at her instigation, they were closed in 1946. Some of them were converted into student hostels; my friend Sanford Gottlieb lived with his wife and child in a former brothel on the rue Blondel, one center of the flesh trade, where evicted hookers walked the pavement outside. The rest of the country followed suit, and the measure soon proved to be a blunder. Driven into the streets, the women were exposed to the cold and rain; without benign madams to manage them, they might be exploited by rapacious pimps and hustlers. No longer could they be examined regularly by doctors, and venereal disease spread. Richard blamed the authorities for failing to introduce social programs to protect the working girls but, in a book published in 1951, conceded that she might have been wrong, and hinted that the brothels ought to be reactivated.

Her diluted apology did little to propitiate Parisians, who abhorred zealous prudes. They could do nothing to reopen the bordellos, but Jean Galtier-Boissière bombarded Richard in his muckraking magazine *Crapouillot,* which means, aptly, "mortar." Her Legion of Honor, he maintained, was bogus; it had actually been awarded to her late husband, an Englishman. He also avowed that, far from being a paradigm of rectitude, she had slept with a German diplomat in Madrid during World War I, when she had been a French spy. Boissière further contended that she had forfeited her French citizenship by marrying an Englishman and had no right to sit on the Paris council. Thus her action against a venerable institution, besides being an abomination, was illegal.

Richard predictably sued Boissière for libel, and, on a sticky morning in June 1952, I went over to the Île-de-la Cité, climbed the steps of the Palais de Justice, found the courtroom and squeezed into the press box. The scene was a Daumier etching: the solemn judges peering down from their podium, the smug lawyers in their black robes looking like ravens. Both in their early sixties, the adversaries were fastidiously attired. Her hair dyed platinum blond, Richard wore a tailored gray ensemble; Boissière was dapper in a tweed jacket and yellow waistcoat. Her liaison with the German, argued her thirtyish attorney, had been a sacrifice for *la patrie:* "Like our courageous poilus in the trenches, she too played her part; furthermore, the enemy diplomat was already in his seventies, which could hardly have amused her." I was mesmerized by Boissière's formidable defense counsel, Maurice Garçon, a member of the Académie Française and a consummate ham. Rising to address Richard's lawyer, he intoned, "*Cher maître,* you are still very young. May I emphasize that seventy is not necessarily a repugnant age; I myself am sixty-nine. Whatever her motives, Madame Richard's dalliance with this German is strictly her affair, but I cannot comprehend why, thirty years later, she would deny thousands of unfortunate girls the same pleasures that she herself once enjoyed."

Within less than an hour the judges ruled, tongue in cheek it seemed, that Boissière had "exceeded the bounds of satire." They condemned him to pay Richard damages of three thousand francs—five dollars. The token sum, commented *Combat,* "represents the monetary evaluation of her virtue."

I collected other minutiae that I might fold into stories. Despite her success, Coco Chanel bunked in an attic at the Ritz and, drenched in her signature pearls, left by a back door every morning for her atelier across the street in the rue Cambon, where she designed handbags, jewels, shoes and dresses for ladies from Delhi to Dubuque. The Eiffel Tower was a lucrative private company that paid its shareholders a healthy dividend—a bit like selling stock in the Brooklyn Bridge, I thought. The Chambre Syndicale de la Savonnerie divulged that only fifteen percent of Paris dwellings had bathrooms, and that French soap consumption was the lowest in Western Europe, which accounted for the popularity of eau de cologne.

Correspondents usually spent two or three years overseas and, unless they moved to another foreign or domestic bureau, were transferred to New York. I saw them come and go. Some were brilliant, others mediocre, still others incompetent.

If *Time* had a Most Valuable Player Award, it would have gone to Frank White. The only correspondent I knew who actually wore a trench coat, he had served in Indochina during World War II with the Office of Strategic Services, the forerunner of the CIA. He worked for the magazine in Paris, South America and West Germany before returning to Paris as bureau chief in 1954. Despite his years overseas, he was a quintessential American who never deprecated his own culture—a tendency common to expatriates. The French scorned anyone who spoke their language poorly; White accomplished miracles in fractured French. Extraordinarily versatile, he could cover everything from sports to military affairs—though he sweated like a rookie over his typewriter. He revered *Time;* the company was his Mother Church. But he had a higher allegiance to his colleagues, which made him an unparalleled leader. He would not recoil from defending dissenters, even against Luce. Once he was presiding over a lunch for Luce in Paris when Israel Shenker, a young member of the bureau, berated *Time* mercilessly for its political tilt. After suffering through the diatribe, Luce thundered to White, "I want that man fired!" White riposted, "Who do you think you are, Hearst?" Shenk stayed.

The McCarthy virus then plaguing America periodically infected the bureau, as exemplified by a new correspondent named Arthur White—no kin to Frank. He arrived with the conviction that every Frenchman was, if not a card-carrying Communist, at least anti-American. His French was nil, and I had to interpret for him; and on every story he would bedevil me with the same refrain: "Is this guy a Commie?" I ignored him. Charlie Chaplin, who had just been denied reentry into the United States on suspicion of Communist sympathies and other allegations, had scheduled the premiere of his new film, *Limelight,* in Paris. I obtained a pair of passes and, on orders, took White along. The French adulated Chaplin, and the theater was packed. Looking around, White mumbled ominously, "Commies, Commies everywhere."

I was more indulgent toward another staffer, George Abell, a scion of the family that owned the *Baltimore Sun*. He owed his job to his wealthy wife, Jane, a superannuated flapper. She had set them up in a château outside Paris, where George, now an aged dandy with little to do, was becoming a nuisance. To get him out of the house during the day, she induced her friend Clare Boothe Luce to coax Harry into hiring him. Every morning George would show up bright and bubbling in Jane's chauffeur-driven limousine, charming everyone, myself included; a gumshoe journalist he was not. A notebook, he explained, would cause a bulge in his impeccable Savile Row suit. He mingled with French aristocrats and rich American expatriates, and swallowed their word as gospel. Once, on a trip to Casablanca, he was wined and dined by a big French landowner, who assured him that the tales of native unrest were grossly inflated. George parroted his complacency in his dispatch; shortly afterward an insurrection erupted.

Another correspondent, Enno Hobbing, bewildered me. He was tall and scholarly—and, as far as I could tell, rarely went out on stories. Instead, he would seclude himself in his cramped office, chain-smoking Gauloises and scribbling away in Harvard Law School record books. Early in 1954 he inexplicably disappeared and, we subsequently discovered, had played a key role in the ouster of Jacobo Arbenz Guzmán, the left-wing president of Guatemala—a CIA coup. Later he returned to the *Time* office in New York to retrieve his old position; as the story goes, the managing editor, Roy Alexander, asked him whether he had been a CIA man. "No," Hobbing responded. Alexander restated the question: "Enno, if you were in the CIA and I asked if you were, what would you say?" Hobbing repeated, "No." Alexander rehired him.

With my work being praised and published regularly, I felt that I deserved to be promoted to the staff, and in January 1953, leaving my wife in Paris, I went to New York to plead my case. For reasons I never totally understood, I was rebuffed.

Perhaps, because of my years abroad, I was deemed unfit for *Time*'s all-American team. The magazine also liked its reporters to be fungible, and my Paris performance, however laudable, was no guarantee that I could adapt to Chicago or Los Angeles. Or maybe, during the egregious McCarthy era, when companies dreaded smears, my reputation as a liberal had stigmatized me. I hung around New York for weeks, but my only nibble came from the editor of the "back of the book" sections. Presuming that my *vie de bohème* in Paris must have made me an art maven, he dangled the notion of my becoming *Time*'s art critic. The possibility enthused me, but, I disclosed, I was partly color-blind. "Don't worry," he said, "we'll get a researcher to look at the paintings for you." The idea evaporated.

I was despondent. My prospects at *Time* were bleak, other news media jobs in New York were scarce and, after Paris, the thought of Atlanta or Cleveland appalled me. But the *Time* organization could be flexible. The chief of correspondents, John Boyle, an old friend from the Paris bureau, offered to send me back to France as a contract reporter—twenty-five dollars a day and no servile chores. I grabbed it.

Meanwhile, my marriage to Claude was unraveling. Having forsaken her dream of becoming an actress, she was covering the Paris theater for *Le Monde*, which delighted her. She was also dedicated to Paris, while I could not conceive of remaining in France forever. For those and other reasons, we eventually divorced.

On my return, Frank White, now the bureau chief, handed me major assignments, frequently to other countries within our domain. One day I was summoned to the American embassy by the consul in charge of passports, Agnes Schneider. A blue-haired spinster, she had been dubbed "Schneider the Spider" for the subterfuges she devised to confiscate the passports of allegedly disloyal Americans. Among her ruses, she would ask to verify some technicality, then slam the passport into her drawer, thus depriving the owner of a vital document. When she requested mine as "a routine check," I declined on the grounds that I needed it for my travels. To appease her, however, I swore under oath: "I am not now, nor have I ever been, a Communist." That, I decided, was the end of the matter—until it reemerged in a talk between Frank White and C. Douglas Dillon, the United States ambassador. Dillon drifted into the issue of "leftist" American journalists in Paris, including me. White sensed that he was uneasy with the topic—as though he had raised it on instructions from some upper echelon—and they switched the conversation to American politics. Dillon was then being mentioned as a Republican presidential candidate—but, he said, his Jewish ancestry would probably be a handicap. My passport dilemma mysteriously faded away.

In 1955, with White's support, I was finally made a full-fledged correspondent. I was listed on the magazine's masthead, and entitled to the fringe benefits that went with the job. It was as though I had been elevated from a noncom to an officer.

4

Le Monde

⁓

*I*n May 1951, as parliamentary elections approached, I was assigned to cover Gaston Palewski, the debonair Gaullist politician and man-about-town. Nicknamed "Monsieur Lavande" for his aromatic lavender after-shave lotion, he was irresistible to women; his innumerable mistresses included Nancy Mitford, who transparently disguised him as the velvety Fabrice in *Love in a Cold Climate,* her sparkling roman à clef. He was visible at nearly every fancy Paris event, from vernissages at voguish Saint-Germain-des-Prés galleries to premieres at the Comédie-Française. Periodically I would spot him in action, looking like a cartoon-strip Frenchman as he bowed to the ladies and brushed his lips across their fingertips. One day I joined him on a campaign trip to Strasbourg, during which a trivial incident kindled my curiosity about a side of French society that until then I had chiefly observed from a distance.

We were chatting idly as the train rattled across the plains of eastern France when an elfin man poked his head into our compartment. Palewski bussed him effusively and introduced us, and his name instantly rang a bell with me. He was Francis Poulenc, the composer, whose ballet scores I treasured. As I basked in the glow of his presence, he and Palewski rambled on, exchanging anecdotes and dropping names that I recognized from the gossip columns. After more embraces Poulenc departed, and I naively asked Palewski how they knew each other. Peering at me down the length of his mottled nose, he explained indulgently, *"Mais mon cher ami, dans le Monde tout le monde se connait."*

By *le Monde* he meant his crowd: a few thousand citizens—well-born, well-heeled or both—who were so convinced of their own superiority that they referred to themselves as "the world," as though they embodied everything that truly counted. In many ways they resembled Chinese mandarins, who called their land the "center of the universe" and dismissed the rest of mankind as barbarians. Also labeled *le gratin*, "the upper crust," they included *le tout Paris*—which was not at all *tout* but a highly exclusive coterie of sophisticated, clever aristocrats, politicians, authors, artists, actors, musicians, even some businessmen. They were the "beautiful people"—the species portrayed by Nancy Mitford as "U," as opposed to the "non-U" multitudes. The worst fate that could befall them was to be forced to move to a provincial town, where the streets were pulled up after dark; where the smart set consisted of the mayor, doctor, priest and newspaper editor; and where, as one woman told me with a shudder, "foreign films are dubbed into French."

During the 1950s, strikes and riots were roiling France, yet, except when it inconvenienced them, the upper classes seemed to be oblivious of the unrest—inspiring alarmist critics to compare them to Marie-Antoinette on the eve of the Revolution. For all their complacent insularity, however, they were dazzling and innovative. Their tone and trends shaped tastes from New York to Tokyo, and foreigners gravitated toward Paris in hopes of imbibing a bit of their panache. Justifying their narcissism, the urbane, prolific jack-of-all-arts Jean Cocteau wrote, "Egotism may indeed be antithetical to civic

virtue, but if it stimulates genius, discovery and that tingling electricity of creation—*alors, vive l'égoïsme!*"

For elite Parisians, though, creativity did not have to be as lofty as writing, painting or composing music. They sought to attain aesthetic perfection in their daily lives—*le savoir-vivre,* which defined virtually every endeavor as an art, from marriage and raising children to hunting, fishing, driving a car and, of course, making love. Versed in the art of eating, they served only haute cuisine at their elegant dinner parties—never such earthy Gallic fare as tripe, snails and frogs' legs, which were for peasants, tradesmen and tourists. Their apartments were façades designed less for comfort than for appearance: airy salons embellished with rare tapestries and recherchés bibelots, and unheated bedrooms furnished with frayed rugs and tattered curtains. Preoccupied with the art of dressing, husbands accompanied their wives to fashion shows and commented on the latest styles. No couturier of any consequence catered to the distinct needs of matrons and adolescents; in theory all Parisiennes were ageless and as svelte as mannequins.

Aesthetic refinement could not be achieved haphazardly, but hinged on complying with rigid canons of behavior that were innate to *le gratin* and that social climbers had to learn. A woman who circulated photographs of her children at a luncheon would be ostracized; nor was it acceptable to wear a jogging outfit to a weekend château party. The rules differed according to rank, however; nobles could get away with violations for which the bourgeoisie would be severely punished. One afternoon I drove over to Saint-Germain-des-Prés for coffee with the Comtesse Louise de Vilmorin, a talented poet and novelist who habitually went around in jeans and an old sweater and smoked cigars in public. She attributed her latitude to her impeccable credentials: "My ancestors were contemporaries of William the Conqueror. If I turned up at the races at Longchamps in a bikini, they would nod and say, '*Comme c'est original!*' "

Obsessive politeness was a mark of breeding. It was de rigueur for a gentleman to kiss a lady's hand and for her to reciprocate with a calculated blush. Every French schoolboy was familiar with the gallantry of Monsieur d'Auteroche, the commander of the French guards at the battle of Fontenoy in 1745, who announced as their English adversaries advanced: "*Messieurs les Anglais, tirez les premiers.*" Courtesy also reached down to lower-echelon Frenchmen. Shopkeepers never failed to welcome their customers with a cheerful, singsong "*Bonjour, m'sieur, 'dame.*" The French purloined an English term for one of their most immutable rituals—*le handshake.* My concierge, my mailman and the waiter at the neighborhood café religiously clasped my hand. I once went camping with a group of French students on a Normandy beach; they shook my hand before we crawled into our tents at night and after we woke up in the morning.

But to the French, politeness was not synonymous with generosity, much less kindness. They could be conspicuously avaricious and rude—as anyone would testify who witnessed them quarreling over a legacy or jockeying for a bus seat. It was precisely to check their baser instincts and lend a measure of order to society that, through the centuries, they developed the precepts of good manners. "Otherwise," a French acquaintance told me, "we would sink into savagery."

The upper crust excelled at conversation, another art. Occasionally invited to soirées, I was awed by nimble wits as they lunged and parried in exhilarating rhetorical duels. Women invariably participated and held their own with men. Often the dialogue was stilted and flowery, but it could also be delicate and nuanced—another reminder that French, with its deliberate ambiguities, had long been the diplomatic lingua franca. Some of the guests were astoundingly erudite; as I tried to keep up with the rapid pace, I frequently felt like the young English bride in Nancy Mitford's novel who finds to her chagrin after marrying a marquis that he expects her to identify Second Empire objets d'art, analyze Braque's early Cubism, quote Verlaine, discuss Giraudoux's latest play and express an opinion on Sartre's recent squabble with Camus.

Within this hothouse, everyone knew what everyone was doing, yet a mask of secrecy had to be maintained to avert gaffes that might transgress the codes of conduct. It was permissible for a husband to have a mistress, and his wife a lover—as long as she did not insinuate him into the conjugal bed. But divorce was a strict taboo that jeopardized the stability of the family, the sacred pillar of society, and had to be avoided at all costs. A conspiracy of silence prevented disclosures that could disrupt the system. A favorite afternoon escapade of the elite, *le cinq-à-sept,* depended on discreet concierges. Jewelers and couturiers kept confidential records; to greet a rendezvousing couple in a restaurant or a hotel lobby was an unforgivable faux pas. Sensitive to human frailty, judges and juries almost always treated the defendants in *crimes passionnels* leniently.

Much of avant-garde French culture blossomed under high-society patronage. The effervescent Comtesse Marie-Laure de Noailles opened her enormous *hôtel particulier* in the Place des États-Unis to impecunious Left Bank painters, displayed their works on the walls of her salon, and financed Dada and Surrealist films. The Comte Étienne de Beaumont subsidized Erik Satie and Cocteau, and commissioned Picasso to decorate his house with murals. Parisians rejoiced in even marginal associations with creativity. My friend Madame Gabrielle Vittini, an indestructible grande dame nearing eighty, who liked to muse on her youth before World War I, recalled to me that she would encounter Proust at *thés-dansants.* "*Ah, le pauvre petit* Proust. If I had known that he was going to become so famous, I would have paid more attention to him."

As heirs to the medieval chevaliers who had defended their domains against intruders, many aristocrats assumed that their status shouldered them with special obligations toward *la patrie.* For that reason, numbers were active in the maquis during the Occupation, but those I interviewed tried to make it all sound effortless—or, in Talleyrand's words, "*Surtout, pas de zèle.*" One of them, who had rescued Allied pilots, sheltered clandestine agents and concealed fugitives from the Gestapo, denied having been heroic. "I supported neither Marshal Pétain nor General de Gaulle," he said. "The Resistance for me was a wonderful adventure—*et fortement amusante.*"

$\mathcal{H}$istory exerted a profound and enduring influence on French social attitudes. The English nobility, in alliance with the common people, had curbed the king's absolute authority; but Louis XIV, who reigned from 1643 to 1715, was resolved to deflect a similar challenge to his crown. He built a massive palace at Versailles and, as befit his power, transformed it into the most magnificent court in Europe. Lured by the splendor of this Xanadu, the rural aristocrats abandoned their fiefdoms and vassals—and, in the process, forfeited the chief source of their strength to become ensnared in a pernicious web of luxury. Versailles augured what Paris was to be two centuries later: the pivot of a highly centralized nation. It also dictated standards of deportment that *le gratin* would subsequently imitate.

Just as the earth orbits the sun, so the court revolved around *le Roi Soleil.* Designated members of his entourage would gather every morning in his bedchamber for *le lever,* at which they helped him to bathe and dress. They watched while he moved his bowels, then anxiously waited until he granted one of them the honor of wiping him. In his vivid if often exaggerated chronicle of palace life, the Duc de Saint-Simon tells of an obscure curé who was so ecstatic at being selected for the task that he planted a kiss on the divine derrière.

Courtiers bent over backward to ingratiate themselves with the king. Once, when he asked the Cardinal de Polignac the time, the prelate answered, "Whatever hour pleases Your Majesty." The better to control them, Louis XIV encouraged aristocrats to compete against each other for his graces, which he denoted by determining where they could stand or sit in his august presence. He decreed whom they could marry, and even chose the names of their children. An aura of contrived, pretentious, suffocating formality pervaded the court. Its pompous decorum, excessive politeness and exquisite etiquette were as meticulously choreographed as a minuet. The penalty for a defiant nobleman was banishment—not to some remote island but to his provincial château, usually a more congenial place than artificial Versailles. To be so exiled, though, could tarnish his family's prestige for decades.

But creativity and frivolity tempered the inflexible atmosphere. Courtiers wrote essays and poetry and attended Molière, Racine and Corneille plays. The main diversion, however, was *affaires de coeur*, with the king in the lead. He erected an ersatz Chinese temple in the spacious gardens for his romps with his first *maîtresse en titre*, Madame de Montespan, by whom he had seven children, and dismantled it to placate her successor, Madame de Maintenon. Following his example, the aristocracy frowned on marital fidelity as woefully prudish—and, even worse, in bad taste. So much so that the slightest hint of a happy marriage was a cause for whispers. Yet propriety compelled lovers to veil their affairs, which only added spice to their trysts. A German visitor to the court remarked: "You may see solid unions in the lower classes, though among people of quality I know of not a single case of mutual affection and loyalty."

Their dissolute lives, coupled with their incapacity to adjust to change, ultimately doomed the courtiers, leaving Versailles a hollow monument to their glorious past. But, to an extraordinary extent, their spirit survived. During the nineteenth century, remnants of the ancien régime nobility began to blend with the rising bourgeoisie, and out of the unleavened mixture emerged *le Monde*—a new privileged class just as circumscribed and self-conscious as the entrenched aristocracy had been.

*D*espite their allegiance to the egalitarian principles of the Revolution, birth continued to matter to the French; the particule "de" in a name impressed even fervent republicans. About four thousand families claimed nobility, and, scanning the stud book, I ran across jawbreaking patronymics that evoked centuries-old dynastic alliances, like Morel de la Colombe de la Chapelle d'Apcher or Briot de la Crochais de la Mallerie. There were also such hybrids as Brindejonc de Bermingham, of English genesis, and d'Oilliamson, originally Scottish Catholic émigrés called Williamson. As members of the leisure class, aristocrats were not supposed to smudge their hands in commerce, but numbers of them worked for chic couturiers, perfume manufacturers, champagne firms, public relations companies, advertising agencies and automobile dealerships, which derived a certain cachet from employing peers as window dressing.

But titles varied drastically—and even a superficial understanding of their importance entailed a grasp of the hierarchy of the intricate and often baffling divisions and subdivisions that made up the nobility. To my amazement, even my left-wing French friends could recite the rankings by heart. Madame Vittini, whom I often consulted, was a genealogical encyclopedia. I had only to refer to a duke, a prince or a count, and she would feed me an indigestible menu of minutiae on his parents, wife, paramours, uncles, aunts, cousins and in-laws. "Unless you comprehend *le Monde*," she warned, "you cannot comprehend France."

The creamiest of *la crème* were the great ducal tribes of the ancien régime, among them the Broglies, Choiseuls, Clermont-Tonnères, Gramonts, Harcourts, Noailles, Polignacs and La Rochefoucaulds, who provided France with many of its illustrious figures. Starting out as petty landowners in Limousin in 1225, the Noailles spawned marshals, admirals, diplomats, an archbishop and, in the nineteenth century, a melancholy woman poet. The Broglies produced, along with prominent soldiers and ministers, Prince Louis-Victor, the Nobel laureate in physics in 1929 for his discovery of the nature of electron waves. Secure in their pedigrees, these blue bloods saw no necessity to conform to convention. The eccentric Duc de Lévis-Mirepoix, who claimed to be related indirectly to the Virgin Mary, sometimes worshiped at a decrepit parish church; when an acquaintance teased him for slumming, he riposted, *"Mais pas du tout!* I simply stopped by to offer a prayer to my cousin."

The vintage patricians shuttled between their ancestral châteaux and *hôtels particuliers* tucked away in the quiet, tree-lined side streets of the Faubourg Saint-Germain, the Left Bank *quartier* scrupulously described by Proust. For many of them the Terror had occurred only yesterday. Ensconced behind the closed shutters of their musty salons, dowagers perpetually mourned for guillotined martyrs while fossilized monarchists optimistically awaited the triumphant return of the Bourbons. Comtesse Jeanne de Pange, who was reared in a devoutly royalist household, recalled her father flying into a tantrum at the mere mention of the Republic.

At a lower level of the peerage were *les hobereaux de province*—country squires who often languished in genteel poverty on their ramshackle estates. Respected for their lineage, they frequently presided over regional fairs and festivals, though numbers of them were even poorer than the local peasantry. If they went to Paris, which they seldom did, they stayed in scruffy hotels and ate in cheap bistros. Once in a while I would spend a weekend with a friend at his parents' château in Britanny, an impressive if dilapidated pile of ivied stones, its only heat a fireplace, its only light the flicker of a few bare bulbs. With no prospect of an inheritance, the young sons of these families faced a bleak future. But they flinched at blemishing their escutcheons in business and, as an alternative, many enrolled in *la petite noblesse de l'épée*, the traditional officer caste whose most celebrated exemplar was Charles de Gaulle. Its civilian equivalent was *la petite noblesse de robe*, a corps of lawyers, teachers and minor functionaries recruited from the landless gentry.

The aristocracy had been abolished at the start of the Revolution as inimical to the ideal of *égalité*, but the ban did not last long. During his decade as emperor, Napoleon conferred titles on more than two thousand of his marshals, generals and officials. He also founded the Legion of Honor as a way of rewarding services to his crown; when one of his aides protested that he was reverting to the ancien régime, he replied, "It is with baubles that men are led. . . . So, to win their esteem, we have adopted such monarchic forms as titles, crosses, ribbons and trinkets." The Legion was to become a surrogate aristocracy—particularly for the bourgeoisie, who could emblazon themselves in decorations. Further complicating the already complex social hierarchy, the restored Bourbon kings ennobled their sympathizers, and Napoleon III bestowed peerages on his courtiers. Several French Jewish bankers, like the Rothschilds, were barons—a title their family had acquired from the emperor of Austria.

After his reign began in 1830, Louis-Philippe devised a scheme to expand his own aristocracy. He was descended from the House of Orléans, the cadet branch of the Bourbons, and regarded by the Legitimists as a usurper. To buttress his cause, he proclaimed that anyone able to produce proof of a Crusader among his forebears would be eligible for admission to his peerage. Hundreds of politicians, bureaucrats, army officers and others rushed to apply, and a team of scholars was mustered to approve their requests. Oddly, however, all the evidence of their progenitors had been dredged up by one Henri Courtois, who socked them each forty thousand francs for his research. But to cast doubt on the king's project would have been embarrassing; and, in 1841, the emblems of the venerable dynasties were exhibited in La Salle des Croisades at Versailles, which by then had been turned into a museum. Nobody questioned their authenticity until October 1956, when Robert-Henri Bautier, an archivist, divulged in a lecture before the Académie des Inscriptions et Belles-Lettres that the coats of arms were spurious.

By chance I read Bautier's paper, and we met at a Latin Quarter café to talk about it. A slim, dark man in his thirties, who clearly relished genealogical detective work, he had obtained the Courtois documents from a Paris family, thinking that they would be useful for his studies of the Crusades. The more he pored over them, though, the more he was persuaded that they were phony. "*Mais quelles fraudes extraordinaires*—the work of a master!" he said. "Even though the script and language did not quite match the period, the parchment and seals were genuine." Investigating further, he learned that Courtois had been a convicted swindler and had mobilized a ring of counterfeiters to cash in on Louis-Philippe's plan. Among them was the insidious Vrain-Lucas, who accumulated a fortune foisting on the gullible such forgeries as Caesar's billets-doux to Cleopatra and a memo from Lazarus to Christ. Calling Bautier's revelations Black Friday for the nobility, the *Journal du Dimanche* headlined its story TITLE MARKET CRASHES. A few aristocrats mumbled about litigation—but most of them put on a brave veneer. "Even if my ancestors were not Crusaders," declared the Comte Emmanuel de las Cases, "we are still a great family."

Had the French monarchy endured, nouveau riche winegrowers, stockbrokers and textile magnates would have been elevated to the peerage, as were affluent English bankers, brewers and tea merchants. But the advent of the Third Republic in 1870 punctured their aspirations—though their bulging pocketbooks gained them entry into *le gratin*, whose snobs sneeringly captioned them *le gratin bien lavé*, the laundered upper crust. Soon they were part of *le tout Paris*.

$\mathcal{A}$s much as they still lamented France's humiliating defeat at Agincourt and denounced Perfidious Albion, upper-class Frenchmen went to strenuous lengths to pattern themselves after English gentlemen. Their paradigm was the immensely popular Prince of Wales, the future Edward VII, a frequent fin de siècle visitor to Paris. They borrowed such English sartorial styles as stiff collars, starched shirtfronts and tweeds for the country, either imported from Savile Row or ordered from the Paris branches of English haberdashers and tailors situated on the rue du Faubourg Saint-Honoré or the rue de Rivoli. The fussier among them shipped their dirty linen to London. Copying English swells, they parted their hair down the middle, wore mustaches rather than beards, and sported silk top hats, canes and monocles, usually made of plain glass. Their clubs bore franglais names, like Le Jockey, Le Travellers and Le Racing. They retained English coachmen to drive their carriages, English trainers to groom their horses, English nannies to care for their children. Many of them affected a lockjaw English accent and in good weather attended garden parties, an English institution, and their wives dutifully served *le fif' o'clock*—afternoon tea. But, while the English tended to be serious if not stodgy, the French subscribed to Voltaire's apothegm: "The pursuit of pleasure must be the goal of every rational person."

During the season, upper-crust Paris hostesses staged fabulous private banquets. Forty or fifty guests, carefully seated according to protocol, would dine at tables adorned with gigantic candelabra and huge floral arrangements. The silver and crystal were heirlooms, and the gargantuan menu might consist of fifteen courses: soup, fish, beef, venison, ham, duck, chicken, pheasant, assorted vegetables, several desserts and a half-dozen superb wines, including champagne. The requisite musicale afterward would prompt some of the men to flee to the drawing room for cigars and cognac—or to slip away to meet *une cocotte* at Maxim's.

Highbrow members of *le Monde* frequented weekly salons to debate classical drama, symbolist poetry or naturalistic novels with such literary lions as Anatole France, Alphonse Daudet, Stéphane Mallarmé and Émile Zola, the foremost *homme de lettres* of the period. Among the darlings of *le gratin* was Tristan Bernard, nicknamed "Bébé," a corpulent, bearded critic, playwright and gadfly noted for his bons mots. Once a theater doorman saw him sneaking out during the intermission. *"Mais cher maître,* there is still another act," the doorman remonstrated, to which Bernard responded, "And that is exactly why I'm leaving." Overwhelmingly anti-Semitic, the social nabobs believed that Captain Alfred Dreyfus had correctly been judged guilty of treason; still, they adored Bernard, who was also Jewish. During the Occupation he was deported to a concentration camp but survived to have a Paris square named for him.

Proust drew the characters for his masterpiece, *À la Recherche du Temps Perdu,* from Parisian high society. He partly based Swann on the magnetic playboy Charles Haas and modeled the haughty Baron de Charlus on the Comte Robert de Montesquiou-Fezensac. Lean and handsome, with wavy black hair and a chiseled nose, Montesquiou traced his ancestry back to the Merovingian kings, who ruled France from the fifth through the eighth centuries. His *hôtel particulier* on the rue Franklin was crammed with precious Persian carpets, Dresden porcelains and Japanese wood-block prints, of which he was a pioneer connoisseur, as well as such absurd mementos as the bullet that killed Pushkin, a chamber pot used by Napoleon at Waterloo and the butt of a cigarette smoked by George Sand. Housed in a glass atrium, his library was one of the most extensive in Paris. His closet contained clothes of every variety, including more than one hundred neckties. In a full-length portrait by his friend James McNeill Whistler, he holds an ivory-tipped cane in one hand and has a chinchilla cloak draped over his arm. An unabashed homosexual at a time when most gay men camouflaged their proclivities, he spoke only about himself in soliloquies punctuated with studied gestures, like tapping a glove on the toe of his shoe. His conversation, wrote a contemporary, was "very refined, very precise, very insignificant." He reveled in his arrogance. "The place of honor," he would say at dinner parties, "is wherever I sit."

If Montesquiou had an equal, it was the Comte Boniface de Castellane, or "Boni," the dapper scion of an ancient Provençal dynasty and a notable paladin of the boudoir. In 1894 he took a step that was then unusual for a French peer: he married an American heiress—Anna Gould, the daughter of Jay Gould, the railroad mogul. The Parisian elite gasped in horror at her ugliness, but she brought him a dowry of some fifteen million dollars, which enabled him to fulfill his fantasy of reliving the past. He would show up at costume balls ridiculously accoutred in doublet and hose, powdered wig, plumed hat and gold sword, and speak in the euphuistic idiom of the eighteenth century. Selecting a site near the Bois de Boulogne, he plundered Anna's coffers to construct the Palais Rose, a pink marble facsimile of the Grand Trianon at Versailles. He engaged hundreds of servants and threw lavish parties that Louis XIV would have envied. His wife tolerated his profligacy until, inevitably, he returned to his *petites amies*. Unaccustomed to Paris ways, she divorced him without a sou but, by now hooked on nobles, married a descendant of Talleyrand. Flat broke and forgotten, Boni ended his days selling antiques to prosperous foreigners.

Paralleling *le Monde* was *le demi-monde*—a galaxy of expensive courtesans variously known as *les dégrafées, les poules de luxes, les grandes cocottes* and, most explicitly, *les grandes horizontales*. More like geishas than ordinary prostitutes, they were shrewd, beautiful and entertaining. Many started out as seamstresses, shop assistants, chorus girls or artists' models, and, to mix a metaphor, climbed the ladder on their backs. At their peak they owned *hôtels particuliers* and country estates; some of them attached "de" to their names. In contrast to scarlet women in puritanical England or the United States, who were hidden from sight, they could be seen at opening nights at the Opéra, the polo matches at Bagatelle, and the procession of private calèches that paraded through the Bois de Boulogne every afternoon. Their liaisons, reported in lurid detail by the press, enthralled the public. They would never be admitted into the company of duchesses and countesses—nor did they expect to be—but they regularly consorted with dukes and counts. Bedecked in furs and jewels, they appeared night after night at their habitual haunts, Le Café Anglais, Le Café Riche, Le Café de la Paix and, above all, Maxim's, where wealthy playboys flung money and themselves at their feet.

Like Oriental concubines, ancien régime mistresses had been an integral part of the court. They had personal retinues and often, at ceremonies, even took precedence over wives. Emulating the king, their lovers acknowledged their children along with their wives'. But nineteenth-century demimondaines enjoyed no such rights. As individual entrepreneurs, they had to shift for themselves and rely only on their charm to conquer and hold their distinguished "protectors."

One of the most noted, Léonide LeBlanc, counted among her many lovers the aged Duc d'Aumale, the fifth son of Louis-Philippe and a towering figure of the time. Once, while traveling to Chantilly, his picture-book palace near Paris, she overheard three society matrons in the railway carriage boasting about their invitations to tea at the château. "And I, *mesdames*," she interrupted, "will be sleeping with *Son Altesse* this very night." Some *cocottes* imposed bizarre demands on their suitors. A Russian Jew who operated under the nom de guerre of La Paiva conceded to an assignation with a financier on condition that they burn twenty thousand-franc bills one by one during their session—but at the decisive moment, the sight of the cash going up in flames rendered him impotent.

The undisputed queens of the demimonde at the pinnacle of the belle époque were Liane de Pougy, Émilienne d'Alençon and Caroline Otéro. They—and others like them—soared to stardom, shone brightly and faded in tragedy.

Liane was playing in a skit at the Folies-Bergère when the Prince of Wales, who happened to be there, applauded her enthusiastically—and made her reputation overnight. She was deluged with gifts from admirers; one of them promised her one hundred thousand francs merely to disrobe for him. Jilted by a lover, she attempted, or perhaps feigned, suicide, which further magnified her romantic image. Suddenly she became a Dominican novitiate, then quit to resume her former life and subsequently wed a Moldavian prince. She remained married to him until his death twenty-five years later, when to atone for her sins she returned to the convent under the appropriate name of Sister Marie-Magdalene de la Pénitence.

A minor actress, Émilienne infatuated the Duc d'Uzès, a giddy teenager who would have squandered his inheritance on her had not his horrified family hustled him off to Africa, where he shortly succumbed to dysentery. Next she enchanted King Leopold of Belgium, an elderly lecher—a triumph that catapulted her into a string of other noble beds. Her lovers showered her with jewels; during a spat with one of them she threw a flawless pearl necklace he had just given her out the window. Eventually she became a heroin addict, renounced heterosexual relationships and died in solitude.

By far the most flamboyant *cocotte* of the era, La Belle Otéro was the bastard daughter of a Barcelona gypsy. She began dancing in local cafés and soon reached Paris, where her sensuous performances made her an immediate sensation. The Prince of Wales and Kaiser Wilhelm both extolled her; a French count constructed a sumptuous mansion for her off the Champs-Élysées. Her chief lover, a boorish German baron, would summon her to bed with a costly jewel. Vulgar, wily and greedy, she bilked millions from her series of paramours. She contended in a dubious autobiography that they fought duels over her and threatened suicide when she spurned them. A reckless gambler, she lost bundles at Monte Carlo until, down to her last centime, she had to pawn or auction off her possessions. She retired to a shabby apartment on the Côte d'Azur, the scene of her past extravagances, and was still residing there a decade after World War II. A French journalist who tracked her down concluded that, in her poignant seclusion, she symbolized the end of an era—and she did.

But a feature of France that never ceased to astonish me was its stubborn resistance to change. Two catastrophic wars, aggravated by economic strife and political turmoil, had eroded its class structure, and it was unimaginable that the old Paris upper crust could remain intact, much less recover. By the early 1950s, however, the snooty salons, dinner parties, château weekends, literary receptions, art galleries and fashion houses were glittering again—and, illuminated by their own brilliance, seemed destined to shine forever.

5

Names Make News

*C*elebrities were constantly popping up in Paris and, obeying *Time*'s doctrine that names made news, I pursued them. They left me with mixed feelings. I was bored stiff by those who automatically assumed that their prominence qualified them to pontificate on everything from child care to the stock market, race relations to global politics. But some of them could be unaffected, attractive and intelligent. I also got a charge out of impressing my parents back home with the illusion that I was chummy with the rich and famous—a fantasy that vicariously thrilled them and justified my living abroad.

Toward the end of 1954, I heard that Ernest Hemingway was staying at the Ritz, which he—with the assistance of the Allied armies—had "liberated" during the struggle for the city a decade earlier. The emblematic American in Paris and incarnation of the Lost Generation, he had recently won the Nobel Prize. I was aware that his wife, Mary Welsh, had been a *Life* reporter and, exploiting that connection, called her to request an interview with him. A day or two later she invited me over for drinks the next afternoon at the Ritz Bar, where he customarily held court. When I arrived, the bartender motioned me to a corner table, and soon Papa lumbered in. He was the spitting image of his Karsh portrait, his shaggy hair hanging over his wrinkled forehead, a grizzled beard shrouding his square chin, a charcoal turtleneck stretching across his barrel chest. Greeting me in a whiskey voice, he gripped my hand with the force of an iron vise, embarked on a series of Pernods and, propelled by my questions, carried on a monologue.

The Nobel Prize? "Oh, that little Swedish thing. Gave it to the mayor of Havana. Win medals, but don't wear them." Journalism? "I freelanced for newspapers before I turned to fiction. Learned a lot. Every reporter needs a built-in shit detector." The Americans in Paris during the twenties? Gertrude Stein was a pretentious egotist, Scott Fitzgerald had doubts about his virility, John Dos Passos squandered his talent. As he rattled on, I gradually felt that the icon of my youth had devolved into a caricature of himself, and my ears glazed over. After a while, visibly fatigued and slightly tipsy, he stumbled to the telephone, rang up his wife in their room and slurred, "For God's sake, come down here and rescue me."

$\mathcal{D}$espite their staunch commitment to republican principles, the French were captivated by royalty—or, more precisely, foreign royalty. Indeed, I often mused on whether they secretly yearned to jettison their bourgeois politicians and restore the Bourbons or Napoleon so that they might enjoy a bit of pomp and circumstance. Even though their motorcades paralyzed traffic for hours, visiting monarchs electrified Parisians, who delighted in displaying France's grandeur in spectacular banquets, parades, ceremonies and evenings at the opera. The daily papers, and especially the popular picture magazines, were packed with features on La Reine d'Angleterre, and, at the time of her kid sister's tormented romance with Captain Peter Townsend, devoted pages to *"les chagrins de la pauvre petite Princesse Margaret."* They went bonkers in 1956, when Grace Kelly wed Prince

Rainier of Monaco, a fairy-tale marriage that ideally linked a commoner with a dynasty that dated back a thousand years.

The French also provided asylum to banished potentates and a spectrum of lesser blue bloods. Ousted in 1952, Egypt's gross, repugnant King Farouk was permitted by the authorities to console himself in a clandestine Paris brothel; the dissolute Emperor Bao Dai of Vietnam, dethroned three years later, dipped into funds that France had granted him during his precarious reign to acquire a casino in Lyon. East European nobles fleeing Communist persecution streamed into the city; the former Russian archduke behind the wheel of a taxi, an enduring stereotype, nevertheless contained a kernel of truth.

In July 1954 I had a fleeting moment with the world's most illustrious aristocrat-in-exile. The Luce empire was then preparing to launch a new publication, *Sports Illustrated,* and to build up a backlog of material for the future, the editors detached me from *Time* to accompany the photographer Toni Frissell on a story about the upper crust summering on the Côte d'Azur. A snobbish New York socialite with gilt-edged contacts, she had arranged for us to cover the Duke and Duchess of Windsor. We wended our way along the coast from our hotel at Cannes to Cap d'Antibes, where their elegant villa was situated on a bluff overlooking the Mediterranean. The day was to be as melancholy as any as I can remember.

Formerly Edward VIII, the duke had forfeited his crown in 1936 for "the woman I love," as he declared in his abdication statement. And here was Wally, in a cotton frock, straw hat and sunglasses, stretched out on a chaise longue under a palm in a garden lush with bougainvillea, frangipani and peonies. Obviously the boss, she ordered David, as she called him, to serve us tea, and he humbly complied. Attired in a navy blue blazer, twill trousers, paisley ascot and suede shoes, the duke bore few traces of the once-handsome Prince of Wales; now, with his sagging jowls and puffy eyelids, he resembled an old poodle. The Windsors did nothing except lounge around, which seemed to me to be hardly worth recording, but Frissell, evidently persuaded that she had a sensational scoop, clicked away at them from dozens of angles. Before long the duke announced that he was departing for a round of golf and proposed that we ride along in his chauffeur-driven Bentley. We motored up the corniche to an exclusive club, where he joined three American multimillionaires. However much his regal glow may have faded, the duke still awed them. Whenever he muffed a shot, as he did repeatedly, they chorused, "Rotten luck, sir." I was alone with him when he hooked a ball into the rough. "Rotten luck, sir," I echoed. "Not you, too," he moaned. "I'm just an awful golfer."

The American movie studios were then flocking to Europe, where the powerful dollar enabled them to produce films for peanuts compared to the cost in the United States. To discourage its currency from leaving the country, the French government also prohibited them from repatriating the fat profits they had accumulated in France, and their only option was to use the blocked funds to shoot on location. As a result, Paris was crawling with Hollywood folk—Bing Crosby, Gene Kelly, Danny Kaye, Ingrid Bergman, Otto Preminger, Billy Wilder—some of whom occasionally furnished me with stories.

The neglected giant among them was Orson Welles, the movie industry's bad-boy genius. As a teenager back in the 1930s, I had been hypnotized by his Mercury Theatre radio dramas, in which he starred with such splendid actors as Joseph Cotten, Agnes Moorehead, George Coulouris, Everett Sloane and Ray Collins, whom he also cast in his screen masterpieces, *Citizen Kane* and *The Magnificent Ambersons*. Though the critics extolled his films, Hollywood rejected Welles as box-office poison. Later he escaped to Europe, where he directed innovative pictures, notably a visually daring adaptation of Shakespeare's *Othello*. Paris intellectuals, always ready to denounce the United States, described him as a victim of American capitalism. He reveled in the idolatry, but he was lonely and bitter and ventilated his grievances to anyone in sight.

Periodically I would drop into the Calvados, a comfortable bar around the corner from the George V hotel. One night I spotted Welles there, sitting by himself and gazing into a drink. He had the torso of a bear and the face of a cherub. Guessing that he might welcome companionship, I sidled onto a stool beside him, introduced myself and, trying not to sound unctuous, said that I had long been an admirer. He started talking in his familiar baritone, the words cascading from his lips in aphorisms.

"Your task, whether in the theater or in films, is to excite the audience," he said. "If that requires playing *Hamlet* on a trapeze or in an aquarium, no matter—you do it." He dismissed all the highbrow stuff about movies as art. "Perhaps the silent cinema could have become art, but the technicians never gave it a chance. Directing pictures is no more an art than, say, practicing journalism: you have a enormous public, you're under pressure to work fast and you can never work fast enough." Welles was gloomy about the future—or maybe about himself: "I rather think the cinema will die. Look at all the gimmicks they're contriving to keep it alive; yesterday color, today three-dimension, tomorrow some newfangled concoction. I don't give it another forty years." Movies were doomed, along with the entire concept of pleasure. "Witness, for instance, the decline of leisurely conversation. People no longer have the time or patience to listen, as they did in the eighteenth century. They're obsessed with being serious, afraid to be frivolous. The only authentic conversationalists left are the Irish, because modern technology has eluded them."

*I*n July 1953 I spent the better part of an afternoon with Audrey Hepburn in her suite at the Ritz—and for me it was a memorable if regrettably brief encounter. Recently turned twenty-four, she was in Paris to tout *Roman Holiday,* her first American picture, for which she had been awarded an Oscar. She had trained to be a ballerina and showed it—gliding into the salon as gracefully as Pavlova, even

doing a little pirouette. I presumed that her coquettish entrance was designed to dazzle me, since I represented *Time,* whose influence could make or break her reputation. Glancing at herself in the mantelpiece mirror, she gestured to me to sit beside her on a brocaded divan. She seemed to be thoroughly poised until she began to fiddle with her hair, fidget with her dress and fumble with her gold cigarette lighter; and I sensed that, for all her cool composure, she was as jittery as a kitten. Little did she realize that I was so smitten by her gossamer beauty that she could do no wrong.

Gradually she loosened up enough to reminisce about her life. Born outside Brussels to a British businessman and a Dutch baroness, she was sent to school in London after her parents divorced. When World War II broke out in 1939, she was vacationing with her mother in Holland. The Germans overran the country, she was stranded there and, like many other kids, ran errands for the Dutch underground. "Please don't write that I was a hero," she implored me. "It would mortify me if anyone who was actually in the Resistance read that. I only did what we all did—the patriotic thing."

After the war, she and her mother settled permanently in London, where she finished high school and went on to study ballet. Lithe and long-legged, she appealed to fashion photographers and became a top model. She also attended acting classes, exhibited potential and began to earn minor parts in British pictures. While shooting on the Côte d'Azur in 1951, she met Colette, the venerable author of *Gigi,* who was enchanted by her fragile, childlike charm and insisted that she be cast as the lead in the Broadway version of the novel. Her overnight success in the play won her the starring role opposite Gregory Peck in the movie *Roman Holiday,* and Paramount signed her up for another. Her contract authorized her to alternate between the theater and films, and she hoped to do both. "I don't know whether I am confused or flexible," she said. "When I'm making pictures, I can't wait until I get back to the stage, and after I've been on the stage for six or eight months, I can't wait until I get back to pictures."

By now, her dark eyes sparkling, she was relaxed and laughing. As she nattered away, however, it occurred to me that Audrey Hepburn was not just another pretty ingenue but clever, intensely ambitious and destined to succeed. Determined to avoid alienating anyone who might help her, she gushed over every movie name I mentioned. The directors, producers and actors she knew were all "wonderful" or "marvelous" or the epitome of fatuous Hollywood jargon: "real." Her priority was work. "Before I marry I want to lay the foundations of a career, and I'm at it around the clock." What did she do for fun? "I'm not much of a going-out person—I mean, I adore going out, though not too often. You need some distraction after a hard day." She conceded that she sometimes seemed to be cold and aloof: "Until I began acting I tended to babble at a mile a minute, and nobody could understand a thing I said. So I taught myself to enunciate clearly and distinctly and exercise self-control. Maybe that's why people take me for snooty, yet I'm really not." Then she added with a luminous smile, "Honestly, what do you think?"

I could have stayed with her for the rest of the day, prattling about one thing or another. But my infatuation was probably one-sided. I left, floated out of the hotel into the Place Vendôme—and never saw her again.

In April 1954 John Huston appeared in Paris. A former child actor, vaudevillian, prizefighter, Mexican cavalry officer, newspaperman, playwright and general roustabout, he had all the ingredients of a colorful story, but I was principally interested in his experience as Humphrey Bogart's director. They had worked together on five classics—among them *The Maltese Falcon, The Treasure of the Sierra Madre, Key Largo* and *The African Queen*—and had just finished *Beat the Devil* on location in Italy, which, it turned out, would be their last venture. I reached Huston, and he agreed to meet me late one afternoon in the George V bar.

While waiting for him, I nursed a Scotch and ogled the high-class hookers. Presently I spied him threading his way through the maze of tables. A lanky man with an angular, weathered face, he wore cowboy boots and a string tie, and was chomping on a stogie. He extended a callused hand, eased himself into a chair, ordered an Irish whiskey neat and asked what he could do for me. I told him that I wanted to pump him on Bogart, who was already becoming a cult figure. Houston nodded and started out in a slow drawl that gathered velocity as he went along.

"Making *Beat the Devil* was a nightmare," he said. "It's from a novel by an English friend of mine, Claude Cockburn, who signed it James Helvick. I bounced the idea off Bogey, who had his own production company, figuring that he could use it for a low-budget picture. Next thing you know, we're in Italy with Bogart, Robert Morley, Peter Lorre and a couple of million dollars involved—a lot of it Bogey's. We were at our wit's end. I had hired Truman Capote to write the scenario; he was getting nowhere and Bogart stood to lose a packet. 'Maybe we ought to scrap it,' I said to him. He just shrugged and replied, 'What the hell, John, it's only money.' That typifies him. He takes enormous, never tiny, risks. Go with him to the track, and he will bet ten bucks while everybody is betting hundreds; but when the stakes are really big, he's a high-flying gambler."

Puffing his cigar, Huston recalled Bogart's gamble on *The Maltese Falcon*. "Fate brought us together. Bogey was already in the major leagues, and I'd never directed a movie in my life. The part of Sam Spade was slated for George Raft, but Raft refused to do a B picture under a novice like me. Bogey was the only other possibility on the Warner lot. He didn't know me from Adam; still, he accepted. Or if he had any qualms, he didn't reveal them. Perhaps his intuition told him that everything would be okay. Anyway, he came on the set and immediately made me feel like I was the world's best director."

From then on they operated on trust. "Bogart is very practical, very instinctive," Huston continued. "He judges a script very quickly, and he's not selfish. We don't hold those nonsensical conferences where everyone shows off. I say to him, 'Wanna do something?' He answers, 'Yeah.' And off we go. In fifteen years he's never turned down one of my projects."

The bar was growing noisy with the pre-dinner crowd, but Huston seemed not to notice. He lit a fresh cigar, signaled to the waiter for a fresh round, then meandered on. "Bogey is your total pro. He has a knack for doing the right thing at the right time, speaking his line and turning at the exact moment. On some scenes I get tricky, and let him do something I would not permit any other actor: look through the camera and advise me. I've even asked him to coach an actor who's in trouble, and he will pitch right in. He'd make a superb director."

Lubricated by the booze, Huston was unstoppable. "Most of the actors I know are either apologizing for being actors or aggressive about it. Not Bogart. He doesn't sit around waiting for inspiration, and he won't discuss acting. For him it's a craft, as if he were a fine cabinetmaker, and he takes pride in it. Also, there's no arrogance or egotism in him; hard as it may be to believe, he even has a streak of humility. He shows up on the set punctually, learns his lines and is ready before everyone else. In 1942 we were filming *Across the Pacific,* and one night his wife of the time stabbed him in a dispute. What bothered him the next day wasn't the fight or the injury—it was only a scratch—but that he arrived late for work."

By now I was on my third drink, which emboldened me to remind Huston that he sounded like Bogart's press agent. He paused and, waving his cigar, recollected a snag during the making of *The African Queen,* costarring Katharine Hepburn. "Bogey doesn't often slip, but he did here. He was playing this mutt dominated by a spinster, and his macho temperament recoiled against it. From time to time he'd go into a sulk. We would have to stop shooting while he had a breather and buttoned himself back into the role."

A challenge, Huston explained, was inducing Bogart to travel. "I've got wanderlust. Hollywood to me is the pits. My goal is to make movies in the most remote spots possible. Bogey, by contrast, likes nothing more than staying at home with his family, his friends and his sailboat. He's not a coward; indeed, he can be very gutsy. It simply makes no sense to him to go to the ends of the earth. Once you've convinced him, though, he will endure all sorts of physical hardship. The heat and humidity were terrible when we were filming *The Treasure of the Sierra Madre* in Mexico, yet he never griped. He didn't complain in Africa, either—despite the snakes, flies, mosquitoes and danger of malaria. His formula for keeping healthy was to knock back three or four Scotch-and-sodas every night, and it worked. He never showed the slightest sign of disease. But deep down he was suffering. One day he snarled to me: 'You sonuvabitch, you like this godforsaken cesspool. I hate it.' "

Back in civilization, on the other hand, Bogart could be intolerable: "He's in the fanciest restaurant in town, and if the bacon and eggs aren't cooked just right, he'll fly into a rage."

Huston had recently proposed to Bogart that they go to Afghanistan and make a film based on Rudyard Kipling's *The Man Who Would Be King.* "Not the least damned interested," Bogart responded. "A very wise decision," Huston deviously concurred, then proceeded to tell Bogart the story. "Soon he was raising questions about it," Huston said, "and I knew I'd hooked him." They started to plan the picture but, for one reason or another, it never came off.

"What is he like off the screen?" I asked, to which Huston gave me a blunter answer than I expected. "Bogey is essentially very gentle, though he bends over backward to conceal it. Nobody I know is better at putting his worst foot forward. Alcohol brings out his wild side. He has the constitution of an ox, and he's not a certified dipsomaniac, but he loves to drink, and after a few he becomes extremely belligerent. It's no secret that several Hollywood and New York nightclubs refuse to admit him. He will attack people—complete strangers—savagely, yet never violently. Once, in some joint or other, he caused holy hell by snatching a girl's panda doll. Then, in the middle of the upheaval, he flipflops, apologizes profusely, smiles, shakes hands, pays damages, and everyone ends up making believe they're great friends. Everyone, that is, except Bogey."

Shortly before, Huston remembered, Bogart had gone on a gigantic bender in Paris. He and his wife, Lauren Bacall, both in their cups, were riding down the Champs-Élyseés in a horse-drawn coach. "Suddenly he jumped into the traffic and vanished for hours. The gendarmes searched everywhere and ultimately found him in some obscure part of town, offering flowers to a prostitute, but he dashed off before they could catch him. Subsequently they located him backstage at the Lido nightclub, plastered and attempting to squeeze into the chorus line. Those are the times when, as much as I worship him, I could slit his throat."

To the extent that anyone exercised any influence over Bogart, it was Bacall. "This is the first true marriage he has ever had," Huston said, "and he loves her profoundly. She isn't out to reform him, but she's given real meaning to his life; not an artificial artsy-fartsy grab at culture but a sincere inclination for the better things. Betty knows good painting, books and music, and she has widened his horizons.

I don't want to exaggerate; he's not about to plunge into Dante's *Inferno* or *Finnegans Wake*. Still, she has changed him. When the campaign for the presidency started in 1952, she backed Adlai Stevenson and Bogey championed Eisenhower. In November he voted for Stevenson. One evening a bunch of us were hanging around, undoubtedly drunk, and the talk got sentimental. Someone asked, 'Is there a moment in your life that you'd like to repeat?' Nobody spoke except Bogey, who remarked, 'When I was courting Betty.' "

It was well past eight as we left the bar and tottered through the bustling hotel lobby into the balmy Paris air. While we were waiting for separate taxis, Huston added a final word. "I forgot to say that Bogey is a natural athlete. Every afternoon following work, the English crew on *The African Queen* would stage a cricket match, and they invited him to participate. His skill astonished them, and they presented him with an autographed cricket bat. Chess, though, is the extracurricular activity he prefers. I can't imagine why, but he's one helluva chess player."

6

The Prince
of Gastronomes

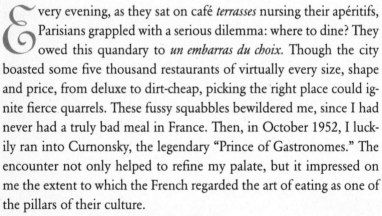

Every evening, as they sat on café *terrasses* nursing their apéritifs, Parisians grappled with a serious dilemma: where to dine? They owed this quandary to *un embarras du choix*. Though the city boasted some five thousand restaurants of virtually every size, shape and price, from deluxe to dirt-cheap, picking the right place could ignite fierce quarrels. These fussy squabbles bewildered me, since I had never had a truly bad meal in France. Then, in October 1952, I luckily ran into Curnonsky, the legendary "Prince of Gastronomes." The encounter not only helped to refine my palate, but it impressed on me the extent to which the French regarded the art of eating as one of the pillars of their culture.

At the time, France's foremost epicures were converging on Paris to commemorate Curnonsky's eightieth birthday; and, among the numerous tributes, eighty restaurants had awarded him a permanent reservation by affixing an engraved copper plaque over his favorite table. For me the events promised to be a unique chance to indulge my appetite. I contacted *Son Altesse*, and he cordially invited me to join him on one of his nocturnal culinary tours. Umpteen thousand calories later I concluded that I had the potential to become, if not a genuine gourmet, at least a creditable bon vivant.

I planned for the expedition by doing a bit of research on Curnonsky. The son of a prosperous landscape painter, he was born Maurice Edmond Saillant in Angers, the capital of the ancient province of Anjou, the fertile area in the Loire Valley. His ancestors, he was fond of claiming, included a saint and a monarchist guillotined during the Revolution. He enrolled in the Sorbonne, intending to study literature, but got caught up in *la vie de bohème,* pursued women and reputedly sired two illegitimate children. His devil-may-care manner prompted his classmates to nickname him "Cur Non"—Latin for "why not?" Early in the twentieth century France and Russia signed a mutual-defense treaty, trendy Parisians went Slavic and he added "sky" to the sobriquet; hence his nom de plume. At the outbreak of World War I in 1914, their suspicions aroused by his exotic pseudonym, the French gendarmes detained him as a suspected Bulgarian spy, and he gained his release only by exhibiting his proficiency in Latin Quarter slang.

His ambition was to become a journalist, and he began to contribute vignettes to the newspapers. The smart set praised his breezy style, their admiration animated him, and presently novels and short stories were rolling off his prolific pen. An urbane boulevardier and witty raconteur, he started to hobnob with belle époque literary lions like Colette, the Nobel-laureate author Maurice Maeterlinck and Georges Feydeau, whose risqué burlesques were all the rage. They would gather at such boisterous restaurants as Weber or Maxim's, on the rue Royale, or retreat to the bucolic Closerie des Lilas, where they read their works to each other or just gossiped. Unable to resist the lure of distant horizons, Curnonsky journeyed on a safari to Africa and subsequently roamed around Asia. He had always been *un bec fin* and, back in France, resolved to consecrate himself to gastronomy.

A confirmed bachelor, Curnonsky focused his inexhaustible energy on his career. He initially flourished after World War I, as the

French sought to forget the recent austerity and resume the good life. The tire company that put out *Le Guide Michelin* inducted him into its team of clandestine inspectors, whose ratings could determine the destiny of a restaurant. He also exerted enormous influence as editor of *Cuisine et Vins de France,* the culinary gospel. Along with a colleague, Marcel Rouff, he crisscrossed the provinces for nearly a decade, collecting anecdotes and more than thirty thousand recipes for their definitive *France Gastronomique,* which ultimately appeared in twenty-eight volumes late in the 1920s. Shortly before, polled by the daily *Paris-Soir,* some five thousand chefs, restaurateurs, hoteliers, gourmets and gourmands had unanimously voted to crown Curnonsky *"le prince des gastronomes."* From then on he was constantly in demand for dinners, inaugurations, wine tastings and other such functions. He could have exploited his position had he not been scrupulously honest; when a margarine manufacturer offered him a handsome fee to endorse oleo as a substitute for butter, he adamantly refused, saying, *"Il n'y a rien que remplace le beurre."*

A staggering array of food and wine *confréries* pervaded France, many of them rooted in medieval guilds or religious orders. One of their chief purposes was to publicize their local products—oysters, raspberries, morels, chanterelles, rare truffles and various kinds of charcuterie. They also operated as benevolent associations, or assembled simply for amusement. Some consisted of complicated hierarchies that reached from masters and fellows down to novices. Attired in gold-braided tunics, ermine-lined cloaks, jewel-studded lavalieres and plumed toques, they would file in stately procession into gargantuan feasts, at which they conferred medals on meritorious cooks, delivered lapidary speeches, explored the nuances of cookery, recited poetry, chanted hymns and prayed to patron saints. They idolized Curnonsky.

He headed the Académie des Écrivains Gastronomiques, a consortium of food chroniclers; the Académie Rabelais, whose members cataloged restaurants; and the Compagnons de la Bonne Table, which campaigned to beautify menus and dining rooms. In addition to presiding over the Déjeuner du Grand Perdreau, a luncheon for editors, he chaired sessions of the Chaîne des Rôtisseurs, a society dedicated to stimulating interest in grilled meat. He was a pivotal figure in the Club de la Casserole, a coterie of ragout enthusiasts, and in the Compagnie des Gentilhommes de la Gueule, a circle of culinary scholars. His other affiliations ranged from the Amis du Poisson, which concentrated on fish, to the Maîtres Cuisiniers de France, a brotherhood of professional chefs. He was also a leading knight of the Chevaliers du Tastevin, the august Burgundian wine fraternity.

But his pride was the Académie des Gastronomes, which he organized in 1928. Patterned on the prestigious Académie Française, it had forty seats, each bearing the symbolic title of an immortal gourmet, among them Epicurus, Virgilio Maro and the brilliant, cynical foreign minister of France under several regimes, Prince Charles-Maurice de Talleyrand-Périgord, a formidable voluptuary. Curnonsky assigned the seats to such friends as Rouff, Maeterlinck and the Marquis de Polignac, of the cognac family. He retained for himself the one named for his icon, Jean-Anthelme Brillat-Savarin.

The French had long been imbued with the belief that man, because of his superiority over all other creatures, was endowed with the gift to transform nature into pleasure. This conviction, which reflected the Cartesian vision of a universal human order predicated on reason, motivated them to design artificial gardens, formulate rigorous rules of etiquette and even conceive stringent codes for the conduct of amorous affairs—lest they succumb to irrational flights of passion. Their obsession with gastronomy evolved out of much the same impulse.

The Gauls domesticated boars and cultivated parsnips; and some anonymous Alsatian peasant conceived the technique of force-feeding geese, the clue to pâté de foie gras. Isolated on their remote estates, where one of their few distractions was eating, early French squires habitually consumed at a single meal mounds of pheasants, partridges and quail and giant slabs of beef, ham and mutton, in addition to puddings and compotes. In 1110, Louis VI, a fabulous trencherman appropriately called *Le Gros*, laid out Les Halles adjacent to his palace, to put its fish, meat and vegetable stalls within easy access of his kitchen, and before long it was the largest market in Europe. The oldest treatise on French cuisine, *Le Viander*, appeared about 1380 under the signature of Guillaume Tirel, chef to Charles VI. Dubbed Taillevent, for his elongated nose, he detailed methods of preparing swan, peacock, turtledove, stork, heron and even whale. His recipes relied heavily on clove, pepper, ginger, cumin, cardamom, cinnamon, coriander, mace, nutmeg, saffron and other spices brought back by the Crusaders from the Middle East. His tome remained the bible of French cooks until 1533, when Catherine de Médicis, the bride of Henri II, came to France with a retinue of Florentine chefs versed in more delicate fare. The contemporaneous Pierre de Ronsard composed an ode to lettuce. Some kings, fearing poison, did their own cooking; food was often the principal subject of conversation at court, where aristocrats competed against each other to contrive new dishes. A stupendous glutton, Louis XIV craved strawberries, peas, beans and especially asparagus, and commissioned Jean de la Quintinie to carve out a twenty-acre plot to raise them exclusively for him. At the king's behest, his official mistress, Madame de Maintenon, opened a school to instruct the daughters of noble families in the rudiments of cooking; they were obliged to wear blue ribbons—and *le cordon bleu* became synonymous with haute cuisine. In 1756, after capturing Minorca from Spain, the Duc Armand de Richelieu celebrated the triumph by creating a sauce that he labeled mayonnaise for the island's capital, Fort Mahón. Louis XVI bestowed his personal blessings on Antoine-Augustin Parmentier, a pharmacist who promoted the potato, which before then had been dismissed as pig fodder.

The fixation on eating well also filtered down to the humble. Mediterranean fishermen concocted bouillabaisse from the remains of their catch, and peasant stoves simmered with *la marmite perpetuelle,* a mishmash of leftovers. One evening I dined with a coal miner and his wife in the sooty town of Roubaix, in the north of France. They were shabbily dressed, and their house had neither central heating nor indoor plumbing, yet we ate a succulent cassoulet. I assumed that they were merely being hospitable, but not at all. "What is more important," my host asked me, "than good food and good wine?"

Nearly every Frenchman was familiar with the martyrdom of Fritz Karl Vatel, the chef and supervisor of the Prince of Condé's household at his château at Chantilly. In April 1671, charged with the awesome task of arranging a fête for the fastidious Louis XIV and an entourage of hundreds, he toiled for weeks. He set the tables with gleaming silver, carpeted the grounds with jonquils and illuminated the paths with lanterns. Then, suddenly, everything went wrong. Only two loads of fish arrived, there was not enough roast beef to feed the unexpectedly large crowd and, to make matters worse, clouds spoiled a fireworks display. Though Vatel was renowned for his poise, the catastrophe crushed him. "I am disgraced," he declared to his assistant. Then he locked himself in his room and ran his sword through his heart. Describing the tragedy in a letter to her daughter, Madame de Sévigné wrote, "You may imagine the horrible disorder that such a terrible misfortune caused." The king's courtiers expressed respect for Vatel's valor but blamed him for ruining the party.

Modern French cuisine originated with Brillat-Savarin, who inherited his aptitude for cooking from his mother, the inventor of *l'oreiller de la belle Aurore,* a flaky pie stuffed with meat, mushrooms and truffles. A lawyer by trade, he became a magistrate and, threatened by extremists during the Revolution, escaped to New York, where he resided for three years, working as a French teacher and violinist in a theater orchestra. Fascinated by American food, he later introduced roast turkey, corned beef and scrambled eggs to France. His interest in medicine inspired his *Physiologie du Goût*, which classified gastronomy as a science and was to remain a seminal work in the field.

The preeminent chef of his time—perhaps of all time—was Marie-Antoine Carême. Born into an impoverished Paris family in 1783, he was about to be committed to an orphanage when a pastry cook adopted him as an apprentice. He taught himself to read and write, and his boss, astounded by his inherent skills, encouraged him to study the architectural prints at the Bibliothèque Nationale. Carême used them as models for his pastries, which immediately became the talk of the town. Talleyrand engaged him to superintend his vast kitchen and, in 1814, took him to the Congress of Vienna, where his phenomenal dinners won key diplomatic concessions for France. During his twelve years under Talleyrand, Carême pioneered new sauces and garnishes, some four hundred soups and such spectacular constructions as colossal cakes mounted on gigantic pedestals. The art of cooking, he stressed in one of his essays, ranked with painting and music: "Our culinary combinations appeal to the sense of sight and color and, through their harmony, they are as seductive as sweet melodies." Convinced that he had been ordained to transmit the benefits of French cuisine to the rest of Europe, he served Czar Alexander I of Russia, the British prince regent, and finally, Baron Nathan Meyer de Rothschild, the London banker. He died in Paris at the age of forty-eight—"burned out by the flame of his genius and the charcoal of his roasting spit," as an admirer put it.

Monarchs, aristocrats and rich entrepreneurs everywhere in Europe were soon clamoring for French chefs. The most illustrious of them, Auguste Escoffier, administered the kitchen at the Carlton in London. He confected *cerises jubilé à la reine* for Queen Victoria's Diamond Jubilee in 1897, and created dishes to honor opera singers—like *pêche Melba* for the Australian soprano Nellie Melba and *soufflé Tetrazzini* for Luisa Tetrazzini, the Italian diva. Kaiser Wilhelm, who employed him, once complimented him on his talent, saying, "I may be the emperor of Germany, but you are the emperor of chefs."

One of Escoffier's aides in the pastry department was a bright young Vietnamese later known as Ho Chi Minh.

*B*efore embarking on Curnonsky's excursion, I consulted my dossier on the history of Paris restaurants. The earliest on record was started on the rue des Poulies near the Louvre in 1765 by a certain Boulanger, undoubtedly a baker. His fortifying dishes, he guaranteed, would cure, or *restaurer*, intestinal ailments, liver trouble and other complaints—thus the genesis of the term. Twenty years later Antoine de Beauvilliers, formerly steward to the Comte de Provence, the future Louis XVIII, opened La Grande Taverne de Londres on the rue de Richelieu. As its title implied, it resembled a traditional English tavern by providing both food and drink. Its success spawned imitators like Le Café Mécanique, named for its intricate system of pulleys and dumbwaiters, and La Galerie de Valois, where enlightened intellectuals congregated to debate the issues of the day. At first, however, few Parisians ate out. Common folk lacked the money, while the nobility and wealthy bourgeoisie maintained immense staffs capable of preparing splendid meals at home. But then the Revolution ravaged the upper crust, leaving scores of chefs idle; and several of them, known as *traiteurs*, founded restaurants. A coffee merchant bought Le Café de Chartres, which was concealed in the arcaded courtyard of the Palais-Royal, and sold it to Jean Véfour, who converted it into Le Grand Véfour. Its regulars were to range from Bonaparte and Josephine to Victor Hugo, Colette, Jean Cocteau and legions of French dignitaries.

By the turn of the nineteenth century, Paris counted more than five hundred restaurants, and they rapidly became an institution. The most popular of them were bargain bistros, a term of ambiguous etymology. According to one version, the uncouth Cossacks who rode into Paris with the Russian Army after Napoleon's downfall in 1815 would storm into cafés and demand instant attention by shouting "*bistro*"—Russian for "quick." Another interpretation was that the word stemmed from *bistreau,* a cheerful innkeeper. As the town expanded, restaurants pro-liferated. Patrician dandies and bourgeois playboys whooped it up with actors, actresses and pricey *cocottes* at Tortoni, La Maison d'Or, Le Café Riche and Le Café de Paris, on the boulevard des Italiens, and Le Café Anglais, with its notorious Chambre Seize. Ideological distinc-tions blurred at La Grille, where leftists and conservatives mingled over veal patties or pickled pork. An enterprising butcher named Pierre-Louis Duval launched an eatery called Le Bouillon, which provided the hoi polloi with inferior cuts of boiled beef—and was the precursor of the fast-food outlet. When France was compelled to cede Alsace-Lorraine to Germany following its defeat in the Franco-Prussian War of 1870–1871, Alsatian refugees flooded Paris, opened brasseries and bequeathed the city *choucroute garnie.*

Restaurants swiftly spread across the Seine to the Left Bank. Situ-ated on the quai de la Tournelle opposite Notre-Dame cathedral, the Tour d'Argent had been a sixteenth-century hostel before it was trans-formed into a restaurant in 1790. It was subsequently bought by Frédéric Delair, whose device for numbering his innovation, *canard au sang,* enabled him to identify precisely which duck was eaten when by luminaries like the maharajah of Jaipur, the emperor of Ethiopia, the president of Argentina and Charlie Chaplin. Another Left Bank landmark, Lapérouse, accommodated gentlemen with se-cluded salons decorated with risqué engravings and plush divans for their *dîners intimes* with compliant ladies—and dishes that pur-portedly stimulated the libido. At Brasserie Lipp, in Saint-Germain-des-Prés, politicians, bureaucrats and journalists would huddle on banquettes beneath beveled mirrors, consuming such *spécialités* as *cervelas rémoulade, tête de veau vinaigrette* and huge schooners of beer called *distingués.* The literati ate, drank and argued far into the night amid the foliage of La Closerie des Lilas, which also lured expatriate Russian revolutionaries, among them Lenin, who played chess when he was not conspiring.

Voguish Right Bank restaurants included Lucas-Carton, in the Place de la Madeleine, and Prunier, which carried the finest fish in Paris. The advent of the railway age spurred the erection of mammoth stations with turrets, clock towers and allegorical statues representing the cities on the line. Each had its restaurant—the most ostentatious of them, in the Gare de Lyon, ornamented with gilded panels, brocaded tapestries, precious bibelots and pastoral scenes of France. Called Le Train Bleu, it was the kind of place to which a proper husband might take his wife for their anniversary. But no respectable lady would dare be seen inside Maxim's, whose Art Nouveau interior was the nightly venue for *les grandes horizontales* and the millionaire noblemen and businessmen who kept them. Fueled by champagne, they went berserk—smashing glasses, juggling dishes, climbing onto tables, swaying from chandeliers, leaping into the fountains in the nearby Place de la Concorde. They flung money around with reckless abandon. James Gordon Bennett, the publisher of the Paris *Herald Tribune,* once handed a flower girl five hundred francs for a bunch of violets, while another American tossed out gold coins to the waiters as though they were pennies. For sheer profligacy, however, nobody matched the visiting Russian boyars; the Grand Duke Serge presented a courtesan with a twenty-thousand-franc pearl necklace neatly laid out on a platter of oysters. The doorman, Gérard, was able to retire to a château in the Pyrénées on his tips.

Severe food shortages crippled Parisians during the German occupation, and they were still suffering when I arrived in France two years after the Liberation. Milk, butter, bread and other staples were rationed, but the French ate remarkably well. They skimped on clothing and entertainment, and, with rents tightly controlled, spent a major percentage of their income on food. Some received parcels from their peasant families or patronized the thriving black market. Restaurants were consistently jammed, usually with men who lived in hotels or *chambres meublées* and dined alone at the same place at the same table with their own napkin.

As a student I shed about twenty pounds at *popotes,* the Latin Quarter's equivalent of the Bowery Mission, where the fare included watery cabbage or potato soup and a microscopic portion of mysterious meat. Out of pity for my ignorance, my French *copains* showed me bistros like Madame Antoine on the rue Vandamme, and Wadja, an artists' hangout in Montparnasse, whose *prix fixe* of *bifteck pommes frites,* with a small carafe of wine, ran to one hundred francs, roughly a half dollar. Regional restaurants—Alsatian, Auvergnat, Breton, Basque—were good buys. So were the Vietnamese, Chinese, North African and Greek spots clustered around the boulevard Saint-Michel. Sometimes I would grab a slice of pâté, a baguette and an éclair, and lunch on a bench in the Jardin du Luxembourg while watching kids playing under the rows of chestnut trees.

Soon I graduated to *"restaurants à nappes,"* so called for their table-cloths, which usually featured an economical plat du jour, like *lapin chasseur, boeuf bourguignon* or *raie au beurre noir.* I was partial to the *escalope de veau à la crème* and fruity house Beaujolais at La Chope Danton, on the boulevard Saint-Germain. Nearby, at Aux Charpentiers, formerly a canteen for carpenters, the clients shared long tables and the pot-au-feu. Occasionally I dropped into the Restaurant des Beaux-Arts, facing the famous school, for its *blanquette de veau* and *tarte tatin.* In the narrow, cobblestoned rue Servandoni, across from the hotel where I resided for years, Chez Louise served a reasonable *canard aux navets.* Late at night I might meander over to Les Halles, in Zola's phrase *"le ventre de Paris."* There, at Au Cochon d'Or or Au Chien Qui Fume, brawny porters in blue overalls packed the bar as slumming socialites wolfed down *soupe à l'oignon, pieds de cochons, boudin* and *andouillettes*—the kind of earthy food they would not dream of having at home.

Scanning menus improved my French. I discovered steak, from the elementary *bifteck* to *filet, bavette, tournedos, entrecôte* and fancy *chateaubriand.* They came dozens of ways—*grillé, au poivre, à la borde-laise* in wine and marrow sauce, or tartare. I learned the difference be-tween *agneau* and *mouton, porc* and *sanglier, lapin* and *lièvre, saucisson* and *saucisse, crevette* and *écrevisse, praire* and *palourde, langouste* and *homard.* My French buddies taught me food argot: *fromton* for *fro-mage, sardoches* for *sardines, pinard* for *vin rouge.* French butchers never discarded anything, and, overcoming my squeamishness, I acquired a weakness for such innards as tripe, sweetbreads, hearts and testicles, which were discreetly known as *cervelles basses.* It would have taken me a lifetime to sample France's three hundred cheeses, but I got to appreciate a few: Camembert, Brie, Livarot, Pont l'Évêque, Port-Salut, Saint-Nectaire, Reblochon, Muenster, Roquefort, Tomme de Savoie and the spectrum of chèvres. I salivated over desserts like *nè-gres en chemise,* a gooey compound of chestnut cream and crème fraîche, and a custard with the nauseating name of *pet de nonne,* or nun's fart. My French doctor, who held that health depended on diet, sternly warned me that *buccins* would irritate my kidneys. The word, I found in the dictionary, meant whelk—which I would have never touched anyway.

Gradually I elevated myself to better restaurants, like L'Escargot Montorgueil, which was esteemed for its snails, and Le Louis XIV, in the Place des Victoires, whose *carte* included a flawless *ris de veau en croûte.* I lived briefly in a quaint apartment around the corner from Chez Allard, a chic bistro on the rue Saint-André-des-Arts, where fashionable politicians and *vedettes du cinéma* could be seen relishing such *spécialités* as *coq au vin.* Often I went to Chez l'Ami Louis, an Art Deco spot near the Marais, for ortolans, game birds eaten head and all. Presumably to convey the impression that their chefs were peasant women adept at "real home cooking," numbers of bistros bore the names of females: Chez Catherine, Chez Jacqueline, Chez la Tante Mathilde or Chez la Mère Émilie. The busy bistros abutting Les Halles aux Vins, the wholesale wine market, coddled clients with hearty steaks and industrial quantities of red wine. I would drive out with *une amie* to the *guinguettes* along the Marne to eat *friture* and dance to accordion music. Or we would dine under the trees at cozy auberges that, in addition to their rural charm, let rooms by the hour.

The cuisine was unrivaled at three-star establishments like the Tour d'Argent, Lapérouse and Le Grand Véfour, but I tended to be intimidated by their snooty headwaiters and sommeliers. Pretending to be a sportswriter, however, I wangled an invitation to Maxim's for the glitzy gala held on the eve of the annual Arc de Triomphe horse race. There, amid its fin de siècle setting, I would freeload on *homard au whiskey* and *noisettes d'agneau Édouard VII*—oblivious to the French, English, American and Irish owners and trainers rambling on about stallions, sires, mares and bloodlines.

At seven-thirty on the appointed evening, my taxi pulled up to Curnonsky's building in a somber Right Bank district. I rode the antiquated cage elevator up three flights, and he greeted me with a firm handshake. As befitted his vocation, he was corpulent. He had a ruddy complexion, moist eyes, thin lips and a faint gray mustache beneath his large nose. Books, newspapers, and magazines cluttered his cramped apartment, its walls covered with menus, sketches, caricatures, framed diplomas attesting to his gastronomic expertise. A few of his disciples were present, among them Robert Courtine, the veteran food critic for *Le Monde,* who was widely touted as his dauphin. As Curnonsky chatted with the others, Courtine explained the prince's routine to me.

He ate only one full meal a day, always in a restaurant except when he was required to attend a function. Following dinner, he would work at his littered desk until dawn, then bathe, go to sleep, awake at three or four in the afternoon, breakfast on a boiled egg and a glass of warm milk, receive visitors and wait for his acolytes to appear for the nightly ritual. "He is industrious and very disciplined," Courtine said. "I envy his stamina."

Curnonsky decreed that our destination that evening was to be Chez Pierre, a small family-owned bistro behind the Palais-Royal, and that Courtine and I would accompany him. I had been there before—though never under such majestic circumstances. No sooner did Curnonsky enter than Pierre Nourrygat, *le patron,* rushed to greet him with a deference that bordered on servility; Madame Nourrygat, seated at *la caisse,* smiled proudly. A reverent hush fell over the room as the prince shuffled to his favorite table. Nobody had telephoned to announce him; customers occupied the table, and they were well into dinner. But the plaque behind the banquette was formal: "Reserved for Maurice Edmond Saillant Curnonsky, elected Prince of Gastronomes, defender of French cuisine and guest of honor at this establishment." Pierre courteously gestured to the clients, and they moved without a murmur of protest. Curnonsky was not ashamed to exercise his prerogatives. He squeezed into his throne, and Courtine and I sat down opposite him.

"To open I would recommend *le fricandeau,*" said Pierre, referring to a cold terrine of braised veal and bacon coated in aspic. "Is it fresh?" muttered Curnonsky. "Absolutely, made this morning," replied Pierre. "*Alors, le fricandeau,*" Curnonsky commanded. For the next course he contemplated *les quenelles de brochet mousseline* and *le turbot poché au beurre.* Finally he opted for *les quenelles.* Then, without hesitation, he selected *un gigot d'agneau aux flageolets.* Pierre automatically uncorked a couple of bottles of crisp Sancerre, which he would follow with an excellent Pommard.

The negotiations over, Curnonsky expounded on drinking: "*Un kir* beforehand but only *une larme de cassis.* Unless the occasion is special, just two wines at dinner, an everyday Chablis, Mâcon or Sancerre with the fish, a vintage Bordeaux or Burgundy with the meat, perhaps a fine cognac or calvados with coffee. By all means, shun what the Americans call *le coquetèle;* it is as subtle and pernicious as opium. Beware of those commercial apéritifs, for example Byrrh or Cinzano; *ce sont des produits chimiques!*"

As we dipped into the fricandeau, Curnonsky reminisced on his culinary education: "Until I was fourteen, I mainly ate to live. Then my parents hired *une bonne* named Marie, who led me across the threshold into gastronomic puberty. They entrusted her with the shopping, and she scoured the markets, smelling the vegetables, squeezing the fruit and examining the fish, meat and poultry with the authority of a government inspector. She had no qualms about haggling and always managed to get the freshest ingredients at the lowest prices. If she didn't stick to recipes it was because she couldn't read; what she knew about cooking had been handed down for generations. I would gaze in astonishment as she whipped up a sauce that melted in your mouth, or snatched *une tarte aux prunes* out of the oven at exactly the right moment. She converted my needs into delights, and taught me the doctrine that has guided me ever since: the secret to a really great meal is simplicity. Give me chicken bouillon, grilled sole, *une noix de veau aux carottes,* a Roquefort and a juicy peach—and you can keep those elaborate dinners that pass for *grande cuisine.*"

Curnonsky hastened to emphasize that simplicity had its limits. "Special dishes are advised for special activities, like making love. It is an indisputable fact that Catherine the Second of Russia bore a son nine months after a dinner of caviar and sturgeon with a certain Stolnikoff. Nor should we neglect *les truffes,* which make women more tender and men more gentle. Be careful not to drink too much champagne before the decisive act, or it may interfere with your performance, but you can drink as much as you wish afterward."

By now we were deep into our quenelles, and the prince into his days with his collaborator as they researched their *Larousse Gastronomique.* "You might say that we were gastronomads. We went everywhere—towns, villages and hamlets so small that they weren't even on the map. To find the best eating places in the provinces, you have to ask the the local doctors, priests, journalists and taxicab drivers. They took us to big restaurants, tiny bistros, little inns. We would taste dishes and accumulate recipes and food lore—like the tale of the jilted suitor from Nancy who attempted suicide by gorging himself with *pâté de faisan*, only to end up with a bad case of diarrhea; or the hundred-year-old Auvergnat who was too drunk on *marc* to attend the funeral of his teetotaling son. In some regions, peasants still skinned rabbits alive, on the archaic theory that it enhanced their flavor."

Stretching his memory back half a century, Curnonsky recalled his travels in China. "In Canton a rich Chinese mandarin invited me and several other Europeans aboard his palatial river barge. First he brought on the girls, one more exquisite than the other; I will leave that part to your imagination. Fearing that we could not handle Chinese food, he went to tremendous expense to propose two separate dinners, each of them sumptuous. I remember them as though it were yesterday. The French menu included pâté, fish, fowl, meat, cheeses, desserts, three kinds of wines and champagne. The Chinese repast ran from bird's nest and shark fin soups to spiced crab, lobster in shrimp sauce, steamed bass, chicken with almonds, sweet and pungent pork, lacquered duck, rice wine and a fiery sorghum liquor. We chose the Chinese meal, and it was delicious. I contend to this day that there are only two civilizations in the world, France and China—*la cuisine et la politesse!*"

Curnonsky had smoked between courses, and continued to puff at his Gauloises as we lingered over coffee and cognac. By about eleven-thirty the restaurant was empty and we rose to leave. "*Très bon, comme d'habitude. Je vous remercie,*" Curnonsky commented to Pierre, who beamed and answered, "*Mais non, monsieur, c'est moi qui vous remercie.*" As we stepped out into the brisk air, the prince took a breath and said to me, "*Vous savez,* after you have dined well, you know it but you don't feel it."

Two nights later Curnonsky took me and another of his faithful to Chez Pauline, a bistro also located near the Palais-Royal. Worshiped there as well, he was escorted to his reserved seat. Again it was

a superb meal, punctuated by Pauline's inestimable *compote de lièvre*. As the dinner progressed, I asked the prince to cite his preferred dishes; and, as I should have anticipated, he responded, "In the hands of a virtuoso, anything can be perfect." We discussed all the hoopla over his birthday, and he was not altogether happy: "*Bien sûr,* I am pleased by the honor, but I don't want to be confused with one of those Americans who vulgarly titles himself the sultan of chewing gum or the emperor of canned frankfurters."

The climax of the Curnonsky festival was to be a glittering banquet on Saturday evening in the main ballroom of the Hôtel Lutétia. More than one hundred guests were slated to attend, among them Antoine Pinay, the congenial French premier. As the date approached, chefs were busily crafting dishes with such appropriate names as *coquilles Saint-Jacques du prince* and *agneau pré-salé à la Curnonsky*. Extravagant messages were also swamping the host committee; one from a gourmet society in Dieppe read: "Cur is our Socrates, our Buddha, our Saint Paul." The newspapers, meanwhile, discerned in Curnonsky's gastronomic experience a manifestation of his patriotism. "He has showed us how to love France's pastures, vineyards, foods, recipes. . . ."

I chose a table at random, and found myself wedged in between a Deauville hotelier and a restaurateur from Dijon, and the talk inevitably revolved around food. We guessed that Curnonsky would have judged the dinner to be below his standards, which was normal, considering the number of mouths being fed: *pâté de bécasse, écrevisses à la nage, jambon braisé aux truffes* and a rather banal ice cream cake called *bombe glacée*. But I was amazed by the repertoire of eighty separate cheeses and even more overwhelmed by the red wine, a superlative 1947 Puligny Montrachet.

The string of accolades to Curnonsky began over coffee, liqueurs and cigars. Climbing to the podium, speaker after speaker exalted him in the best French rhetorical tradition. The prize for oratory should have been awarded to a rotund, red-faced figure from some provincial gourmet club. Clad in a cutaway coat and tricolor sash, he lifted his flute of champagne and declaimed in a vibrato voice: "It is not without profound emotion that I solemnly toast *notre cher confrère et ami,* whose heroic stomach has contributed so much to the advancement of France's glorious cuisine."

It was the last time I saw Curnonsky. Despite all his honors, he had been broke. His health, once so robust, was failing, and he had been forbidden everything but toast and milk. In 1956, depressed by the gloomy diet, he jumped to his death from his apartment window. Addressing a suicide note to a friend, he cautioned: "Avoid the left leg of the partridge, since it perches on that limb, which makes the blood circulation sluggish." Had I been delegated to draft his epitaph, I would have quoted Brillat-Savarin's dictum: "Tell me what you eat, and I will tell you who you are."

7

In Deepest
Beaujolais

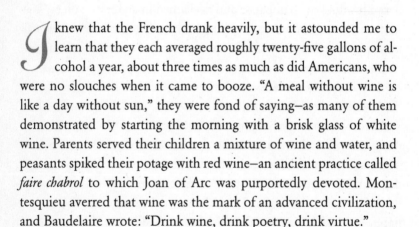

$\mathscr{I}$ knew that the French drank heavily, but it astounded me to learn that they each averaged roughly twenty-five gallons of alcohol a year, about three times as much as did Americans, who were no slouches when it came to booze. "A meal without wine is like a day without sun," they were fond of saying—as many of them demonstrated by starting the morning with a brisk glass of white wine. Parents served their children a mixture of wine and water, and peasants spiked their potage with red wine—an ancient practice called *faire chabrol* to which Joan of Arc was purportedly devoted. Montesquieu averred that wine was the mark of an advanced civilization, and Baudelaire wrote: "Drink wine, drink poetry, drink virtue."

The worst time to venture out on the highways was the middle of the afternoon, just after motorists had finished their bacchanalian lunches. Collisions were a perennial menace, but the gendarmes balked at arresting drunk drivers. Nor would the legislature enact a law to penalize offenders on the grounds that, while such a statute might save lives, it represented a grievous threat to liberty and the pursuit of happiness. So, as usual in France, individual freedom prevailed over civic responsibility. In reality, however, the French were seldom blotto—or, as they liked to quip, "Always faintly tipsy, never really intoxicated."

But several French medical researchers maintained that the nation would be healthier if it consumed even more alcohol. One of them, Dr. Gabriel Seynat, who by no coincidence owned a Bordeaux vineyard, asserted that the minerals and vitamins in wine "soothe the nerves, reduce fatigue, build up energy, strengthen muscles, stimulate the brain and induce a sort of euphoria that bolsters self-confidence." To accentuate his argument, he pointed to the splendid victories achieved by Napoleon's wine-sodden grenadiers. He also echoed Marshal Joffre's adage that the most effective weapon of the *poilus* during World War I had been *le pinard,* and suggested that France's sluggish conscript troops could be reinvigorated by doubling their daily ration to a liter. Seynat's idea elated the country's two million vintners and, in 1954, they lobbied the government to buy up the huge surpluses they had accumulated through state subsidies for distribution to the aged, the infirm and *"les économiquement faibles,"* the official term for the poor.

All this alarmed Pierre Mendès-France, the reformist premier. Revealing that cirrhosis of the liver, in addition to claiming sixteen thousand lives a year, was freighting French taxpayers with astronomical hospital costs, he launched a campaign to curb wine and set the example by publicizing himself drinking milk, a taste for which he had picked up during a stay in the United States. Among other programs, he announced a plan to furnish schools with free milk—thereby spurring a wave of protests. He was criticized by mothers, who firmly believed that milk caused *mal au foie,* a national affliction. His opponents accused him of pandering to the dairy interests of Normandy, his constituency; and patriots contended that, by assaulting wine, he was blemishing one of France's revered symbols. The ruckus delighted polemical Parisians and did nothing to discourage them from packing the city's countless cafés—like Chez

Fraysse, a minuscule *café-tabac* on the rue de Seine, not far from the École des Beaux-Arts.

I first went there late one afternoon with the fabled Paris photographer Robert Doisneau, who thrived on collecting local color. It was *l'heure de l'apéritif,* and the faithful—all male—hugged the zinc bar, chatting and nursing their wine amid dense clouds of Gauloise smoke. Albert Fraysse, *le patron,* a paunchy figure in his fifties, was a caricatural Frenchman with glazed eyes, a hint of mustache below his bulbous purple nose, and a charred cigarette butt stuck in the corner of his mouth. His wife, a dowdy woman with a scowling face, jealously guarded *la caisse* as Albert, a leather apron wrapped around his bulky waist, lumbered up and down behind the counter, filling and refilling glasses and occasionally sharing *une tournée.* He looked at me warily when Doisneau introduced us, as though he were pondering whether to admit me to his exclusive circle, and finally held out a damp hand. Doisneau ordered us *kirs,* the blend of *vin blanc* and cassis that immortalized its inventor, the epicurean Canon Félix Kir, the mayor of Dijon, doyen of the National Assembly and a certified Resistance hero. Then he steered me to a quiet table for a briefing on the café and its cast of characters.

Albert, he explained, had begun his career as *un valet de chambre* to a millionaire, migrated from his native Midi to Paris, where he married and, in 1928, sunk his modest savings into the Left Bank café. His life was humdrum apart from the periodic domestic crisis—like the time he sighed that he needed a break, procured a shotgun and cartridges, and vanished one morning to hunt rabbits. That night, over his *digestif,* a tactless client mentioned to Madame Fraysse that he could have sworn that he had seen her husband that very evening in a restaurant with *une jeune personne;* then, realizing his gaffe, swiftly added that she must have been "*une cousine.*" Albert never again went hunting, though he presumably continued his trysts; his towel, some regulars discreetly noticed, was invariably dry after his weekly excursion to the public baths.

France's two hundred thousand cafés—one for nearly every thirty adults—were an entrenched institution. In dreary provincial towns and villages, which shut down after dark, they were social centers for shopkeepers, peasants and bored adolescents. For Parisians *le café du coin* provided a convenient escape from their cramped apartments—places where they could gather with friends and colleagues for conversation, the national diversion. Cafés were venues for young lovers and illicit couples; pimps and prostitutes operated out of cafés. Books had been written, music composed and revolutions plotted in cafés. Many of them catered to distinct clienteles, for whom going elsewhere would have been treason. Or as the fin de siècle playwright Georges Courteline once observed, "A Frenchman may change his religion, but never his café."

The intelligentsia, genuine and counterfeit, assembled at Le Flore and the Deux Magots, in Saint-Germain-des-Prés, oblivious to the tourists craning their necks for a glimpse of "*les existentialistes.*" Another watering hole for the smart set was the snug bar of the nearby Hôtel Pont-Royale. Politicians and journalists with fat expense accounts met to swap information at Chez Lipp, a belle époque brasserie, also in Saint-Germain-des-Prés. Expatriate artists congregated at Le Sélect, Le Dôme, La Rotonde and La Coupole, on the boulevard du Montparnasse. Farther up the boulevard stood La Closerie des Lilas, a rendezvous for the upper crust. Sorbonne students loafed on the terrace of Chez Dupont, in the Latin Quarter; playboys, couturiers, mannequins, aspiring actresses and demimondaines on the make frequented chic powder boxes on the streets off the Champs-Élysées. The rich sipped whiskey *sur les rocks* and champagne cocktails in the bars of such fashionable hotels as the Crillon, the Ritz and the Bristol, while, in the sooty industrial suburbs, workers spent their evenings playing *belote* at *le plus proche,* the neighborhood pub.

By contrast, Albert attracted a mixed crowd, chiefly from the *quartier*. A carpenter or garage mechanic in overalls might rub elbows with a professor or an architect in a double-breasted suit. As we sipped our *kirs*, Doisneau identified Roland Philippe, a hardware salesman, standing next to Jacques Valence de la Minardière, a tweedy minor aristocrat who bred racehorses—and ill-advisedly bet on them. In an effort to instill a spirit of camaraderie in his customers, Albert had commissioned Georges Bouisset, an impecunious housepainter of dubious talent, to brighten a dingy salon in the rear with a garish mural titled *Les Compagnons du Chez Fraysse*. But the only bond that unified his clients was their dedication to his fruity Beaujolais.

The year before, to reward them for their fidelity, Albert had proposed that they accompany him to the Beaujolais to help him choose his wines. Not only would it be a pilgrimage to the source of their inspiration, but he would benefit from their opinion rather than relying solely on his wholesaler. They happily organized a motorcade and spent a weekend rollicking around a half-dozen vineyards. Three of the five cars in the cortège sustained slight accidents; still, they hailed the trip as *"un grand succès"* and the start of *"une grande tradition"* that would have to be repeated. Through Doisneau they asked me to join them on their next journey, a kindly invitation, considering that I was, as an American, a Philistine by definition.

American tourists flush with powerful dollars were then beginning to invade France, and many treated wine like beer. One group, after essaying a rare Vosne-Romanée, reportedly washed out their mouths with Coca-Cola—which at the time was making its debut in France. There were also poseurs, with their vocabulary of fatuous wine jargon. But French experts esteemed American connoisseurs. Thomas Jefferson, they recalled, had treasured Château Haut-Brion and transported a shipload of it back with him to Monticello, his mansion in Virginia, when he left his post as minister to Paris. In 1935 the New York banker Clarence Dillon had bought the famous

Bordeaux estate and bequeathed it to his son Douglas, who subsequently became the United States ambassador to France. Following World War II a consortium of millionaire Americans, including David Rockefeller, invested in Château Lascombes, another venerable Bordeaux vineyard. One of the world's most respected authorities on French wines, Alexis Lichine, was an American.

In preparation for our junket I boned up on the Beaujolais, a narrow corridor about thirty-five miles wide and seven miles long, which comprised some sixty million acres astride the Saône River. Ranging in size from two to twenty-five acres, the region's four thousand vineyards had been meticulously manicured for centuries, often by the same family, and were more valuable than Paris real estate. The granite soil and Gamay grapes magically combined to yield about one hundred million bottles a year, predominantly red. Beaujolais is at its best when very young—a trait that, during the early 1950s, prompted dynamic entrepreneurs to promote Beaujolais *nouveau*. They hired press agents, pretty models, film stars and other entertainers, and extravagantly touted the wine in France and overseas. The arrival of *nouveau* was advertised as a major annual event, and the craze quickly caught on. It bore no relation to the days before World War II, when Beaujolais had had a limited audience. Vintners would bottle a small fraction for themselves and their friends and sell the remainder in barrels to *négociants,* who shipped vast quantities to Lyon, the magnificent gastronomic center to the south, where, as the maxim went, "Three rivers bathe the city: the Rhône, the Saône and the Beaujolais." So abundant was Beaujolais in Lyon then that, Lichine noted in his classic *Wines of France,* a quart *pot* fetched fifty centimes—the price of a pack of cigarettes.

The pride of the Beaujolais was its nine *crus,* or growths: Saint-Amour, Chenas, Moulin-à-Vent, Chiroubles, Fleurie, Morgon, Brouilly, Côtes de Brouilly and Juliénas, named in honor of Julius Caesar. The area's different communes also produced the less distinguished

Beaujolais-Villages. All, aside from simple Beaujolais, were designated *appellations controlées,* a complex protocol based on geography as well as their alcohol content, which endowed them with durability. Nobody ranked them as exceptional; but they were comparable to *les petits* Bordeaux. Eventually Beaujolais became one of the world's most popular wines, featured on dinner tables from Alaska to Zanzibar.

Nothing infuriated Albert's acolytes more than to hear oenologists denigrate Beaujolais as inconsequent tipple. They were equally incensed by depictions of Beaujolais as just an adjunct of Burgundy. "The Beaujolais," one of them told me in an explosion of viticultural chauvinism, "is independent and indivisible—and one of the loveliest spots in the world. First God created the Garden of Eden, then the Beaujolais."

Brimming with excitement, our expedition convened at Chez Fraysse on a gray, chilly Saturday morning in December. The members were variously dressed—some, like myself, in jackets and sports shirts, others in coats and ties. We exchanged ritual handshakes, opted for either warm croissants and *café noir* laced with calvados, or *un coup de blanc pour la route.* They checked to make sure that they had not forgotten their *tastevins* or, for a few, stomach pills. Maurice Tutovich, a normally robust plumber, telephoned at the last minute to withdraw owing to a sudden *crise de foie.* Albert had mapped out our itinerary and warned that, with barely two days at our disposal, we would be lucky to cover Fleurie, Brouilly and Côtes de Brouilly. He entrusted the café to his wife and daughter, and, within the hour, our cavalcade of six vehicles—my midget Peugeot among them—had rounded the Place d'Italie, passed the Porte d'Italie and was cruising southeast on Route Nationale 6, the archaic and congested artery that connected Paris to the Côte d'Azur.

As we crawled through the wintry landscape, I concluded that we were not about to smash any speed records. It was well after noon when we reached Saulieu, a medieval town on the Burgundy border, where we filed into Le Relais Rabelais for what they regarded as a standard lunch—*charcuterie assortie, quenelles de brochet, gigot aux flageolets, pommes frites, salade, le plateau de fromages* and thick black coffee, paralleled by enormous amounts of crisp Sancerre and fresh Brouilly. Out of force of habit, Albert unsteadily clambered to his feet, brushed aside the waiters and demanded to pour the wine himself. By four o'clock, the table was heaped high with empty plates and bottles, and we groggily resumed our voyage.

Two hours later we pulled into Mâcon, the gateway to the Beaujolais. We halted briefly to assuage our thirst at Le Rocher de Cancale, a pedestrian hostelry on the banks of the Saône. Doisneau and I prudently ordered Perrier, but the sturdier among us could not forgo *encore un coup*. Soon we were inching our way through the late-afternoon mist into the Beaujolais—a picture-postcard panorama of fertile fields and rolling hills, church spires rising above stone hamlets, peasants attired in berets, smocks and sabots, their wives in ankle-length black skirts and veils. During the 1930s, fascinated by its Arcadian charm, several Parisian writers and artists had founded a utopian colony there. One of them, Gabriel Chevalier, captured the bittersweet mood of village life in *Clochemerle*, which was to be made into a movie in 1958 starring Fernandel, the great comic actor.

Under Albert's direction we zigzagged for fifteen miles through a skein of back roads to Fleurie, a town of nine hundred souls, all of them associated with wine. After much difficulty we located the Château des Labourons, which was less impressive than its name. Formerly one of the district's most reputable properties, it belonged to Bernard de Lescure, an engineer who had recently inherited it from an uncle, along with a pile of problems. It had been neglected for decades; he was deep in debt; and, worse still, the cool, rainy summer had damaged his latest crop. Fleurie was a favorite at Chez Fraysse, however, and Albert bid for an earlier vintage. Unfortunately, Lescure had reserved most of it for himself and his friends,

and could spare only a thousand bottles. "*Mieux que rien,*" Albert mumbled. As is customary in wine deals, the transaction was consummated on a handshake and the tacit understanding that Albert would ultimately receive the bill.

Before our departure, Lescure disappeared and returned with an illegibly labeled bottle. "Taste this," he said, dispensing some of it into each of our *tastevins*. It was a 1947, a memorable year, *en principe* a bit old for a Fleurie—but still superb. A unanimous murmur of approbation went up from our party. We drifted into the bracing night air, staggered to the edge of the road for a leak, climbed into our cars and floated off.

Jacques de Valence, the horse breeder, had generously arranged for us to sleep at his ancestral château close to Roanne, a factory town west of the Beaujolais. Getting there meant a detour, but it was free lodging and might be amusing. The family were *hobereaux de province,* rural aristocrats, many of whom enjoyed more status than money. They proudly traced their lineage back to the thirteenth century and had, like the rest of the nobility, suffered during the turmoil of the French Revolution. Repeatedly attacked, burned and demolished, the château had been reconstructed in a jumble of incongruous styles, from Romanesque arches to neo-Gothic turrets. We were cordially welcomed by Jacques's brother, Count Guy de Valence, who lived there permanently. Jacques had described him to me in Franglais as "*un gentleman farmer,*" and he fit the image precisely in his checkered shirt, corduroy trousers, tattersall Irish cap and Wellingtons.

We trailed Guy into his cellar, where he gave us each a glass of wine siphoned from a barrel. It was *primeur,* or new—and abominable. As guests, however, we were required to be courteous, and Albert tactfully predicted, "I assure you, it *will* be good." We politely concurred and repaired to a buffet much too skimpy to absorb our day's consumption of wine. Then, retiring to a low-beamed den, its walls blanketed with medals, antique guns, animal heads, stuffed birds and other trophies, we sank into heavy couches before a roaring fire. Guy circulated *marc,* a high-octane liquor distilled from the debris of crushed grapes. The discussion of course fastened on wine, the only topic we had in common. Chronic cranks—or perfectionists—my fellow travelers deplored everything from the traffic in fraudulent wines to the big chains that undersold individual merchants. Albert lamented the foul weather. I dozed.

It was well after midnight when we wearily ascended the stairs. The bedrooms were as icy as igloos, but, as a form of antifreeze, Guy had thoughtfully placed pitchers of *marc* on our night tables. We were down at about seven-thirty in the morning for a breakfast of bread, butter, compote, ham, salami—and, of course, wine. For reasons that bewildered me, my request for café au lait seemed to inconvenience our host. An hour later we were at La Grande Grange, owned by Henri Chamussy, a wealthy textile manufacturer who shuttled back and forth between the Beaujolais and his plant in Lille, and produced wine as a hobby.

A corpulent man with an amiable disposition, he puffed a pipe as he squired us around. He turned out between fifty and sixty thousand bottles a year under scientific conditions in a cellar that resembled a laboratory. To hasten fermentation, he filtered his wine through infrared tubes and stored it in giant, glass-lined *cuves.* A web of stainless-steel machines sterilized, filled and labeled bottles; but despite his technological innovations, he clung to an antiquated superstition and would bottle his wine only once a month, as the moon was waning. "I don't know why," Chamussy replied when I asked him. "It has always been done that way, and I suppose it always will be."

We sampled his wine, pronounced it worthy, and Albert purchased a thousand bottles. Chamussy then showed us his personal *cave*, which held four rows of barrels, or *pièces*—enough, he mused, for his own daily three or four bottles.

By now it was almost eleven o'clock. As we wobbled through a drizzle to our cars, Maximilien Vox, a member of our band, burst into a dance, declaiming, "It's beautiful! Nowhere else on earth would twenty or thirty men go as far as we have for a glass of wine. '*Seulement en France! Quelle sincérité! Quelle franchise! Comme c'est beau!*'" Doisneau cautioned me that he was an awful windbag, and to expect to hear more from him—as we did.

Our appetites whetted by the wine, we were starving. But Albert had scheduled a visit to the Château des Tours in Brouilly, a vital region for his clients. They drank mostly at bars rather than at meals, and preferred a relatively light Beaujolais like Brouilly, which did not have to be sponged up by food.

Shortly after our arrival, the scholarly proprietor, Jean Marduel, treated us to an interminable lecture on the history of wine that began with the Phoenicians, the Greeks, the Romans and the Gauls, and segued into the drinking habits at the court of Versailles. He propounded a theory I had never heard: that the Crusaders had trekked to the Middle East not to search for the Holy Grail but in quest of new varieties of grapes—and there discovered Gamay, a staple of Beaujolais. His vineyard, he estimated, was the oldest in the district, reaching back to the reign of Charles the Bald in the ninth century. One of the few Brouilly vintners to export to the United States, he labeled approximately sixteen thousand bottles in English.

Marduel brought out all his reds, year by year, and decanted them for our appraisal. Then he recommended his *blanc*, but Albert's brood had a peculiar prejudice against whites, apart from a super

Sancerre or Chablis. They rejected his *rosé*, not a wine for he-men. As one of them laughed, "*Le rosé* is for ladies—*pas sérieux.*"

After emptying our bladders at a nearby hedge, we drove down a gentle terrain of vine-covered slopes to the valley of the Saône. Our destination was La Maison du Beaujolais, one of those places scattered across France, designed and managed by local chambers of commerce to champion regional specialties. It was decorated in faux rustic, with stands in the lobby featuring such souvenirs as emblems, banners and bumper stickers, miniature wine bottles, key rings in the shape of clustered grapes, corkscrews with handles carved out of gnarled vine roots. Not exactly celebrated, *la cuisine Beaujolaise* tends to be crude peasant fare. We were famished, though, and stormed into *la salle à manger.* There the pièce de résistance was *andouillette,* an aromatic sausage concocted from pig tripe, calf membranes and other esoteric innards cooked in pork grease and dosed with a variety of spices. The party grew increasingly boisterous as more and more wine flowed. One of our companions, who tried to keep score, calculated that altogether we must have polished off at least thirty-seven bottles. His vocal chords thus oiled, the appropriately named Monsieur Vox improvised a postprandial toast in emotional cadenzas, extolling the glories of France, its literature, theater, art, republican values and virtually everything else but the valiant defense of Verdun against the Boches.

Our final target, the Château de Thivin, was nestled in a hillside overlooking the Saône, in the Côtes de Brouilly. Though saturated by the liquid lunch, we could not resist one last fling. Claude Geoffray, the owner, escorted us into his cave and along an aisle lined with thirty-five immense *tonneaux.* He tapped them one by one, and handed the *tastevin* to Albert, who frowned and said, "There have been better years." Albert shuffled back to the twelfth barrel, sipped again, meditated for a moment and asked us for our verdict. We each had a swig, nodded assent, and he said to Geoffray, "Give me three hundred cases."

As our expedition wound down, it occurred to me that Albert's habitués had never raised their pinkies, swirled their glasses or judiciously held them up to the light for examination. They smoked ceaselessly and swallowed their wine in a gulp or two instead of sniffing it, rolling it around their tongues and spitting it out, as professionals supposedly did. Nor did they resort to any of those precious adjectives cherished by snobs, such as "naive," "diffident," "presumptuous," "frivolous" or "ephemeral." Trusting their instinct, they knew what they liked and liked what they knew—but their expertise was formidable.

Luckily we emerged from the Beaujolais without so much as a crumpled fender. Prior to driving back to Paris we had consulted *Le Guide Michelin* and decided to dine at Le Cerf Volant, in Auxerre. As I entered the restaurant, I spied Albert, a napkin tucked into his collar, ordering bouillon, a grilled *bifteck*—and a large bottle of Vichy. No wine? "*Surtout pas*," Albert insisted. No sooner did he break a crust of bread, however, than he weakened, beckoned the waiter and growled, "A Côte de Brouilly—but just one."

After a single taste, Albert recognized the vineyard and purred approvingly, "Chez Geoffray." "You're certain?" we challenged, and summoned the sommelier, who confirmed the wine's origin. "Bravo!" exclaimed one of our members as we applauded. Shrugging, Albert muttered the Gallic equivalent of "Aw, shucks"—"*Mais, voyons. . . .*"

8

Crime and Justice

⟨ornament⟩

The French press was glutted with crime news, graphically crafted by writers who, fancying themselves to be potential novelists, rarely allowed the truth to cloud their imagination. I browsed through their accounts every morning over my café au lait and clipped the best of them as source material for my own stories. They were invaluable for the insights they provided into a subject that preoccupied me: the differences between the United States and France. As befitted a dynamic industrial society, the American underworld was highly organized. Murder Incorporated and the Mafia operated as gigantic enterprises, and such racketeers as Al Capone and Bugsy Siegel were, in their way, big businessmen. The conquest of the West had also left a legacy of violence that was reflected in armed desperadoes like John Dillinger and Pretty Boy Floyd. But except for the small-bore Corsican gangsters involved in prostitution and narcotics smuggling, the French tended to commit felonies less for profit than to settle personal grudges. In short, they were still back in the era of the poniard. That obsolete quality enchanted me, and I seldom missed a chance to cover a case.

In August 1952, for example, I was driving down to the Côte d'Azur and stopped in the lovely old town of Nîmes to visit its famous Roman ruins. That evening I was sipping a Pernod at an outdoor café when the *patron* mentioned with dismay that a woman had just been arrested for setting fire to the Théâtre Municipal, which had been erected in 1798 and was, he boasted, *"un monument historique."* In addition to performances by its permanent company, it featured touring troupes—among them, recently, Sidney Bechet in a concert of *le jazz hot.* After dinner, with nothing more exciting to do, I strolled over to gaze at the town's pride; all that stood were four charred walls and its neoclassical columns. Arson ranked low on the agenda of French crime, and, out of curiosity, I explored the incident further.

I knew from my travels around the provinces that I could always rely on the local newspapermen, and the next morning I located one who was on the story. Welcoming me cordially as *"mon cher confrère américain,"* he invited me to accompany him to the police headquarters. At the end of the afternoon we repaired to a café, where, with the help of a couple of thirsty gendarmes, we stitched together a credible narrative in which we facetiously proposed that the Théâtre Municipal might be renamed the Opéra-Comique.

The woman under arrest, one Éva Closset, was a former prima donna of ambiguous age who had been bombarding opera directors throughout France with letters touting her young protégé, José Faes, as the new Caruso. Finally she heard from Francis Lenzi, the manager of the Nîmes opera, who had a vacancy. Soon José was singing in the chorus of Halévy's *La Juive,* and went on to Massenet's *Manon* and Bizet's *Les Pêcheurs de Perles.* He dreamt of stardom until Lenzi began to detect sour notes coming from his direction. Nîmes was not exactly La Scala, but the maestro had standards to maintain and politely dismissed José with a handshake and a goodwill bonus.

Within an hour Éva stormed into Lenzi's office, begging him to grant José another audition. "But he is completely without talent," the director protested. "He sounds like a cross between a duck and a frog." Éva pleaded, and Lenzi acquiesced. With that she flung open the door and José, who had been eavesdropping, barged in with a Puccini aria on his lips. The first notes confirmed Lenzi's original judgment. "No pitch, no caliber, *rien—zéro,*" he said. "If I am not appreciated here, I'll go elsewhere," blustered José, and stalked out.

Late that night, braced by a stiff cognac, Éva returned to the closed theater, carrying a bottle of the alcohol she used to fuel the tiny stove in her shabby hotel room. She assured the watchman that she was simply collecting José's belongings, crept backstage, doused the scenery, applied a match and scurried out. It took the sweating firemen four hours to extinguish the blaze.

At first the detectives encountered only shrugs. Then they received an anonymous letter. "The fire is a woman's revenge," it said, depicting how it had been started. Éva had written the letter in a perverse effort to call attention to herself and was promptly hustled off to the police station. Summoned to identify her, José melted in tears. Éva threw her arms around him, sniveling, "I did it for you, *mon chéri, mon seul amour.*" José growled, "You've ruined my career."

My dispatch made four paragraphs in *Time.* Subsequently I learned that Éva had been sentenced to two years in jail, where she was teaching arias to her fellow inmates.

I never ceased to be intrigued by the way *crimes passionnels* spellbound the French. They worshiped reason and cherished moderation as the traits that made humans superior to animals. But they would drool over the sight of wives, husbands, mistresses and lovers enmeshed in sordid imbroglios, as though these tragedies were real-life theater. On the principle that man was innately imperfect, the press and the public invariably sided with the defendant, who could thus anticipate leniency from judges and jurors. A case in point was *l'affaire Chevallier,* which was hyped up as one of the most sensational in the annals of French jurisprudence.

The drama began in August 1951 in the charming Loire Valley town of Orléans. Then forty-three, its energetic mayor, Dr. Pierre Chevallier, seemed to be destined for a brilliant political future. His heroic record in the Underground had earned him a seat in the National Assembly, where despite its size, his little splinter party, the Union Démocratique et Socialiste de la Résistance, played a pivotal role in the formation of coalition governments. He had just been elevated to his first cabinet post and, returning home from Paris late that night, ecstatically announced the news to his wife, Yvonne. But instead of sharing his enthusiasm, she revived their long-standing squabble over his liaison with Jeannette, the redheaded wife of Léon Perreau, their neighbor. The next morning, still embittered, Yvonne reminded Chevallier that they had been married for twelve years and implored him on bended knee to abandon his paramour—if not for her, at least for the sake of their two sons. He contemptuously repulsed her, whereupon she fished a pistol from a closet, pumped four bullets into him, left her sons in the care of the concierge, went to the police station and confessed.

Yvonne's ordeal from then on illustrated the peculiarities of France's legal process. Based on the Napoleonic code, which had been designed to protect a dictatorship, its essential purpose was to enforce order. For the French, consequently, the concept of an independent judiciary was totally alien. As bureaucrats appointed by the state, judges were expected to serve the state; or, as a Paris attorney explained to me, "The objective of our courts is to convict the guilty, not to acquit the innocent." The pillar of English common law, habeas corpus, was also unknown—an Anglo-Saxon eccentricity. Anyone could thus be held indefinitely—just as, under the ancien régime, the king had only to issue a *lettre de cachet* to have a dissident incarcerated. The bail system existed on paper but, without bondsmen to extend credit, it was a fiction. So a suspect's fate hinged on *juges d'instruction,* investigating magistrates whose function it was to determine whether the evidence merited a trial. Invariably they were young, inexperienced and underpaid, and often lacked a car, even a telephone. They regularly colluded with the police, who in their zeal to bring in indictments counted on shady informers. Yvonne was to languish in jail for more than a year while her *juge d'instruction* conducted his inquiries.

As her trial approached, the French press plunged into a feeding frenzy. Reporters, psychologists, sociologists, criminologists and other commentators advanced an array of theses on the Chevalliers' relationship. Characteristically, in class-conscious France, much was made of their divergent backgrounds: she a peasant's daughter, he the scion of an illustrious dynasty. In 1937, when they first met in an Orléans hospital, she was merely a nurse, he a full-fledged physician. Their temperaments also differed drastically. Timid and reclusive, she preferred the company of her family to his coarse political cronies. Thus, the mavens asserted, their marriage was doomed from the start. But most opinion blamed Chevallier for his misbehavior. For a Frenchman to cheat on his wife was acceptable, on condition that he exercise tact; Chevallier, however, had been indiscreet and ruthless. As much as they prized him as mayor, the citizens of Orléans overwhelmingly supported Yvonne.

Assuming that she could not get a fair hearing in her hometown, the authorities shifted the venue to the Palais de Justice in Reims, the splendid cathedral city eighty miles northeast of Paris. The trial was scheduled to begin on November 5, 1952, yet nearly everything that would emerge in court had been ventilated for weeks beforehand in the Paris newspapers. They had been publishing voluminous front-page accounts under such banners as YVONNE: MAD WITH JEALOUSY and YVONNE'S CRIME: HER INABILITY TO LOVE. No chronicler matched Jean Laborde of *France-Soir*, the mass-circulation daily, from whom I shamelessly cribbed for my dispatch. Torrents of colorful prose cascaded from his prolific pen. Among his many scoops, he obtained Yvonne's private letters—in which, along with other inner thoughts, she pathetically professed

her undying love for Chevallier. By then I had accumulated enough stuff for a dozen stories, but, unable to resist the temptation to see for myself, I boarded the train for Reims and found a spot in the packed press section.

The presiding judge, Raymond Jadin, draped in crimson, ermine-trimmed robes, peered down from the bench while the competing lawyers, in black, exchanged chitchat. Clad in a sober gray suit, Yvonne sat in the defendant's box, visibly weary after her detention—and looking, in Laborde's syrupy phrase, as pure as *"une vierge vestale."* Jeannette and her husband were also there, their smug expressions suggesting that they felt no responsibility for the calamity.

In theory, French judges were supposed to be impartial arbiters who, to guarantee the rights of the defendant, weighed the arguments of the opposing sides and interpreted them for the jury. But in practice they examined the defendant and all the witnesses and had no compunctions about displaying their sympathies. Judge Jadin was openly biased in Yvonne's favor. He courteously addressed her as *"madame"* rather than the formal *"accusée,"* and even apologized to her for posing intimate questions. From the outset he had promised that, to reduce the strain on her, he would keep the trial short. He also made no secret of his desire for an acquittal, since a conviction mitigated by probation or a suspended sentence would have denied her custody of her children. After barely sixteen hours of testimony, the jury retired to deliberate as throngs outside the courthouse clamored, *"Libérez, Libérez!"* The verdict was, of course, not guilty. A friend of mine, encapsulating the decision in crystalline logic, said: "It means that adultery is punishable by death."

But, over the ensuing months, many of Yvonne's firmest champions began to have second thoughts about her. Even Laborde, who had been her paladin during the trial, voiced his misgivings in a book he later wrote: "Was Pierre Chevallier truly the monster she portrayed? Alas! We have only her word for it."

Yvonne returned to her parents, then attempted to live in Orléans, but the stigma was too much for her, and, after a year, she left France with her sons for a job in a clinic in French Guiana, near Devil's Island. If she elected to exile herself to that wretched spot as atonement, it was worse than the suffering she would have endured had she been convicted.

Few episodes illuminated the deficiencies of French justice more vividly than did the spasmodic case of Marie Besnard. Charged with administering lethal quantities of arsenic to several relatives and friends, she went through a series of trials, each of them a bungle.

Besnard had been a paragon of respectability in Loudun, her hometown in south-central France. Her second husband, Léon, ran a prosperous rope business, while she was a stalwart of the Church and had been, as neighbors glowingly said of her, "the only parishioner who could receive communion without having first confessed." Childless, the Besnards owned houses, farms, a hotel, a café and other real estate worth millions, as well as a cache of gold concealed from snoopy tax collectors.

Their affluence naturally made them the target of envy. Like small towns everywhere, Loudun thrived on gossip, much of it ugly. Behind lace curtains or over cards at the local café, tongues wagged about Léon's affair with Louise Pintou, the frumpy postmistress, and Marie's flirtations with Alfred Deitz, a former German prisoner of war who worked for them. Tales of Marie's purported transgressions inevitably bounced back to Léon, and, one evening in October 1947, he grumbled to her, "I'm a laughingstock. Everyone says you're cuck-olding me." Marie pacified him with a copious dinner of soup, roast beef, vegetables, coffee, two wines, a *tarte aux fraises* and a *digestif*. Late that night he vomited, but the doctor diagnosed his ailment as one of his *crises de foie*. Within a week he was dead.

Persuaded that the doctor was mistaken, Louise Pintou confided to the gendarmes that Léon had called her to his bedside and, with his last breath, gasped, "Marie poisoned me." At first, knowing that she had been quarreling with Marie over money, the cops brushed off her charge as vindictive. Shortly afterward, however, Marie's mother died at the age of eighty, ostensibly of the grippe, and rumors of foul play rippled through Loudun. Eager to make his reputation, the young *juge d'instruction*, Pierre Roget, instantly fastened onto the case. Loudun was only forty miles from his office at Poitiers, the Vi-enne *département* capital; but instead of going there to inspect the scene of the crime for himself, he trusted dubious police reports. He ordered Léon's corpse exhumed and examined by Dr. Georges Beroud, a Marseille toxicologist, who discovered the body to be per-meated with enough arsenic to kill an elephant. On July 21, 1949, Roget consigned Marie to the grim Pierre-Levée prison at Poitiers, where she was to wait for thirty-one months as he filled his dossiers with an assortment of bits and pieces.

He had no difficulty inducing witnesses to talk, and they were unanimously hostile to Marie. A junk merchant, Gaspard Tillier, swore that Léon had told him: "If I die suddenly, make sure that they perform an autopsy." Jeanne Malicot, who dabbled in astrology, re-called Marie asking her to forecast when Albert Deitz, her lover, would return from a trip to Germany. The town's midwife, Mathilde Rossignol, repeated Marie's advice on how to handle an unwanted spouse: "Don't cry. Get rid of him. Arsenic leaves no traces."

Roget now commissioned Dr. Beroud to disinter and analyze the corpse of anyone who had been associated with Marie within recent years. Beroud dug up fourteen bodies besides Léon; and, as each emerged, the newspaper headlines blared: *ET UN AUTRE POUR MARIE!* They included that of Auguste Antigny, her first husband; Léon's aunt Émilie Lecomte; his sister, Lucie Bodin; cousins Pauline and Virginie Lalleron; and the Rivets, neighbors.

Beroud shuttled jars of viscera back and forth between Poitiers and his Marseille laboratory. The operation was a model of ineptitude. Clumsy cops mixed up or lost several jars; in one instance—either in error or as a prank—Beroud received a shipment of apricot jam. But Roget persevered, and, when he found that all the victims had bequeathed Marie inheritances ranging from two or three thousand to more than one million francs, he moved to indict her for homicide.

The "trial of the century," as the press labeled it, unfolded in Poitiers on a damp, frosty Saturday morning in February 1952. Marie had retained as her counsel Albert Gautrat, a suave, cunning, silveryhaired veteran of the Paris bar, who staged the kind of stunt that had won him renown. Showing Beroud a fistful of test tubes, he asked, "You claim to be able to identify poisoned organs with your naked eye, *n'est-ce pas*? Which of these, then, belong to the deceased?" Without hesitation Beroud gestured at two. Gautrat paused, then replied with a triumphant smirk, "*Mon cher docteur, je vous remercie infiniment,* but I regret to inform you that all contain pig tripes." Stupefied, Beroud snarled, "Ah, you Parisians with your tricks. . . ."

Depending on their sympathies, the spectators erupted in hisses or cheers. The flustered judge ended the trial and sent Marie back to her cell. Except for periodic items, like the time she slipped and fractured her leg, the news media forgot her. Eventually, the Ministry of Justice announced that the trial would be resumed in Bordeaux, where the mood was calmer, and transferred her to a prison there. Assigned to the story, I boarded the night train late in March 1954. The hotels, restaurants and cafés were crammed to capacity with journalists and crime buffs. Some, to my astonishment, could recite chapter and verse on such celebrated cases as that of the exquisite Marquise de Brinvilliers, who in the seventeenth century eliminated her parents, brothers and sisters by feeding them tainted mush-rooms, or Marie-Fortune Lafarge, a Paris milliner guillotined in 1840 for poisoning her husband.

In preparation for the new trial, the prosecutors had mobilized France's most distinguished toxicologists, among them Professor René Piedelièvre of the University of Paris Medical School. They also brought back the witnesses from the previous fiasco and, to ease the burden on themselves, elected to concentrate on only six of Marie's alleged prey.

The sessions opened on a chilly morning in the Palais de Justice, an anomalous amalgam of classical and baroque styles, built in the late nineteenth century. A hush fell over the gloomy courtroom as Marie, guided by four policemen, limped to the defendant's box. Now fifty-seven, she was haggard after five years in jail. Wearing a dowdy frock, she squinted at the chamber through thick glasses. Again headed by Gautrat, her team of eight lawyers, two of them women, were lined up in front of her; to her left sat the austere pros-ecutor, Jean Steck, and his battery of aides. The jury, bursting with self-importance, comprised seven men and three alternates, attired in their Sunday best. Nearly one hundred reporters occupied the dozen tables in the press section, and a horde of paparazzi, their flashbulbs popping, jockeyed for angles. Some three hundred citizens scram-bled for seats while, in the drafty corridor outside, hundreds more waited for vacancies.

"*La cour, la cour!*" the bailiff declaimed as Henri de Pourquerie de Boisserin, the chief judge, entered. A lean man with a nose as aristo-cratic as his name, he climbed to his dais, smoothed his scarlet gown and imperiously stared around the room. Two deputies took their places beside him, and the proceedings opened against the "Devil of Loudun," as the papers now branded Marie—a reference to the time in the Middle Ages when the town was supposedly plagued by Satan.

Leading off for the state, a psychiatrist described her as "not un-intelligent but extraordinarily unemotional." The earlier witnesses reiterated their testimony; and an inmate who had been planted in her prison cell disclosed that Marie had contemplated the idea of importing a Corsican gang from Marseille to assassinate her malicious neighbors. A string of forensic scientists expounded in scholarly jargon on the effects of arsenic; and ultimately Professor Piedelièvre, the master toxicologist, said, "I can positively affirm that the cadavers in question contain abnormal amounts of poison."

Gautrat reveled in demolishing experts. Swaggering across the courtroom, he compelled them to acknowledge that they were merely indulging in abstractions. Then his own specialist, Dr. Jean Keilling of the National Institute of Agronomy, unveiling charts and statistics, demonstrated that arsenic already in the soil could penetrate a corpse after burial—a strong argument in Marie's favor. Jean Steck, the prosecutor, whispered audibly: "I am baffled." Now, his case virtually wrapped up, Gautrat said: "Madame Besnard must be released until credible evidence against her is available. Should the court disagree, I would consider my duty to be terminated and pass on her defense to others." It was an ultimatum: if Gautrat quit, the trial would again be adjourned, sending Marie back to prison and leaving the government looking ridiculous. France's foremost attorney, Maurice Garçon, cautioned in a front-page article in *Le Monde:* "This abysmal affair, which has so besmirched our honor, ought to alert us to the necessity for urgent reform of our methods."

Stung by what he regarded as a personal rebuke, Judge Pourquerie reluctantly ruled that, after nearly five years, Marie's further detention "no longer seems to be required." He declared that she would be retried, but it was clear that she would never again appear inside a courtroom. Clutching an ivory crucifix as she stood in the wintry sunlight, Marie told reporters: "I owe my freedom to my dear departed ones in heaven, who have been standing guard over me with their sacred shields." Then, for the cameras, she embraced Gautrat and her lawyers, got into a green Citroën and was driven off to a convent.

I hung around Bordeaux for a few days, eating oysters and sampling wines, and went back to Paris with a superb gift from a French colleague in my valise—a bottle of Margaux 1948.

Early in August 1952 a crime occurred in Provence that, had it not been so gruesome, might have provided Marcel Pagnol with the ingredients for one of his bittersweet films on the region. The victims were the noted British biochemist Sir Jack Drummond, his wife, Ann, and their ten-year-old daughter, Elizabeth. They had motored up the winding Rhône Valley from the gaudy beach resorts of the Côte d'Azur through a rolling landscape of wildflowers and vineyards. Their destination was Digne-les-Bains, a little town nestled in the foothills of the Alps, where they planned to attend the annual Lavender Festival, which featured a church pageant and a bullfight. At the time, British tourists could carry only limited funds abroad, and, to economize, they had been camping out next to their Hillman station wagon. Late one afternoon they located a suitable site about one hundred yards from a farmhouse owned by Gaston Dominici, a peasant of seventy-five, who lived there with Gustave, his son, Gustave's wife, Yvette, and their two young children. The Drummonds ate a picnic dinner and were asleep by nine—Jack and his wife under the stars, Elizabeth in the rear of the car. At six the following morning, Gustave and his older brother, Clovis, who had come over to work in the fields, stumbled onto their bullet-riddled bodies. They cycled to the nearby hamlet of Lurs to telephone the police.

Given Drummond's prominence, this was no routine case, and shortly afterward Commissioner Edmond Sebeille arrived from Marseille with a squad of ace detectives and improvised a headquarters in the decrepit Digne courthouse. By then news of the murders had spread like wildfire, and tourists, neighbors and reporters had been tramping over the terrain for hours, obliterating whatever clues existed. A nervous chain-smoker in his forties, Sebeille knew that he would run into a stone wall of silence from the traditionally insular peasants; still he forged ahead. His men combed the area, interrogating peasants, tourists and drifters. They sorted through anonymous letters, answered crank telephone calls and arrested several suspects, all of whom had airtight alibis. Out of desperation, they even heeded the advice of a spiritualist and mounted a midnight vigil in hopes of nabbing the culprit as he returned to the scene of the crime. Weeks dragged on without progress, and Sebeille, his reputation at stake, issued daily bulletins promising an imminent breakthrough. Nobody believed him. A proposal by a group of British politicians that Scotland Yard be invited in as consultants sparked an indignant reaction from French officials, who claimed that such a step would be a flagrant violation of France's sovereignty. Meanwhile, with nothing substantive to report, the press hallucinated. A London tabloid, for instance, maintained that Drummond had been a British spy and was liquidated by French intelligence agents over some rivalry or other that dated back to World War II.

The more he studied the case, the more Sebeille became convinced of Gaston's guilt and dug into the old man's past. The illegitimate son of a manual laborer and a maid, Gaston was raised in an orphanage and started working as a hired hand. After completing his obligatory military service in Lyon, the only journey he ever made beyond the region, he went back to the fields and soon saved enough to buy a few goats. In 1903 he married his boss's daughter, who was to bear him nine children. Her dowry swelled their mattress, but fifteen years elapsed before he could purchase a bit of land. For him that was a proud achievement: he had hurdled the rigid class barrier and become a property owner.

As he matured, Gaston began to resemble a picture-book Provençal peasant. His curly black hair had turned white, his scraggly mustache drooped over his tobacco-tarnished lips, his skin was leathery from days in the searing sun and his vast wine consumption had left his eyes moist and his ruddy face a maze of blue veins. Whatever the weather he wore the same corduroy pants, collarless shirt, frayed vest, gray sash, battered fedora and sabots. He had the strength of a man half his age, and still pastured his goats at dawn and pruned his own fruit trees. But he was highly volatile—or, as the locals labeled him, "*soupe au lait,*" simmering milk that periodically boiled over. Once he single-handedly captured a bandit who had killed two elderly women in an armed robbery, yet he was just as capable of pulling a knife on a friend in a trivial dispute. His language was foul and he terrorized his family, refusing to permit them to eat before he had finished and doling out his money like a miser. Like his neighbors, he had been shaped by his rugged environment. They shivered in winter and sweated in summer as they eked out a marginal existence; and, with no diversions other than drinking, hunting and sex, they were understandably uncouth. While they were not as destitute as they seemed to be, they resented outsiders, French or foreign, whom they imagined to be rich, urbane—and above all, different.

Acquainted with the species, Sebeille proceeded slowly, seeing Gaston two or three times a week. They would drink, smoke and chat, but the peasant perceived that the apparently casual visits were a device to soften him up. "You think you'll get the killer?" he teased Sebeille. "*Eh bien,* I doubt it. He is a lot smarter than you—and more vicious." As their conversations continued, however, Gaston grew maudlin, repeating, "I can't help weeping when I think of that little girl."

Sebeille, now sensing that he was close to an answer, played the Dominicis off against each other. Learning that Elizabeth had still been alive when Gustave discovered her, he detained him for failing to assist a person in danger while creating the impression that he was the prime suspect. At that point Gustave's wife, Yvette, burst into Sebeille's office, wailing, "My husband is innocent. We have two kids. He shouldn't have to pay for Gaston's crime. If he doesn't denounce his father, I will." Confronted with her warning, Gustave conceded:

"*Oui, c'était mon père.*" His brother Clovis, told the news, lashed out at Sebeille: "A fine job you've done. Nothing remains of our family."

French law prohibited a child from testifying against a parent, and now Sebeille's task was to extract a confession from Gaston himself. He questioned him through the night before revealing that his sons had incriminated him. "Don't make me laugh," Gaston replied. "I've never heard anything so preposterous." Sebeille brought in Gustave and Clovis, but Gaston refused to buckle, and the grilling persisted into the next day. Exhausted, the commissioner left for a nap. "*Ce type-là, il est formidable,*" he remarked with begrudging respect. "He's a force of nature, a package of dynamite."

Sebeille consigned Gaston to the courthouse jail, and that night the old man dined with the warden, a childhood chum. They talked about one thing or another, including Gaston's obsession: sex. Then, during a lull, Gaston said softly in Provençal patois, "*Es iou*"—it's me. His startled friend knew what he meant. An hour later Sebeille appeared. "Can't sleep, *pépé*?" he asked. Gaston rose, shook his hand, knocked the ashes out of his pipe and said with a sigh, "You win, *mon petit.* Let's get it over with quickly." They sat down, and Gaston told his story.

On that August evening more than a year before, Gaston had spied the Drummonds as they went to sleep. He had been transfixed by the sight of Ann in a thin red dressing gown. Past midnight, he went to the barn, took Gustave's surplus American army carbine off a shelf and quietly walked out into the moonlight. He crawled through the grass toward the camp, uncertain of what he was doing. "All I could think about," he explained to Sebeille, "was that woman."

He was only a few feet from her when Drummond awoke. Gaston raised the weapon and Drummond, lunging forward, put his hand over its mouth. Gaston fired and Sir Jack reeled, his hand bloody, then rushed toward the car and his child. As he ran, Gaston fired again, sending him spinning into the road, presumably dead. By now

Ann was up and screaming, and Gaston coldly shot her. Hysterical, Elizabeth had meanwhile climbed out of the vehicle and was running toward a nearby river, Gaston in pursuit. He cornered her on the shore, but his weapon was empty, and, as she cowered with her arms over her head, he beat her senseless with the butt. He tossed the rifle into the river, then threw a blanket over Ann's body and a cot over Drummond's corpse.

Gaston returned to his house, got Gustave, and together they went back to the site to retrieve the shell casings and destroy other clues. At dawn, as if nothing had happened, Gaston led his goats into the hills. When Clovis joined him, Gustave mumbled, "Papa did something stupid. Don't tell a soul." The family remained mute for fifteen months until Yvette talked to Sebeille.

In accordance with procedure, Sebeille turned the case over to the *juge d'instruction,* and it rapidly fell apart. Gustave retracted his allegation against his father, then retracted his retraction. Similarly, Yvette repudiated the version she had given to Sebeille, while Clovis stuck to his story. Gaston disavowed his confession and, to complicate matters further, eluded his police escort, clambered to the edge of a railroad bridge and threatened suicide. Harassed by reporters, the magistrate allowed, "*Il y a une certaine confusion.*"

But the Ministry of Justice, under political pressure, resolved to hold the trial anyway, and late in November 1954, more than four years after the crime had occurred, a mob of four hundred converged on Digne. The Marie Besnard affair had ended eight months earlier, releasing the usual contingent of French crime reporters. They jammed the press box in the small courtroom along with at least a dozen British and a few American correspondents, myself among them. Present as well were such preeminent literary figures as Jean Giono, the Provençal novelist and poet, and the playwright Armand Salacrou, who had contracted with *France-Soir* to do a series of impressions. For weeks the newspapers had been stoking the story under combustible headlines—THE MOST IMPORTANT CASE OF THE

CENTURY and THE CRUELEST MURDERS IN HISTORY. Flaunting their intellect, writers were citing Victor Hugo, Balzac, Maupassant, Kafka. It was just the sort of judicial drama the French adored; remarked Pierre Scize in *Le Figaro:* "By comparison the Paris theaters are dull."

The trial, Chief Judge Marcel Bousquet presiding, began as decorously as a minuet and deteriorated into a carnival. One witness, a traveling salesman, laboriously imitated the shots he claimed to have heard in the night: "*S'il vous plaît,* Judge, listen carefully, *tac-tac-tac,* not *tactactac.*" A gendarme who had arrived at the site on the fatal morning recollected seeing "either a dead woman or a cadaver." But the climax was a shouting match among the Dominicis. "My father is innocent!" Gustave yelled. "The whole family's innocent. I only accused him only to avoid being charged myself." Clovis dissented, "Papa did it in a moment of madness. He deserves to be pitied." A married daughter, Augusta Caillat, launched a diatribe against Clovis: "You pig, you coward, you are dishonoring us all." Flanked by two policemen, Gaston chided his children, "Tell them the truth. I didn't do a thing." Judge Bousquet, who had been badgering Gaston from the start, barked at him, "Silence, Dominici!" Gaston replied, "Since you've obviously made up your mind that I'm guilty, why are you going to the trouble of trying me?"

The circus spilled over into Digne's restaurants and cafés in the evenings as attorneys, journalists, witnesses and policemen discussed the case. Only the seven jurors, confined to a hotel, were excluded from the fun—though no regulation prevented them from reading the newspapers. On the eve of his summing up, the prosecutor, Callixte Rozan, was hospitalized with a severe attack of laryngitis. Judge Bousquet, calling a recess, murmured, "I've seen some trials in my day, but this one, *alors.*"

Even before its conclusion the case was being derided as an embarrassing farce. "This sloppy trial epitomizes everything that is wrong with our judicial system," wrote Maurice Garçon, and the novelist François Mauriac echoed: "The main defendant in every

French court today is the court itself." Albert Gazier, a member of the National Assembly, delivered an oration, saying, "What has happened to France, the crucible of the Enlightenment, the birthplace of the Rights of Man?"

After two spastic weeks, the jury deliberated for three hours and pronounced Gaston guilty of premeditated murder. He listened soberly as the judge condemned him to death, but he knew that, in reality, persons over seventy were never executed—and that the sentence would be commuted to life. For someone who had spent his years in the sun, the prospect of being caged must have been sorrowful, but he faced it with his perennial bravado. As the gendarmes trundled him off, he said to the reporters gathered outside the courthouse, "I won't be too unhappy. At my age, all a man really needs is tobacco and red wine."

9

The Last
Penal Colony

*P*ursuing crime and justice had stimulated my interest in the penal settlement in French Guiana, which abutted on Brazil, in the northeast corner of South America. The sensational newspaper stories I had collected on the place described it as a ghastly inferno, but I knew little else about it until October 1953, when I went to Bordeaux for what turned out to be a poignant assignment.

Early on the morning after my arrival, I took a taxi to a dock outside town to watch the *San Mateo* navigate down the Gironde estuary, its whistle shrieking over the sleeping city. The black-hulled ship carried a cargo of sugar, spices, rum, timber—and eighty-eight men. Gaunt and stooped, their faces wrinkled by age and the tropical climate, they slowly descended the gangplank and, flanked by gendarmes, assembled in formation on the wharf. They wore bleached denims, heavy boots and cotton caps or tattered straw hats. Most of them were chained wrist-to-wrist in groups of three or four; the others stumbled along on their own, all their belongings in flimsy cardboard valises and faded musette bags slung over their shoulders. Since its creation a century before, some seventy thousand felons had been committed to the French prison colony's eight camps, including Devil's Island of Dreyfus notoriety. Only about two thousand of them ever returned to France; these were the final remnants.

Those in fetters had terms to complete, and the police, exhibiting unaccustomed politeness for French cops, steered them to waiting vans. They were to be conveyed to Paris, where they would be kept in Fresnes, a suburban jail, while a special panel of judges examined their cases. The others were free—or as free as they could be in their sixties or seventies, without money, jobs and, in many instances, families.

Predictably, a throng of French reporters had gathered for the event, and I joined them. The released inmates, it instantly occurred to me, could not adjust to their emancipation quickly. As though they were still under surveillance, they saluted deferentially when we introduced ourselves and shook their hands, and thanked us profusely when we offered them cigarettes. We escorted them to a nearby café, bought them drinks and interviewed them. Their replies suggested just a hint of the ordeal they had endured.

Nearing eighty, Theodore Roussel had been convicted in 1900 for armed burglary. "I have only myself to blame," he said in a cracked voice. "I was a stupid, stubborn kid and got mixed up with the wrong crowd." Adrien Rebut, sixty-seven, had been nabbed in a jewelry store holdup in Deauville in 1908 and sentenced to twenty years. He tried and failed to escape four times, was given another five years for each attempt, and altogether spent more than four decades in Cayenne. Bewildered, he sniffed the air and rasped, "Of course it's great to be out, but all that's left for me now is to die in peace." André Blanchard, who had been a poilu of eighteen when he deserted under fire during World War I, was as emaciated as a skeleton. "I have no prospects," he lamented. "Who will want me when they know of my disgrace, and where I've been since then? I pray that the good Lord will care for me."

Only Émile Le Clerc, at fifty-three the youngest of the batch, exhibited a modicum of vitality and a faint glimmer of hope. A former vineyard worker, he was arrested in 1933 for strangling his unfaithful girlfriend. "I'm going to get myself a new suit and return to Burgundy. With the harvest approaching, maybe I can find work. I haven't heard a word from my brothers or sisters for years, but perhaps a cousin will remember me kindly."

As usual, *Time*'s editors demanded reams of material, most of which would end up on the cutting room floor. I rushed back to Paris and researched as much as I could on the history of the penal colony before filing my dispatch.

A tangled terrain of mangrove swamps and dense forests crisscrossed by inland waterways, Guiana was touted by European geographers as the fabled El Dorado. British and Dutch explorers searching for gold each claimed a portion of the region for their respective nations; in 1604 the French planted their flag in Cayenne, the future capital of their sector. Pirates briefly based in its bays and coves before shifting to the Caribbean, where the targets for marauding and looting were more lucrative. Over the ensuing years a variety of programs calculated to make the area profitable collapsed. In 1763, lured by inflated promises of wealth, fourteen thousand French immigrants disembarked in the first phase of an ambitious colonization project; within two years ten thousand of them had succumbed to fever, and the others limped back to France. Jesuit missionaries also abandoned their endeavors to convert the Indians. Sugar, spice and coffee plantations, utilizing African slaves, thrived for a while; cayenne pepper became one of the world's most valuable commodities. But in 1848 France banned slavery throughout its empire, and soon the plantations, bereft of manpower, were a shambles. A year later only ten acres of Guiana were under cultivation. At that juncture the French government, seeking to salvage the territory, conceived of importing white convict labor, as Britain had been doing in Australia for decades.

Guiana had previously been used as a place of exile for a few illustrious culprits, among them Charles Pichegru. He had played a crucial role following the Revolution as one of Bonaparte's generals in the defense of France against a coalition of its European enemies, an exploit for which he was awarded the title of Sauveur de la Patrie. Consumed by grievances of one sort or another, he participated in a plot to restore the Bourbon monarchy, was apprehended and, in 1797, banished to the distant site. Launched with much fanfare, the new enterprise was designed to handle masses of inmates: punishment, so to speak, on an industrial scale. By 1852, known as *le bagne,* a word that connoted hard labor, it held more than two thousand men.

The deportation of convicts, the venture's promoters argued, would ease the pressure on France's congested jails and reduce the burden of their support, to the benefit of the taxpayer. They also maintained that the fear of expatriation alone would suffice to deter crime and thus protect French society. Its champions even moralized that the settlement could serve to rehabilitate offenders—a dubious thesis. Under a complex system labeled *doublage,* a prisoner confined for fewer than eight years was required to remain in Guiana for an equal period of time, and one condemned to a longer stretch had to remain forever. This concept reflected the rosy belief that *libérés,* inmates who had been liberated but were barred from returning home, would, if granted land and tools, contribute to the Guianan economy and become useful citizens. So a sentence to Guiana was, in effect, a life sentence.

The penitentiary was usually populated by about three hundred guards and seven or eight thousand prisoners, the overwhelming majority of them French, with a smattering of Algerians, black Africans, East Europeans and English added. They were classified according to their felonies, an arbitrary, imprecise and tragic process that often stemmed from miscarriages of justice. A young peasant who knifed someone in a drunken brawl and should have been convicted of manslaughter was instead found guilty of homicide, deported and, under the rigid bureaucratic procedure, put into the same category as serial killers. The same fate might befall an otherwise respectful son

who, in a rage, killed his father for abusing his mother. A veteran thief who warranted only a couple of years in the slammer appeared in court with such regularity that the judge, out of sheer impatience, would send him to Guiana, where he was thrown in with murderers.

Most of the convicts were consigned to Saint-Laurent, Saint-Jean and Saint-Louis, camps along the Maroni River, on the border of Dutch Guiana, a region infested by mosquitoes and poisonous insects. Mobilized into gangs, they toiled six days a week in the blistering heat and humidity from dawn until dusk, with a half hour off for a lunch of gruel and a siesta. They cut sugarcane, chopped down trees and hacked roads through the jungles, and were frequently flogged by guards for dawdling. Their ranks were chronically being thinned by malaria, dysentery, tuberculosis and diseases that defied diagnosis. With authorization they could hire themselves out to planters or officials as houseboys or gardeners, which enabled them to pick up a bit of money. They slept in rows of wooden bunks in ramshackle, mildewed barracks and were awakened in the morning by the blare of a bugle or the clang of a gong. Feuding factions armed with improvised weapons pervaded the camps. Periodically one of the turnkeys would stumble onto a corpse—the casualty of some nocturnal altercation. More often the bodies belonged to men who, in desperation, had committed suicide.

The worst spots were the Îles du Salut—incongruously, the Salvation Islands. Mounds of rock seven miles from the coast, they were reserved for hard-core murderers, rapists and captured escapees. Rigorous regulations compelled the inmates to rotate between three months of strenuous labor, such as hauling logs or breaking boulders, and three months locked into separate cement cells. Many of them welcomed the work as relief from the interminable loneliness of their coops. The cages were covered with iron grates and catwalks, along which guards in espadrilles would tread quietly, constantly looking for the opportunity to pounce on infractions like tapped messages to neighbors at night. The slightest violation was punishable by a month or more in a suffocating oubliette on a diet of stale bread and water.

Lurid press accounts to the contrary, Devil's Island was relatively comfortable—at least by Guianan standards. Incarcerated under *"le régime politique,"* its denizens were not constrained to work, and could read, write, fish, doze in the shade of coconut palms—or, as Dreyfus did for hours on end, simply gaze out to sea. They occupied individual huts and, if they could afford it, were permitted to engage servants from among the ordinary convicts. Seldom did the tiny island contain more than fifteen or twenty prisoners—chiefly traitors, terrorists and spies fortunate enough to have been spared the guillotine. Apart from Dreyfus, its guest of honor was Georges Ullmo, a navy lieutenant in his twenties. On the eve of World War I, in need of money to keep his profligate girlfriend happy, he naively placed an ad in a Frankfurt newspaper offering secret documents to the Germans; to his surprise, the French police were the first to respond. He lived in Dreyfus's former hut, subsequently got sprung and made his way to British Guiana, where he was last sighted running a bicycle shop.

Uncontrollable eccentrics of nearly every species fetched up in the colony. One of the most obstreperous of them, Paul Roussenq, was a conscript in Tunisia in 1908 when he set fire to a French army building. At his trial he testified that he had been "bored by the monotonous African heaven"—an improbable alibi that earned him twenty years. Shortly after his arrival he proclaimed himself to be an anarchist. He would bombard the warden with letters saying, "*Roussenq vous dit merde*," and etch graffiti on the walls declaring, "*Roussenq crache sur l'humanité.*" For each truculent gesture he was shunted into solitary on the Îles du Salut, but he refused to behave. He got thirty days for deliberately ripping up his clothes, thirty days for punching a guard, thirty days for faking illness, thirty days for defecating in the mess hall, thirty days for swinging and screeching like an ape from the grate above his cell. Earmarked "*un inco*"—an incorrigible—he accumulated more than three thousand days of penalties. Ultimately the warden ran out of disciplinary measures. One night Roussenq inexplicably vanished, triggering rumors that the frustrated warden had covertly helped him to abscond.

Gangsters would show up with hefty wads, buy themselves cushy jobs as nurses or orderlies—and, in some instances, even become guards. There were also white-collar criminals who adapted in their assorted fashions. Edmond Duez, a rich Paris stockbroker, had speculated heavily on the Bourse and, in 1911, lost fifteen million francs in a sudden crash. To cover his debts he stole the equivalent from his customers, for which he drew ten years. Rather than soil his hands at hard labor, he wangled a sinecure as the staff accountant. Talented at juggling figures, he balanced the ledgers, and soon officials were addressing him as "monsieur." He acquired a perverse affection for Guiana, elected to stay following the end of his term and invited his wife, Isabelle, to join him. They purchased the fertile Île des Mères, carved out a farm on which they raised chickens, cows, hogs, sheep and vegetables, and did a brisk business provisioning passing ships. Fervent patriots, they unfurled the French flag over their tiny domain and would declaim to visitors, "*Ici, dans ce coin perdu du monde, nous sommes la France!*"

Isidore Hespel, banished for driving the getaway car in a bank heist, was a model inmate—until his volatile temper doomed him. A mechanic by profession, he learned to operate the guillotine and was eventually appointed executioner, a post that gave him privileges, like the right to live in his own bungalow, employ servants, receive supplementary rations and sport a mustache. Indeed, he was better off than he had been back in Clermont-Ferrand, his hometown in France. But one day Hespel killed another convict in a quarrel over money and was sentenced to death. The evening before his decapitation he scrupulously tested the guillotine, oiling its pulley, greasing its rope and sharpening its blade to ensure that it would function smoothly the next morning.

Thumbing through old newspapers, I was intrigued by an episode that made banner headlines in 1931. Fourteen blacks from Guiana, including two women, were brought to France to stand trial in Nantes, the Breton port that had once flourished as the hub of French commerce with the West Indies. Arrested three years before for slaughtering scores of Cayenne's citizens, they had been languishing since in a damp jail and suffered from influenza and bronchitis. They were as weird a bunch as ever appeared in a French court. Bearing such exotic names as Mith, Mars, Avril and Parnasse, they were attired in swallowtail coats and striped trousers, top hats, suede gloves and varnished shoes with spats; one of them wore a silver medallion inscribed with his slogan: *"La vie est belle."* Dispensing with interpreters, they spoke softly, almost inaudibly, in a kind of calypso French, relating a bizarre, chilling tale involving politics, corruption, witchcraft and primitive cruelty.

It had started with a white *libéré* known as "Papa" Galmot, who had been deported for gross fraud in connection with his race for election to the French legislature from his native Périgord. A dwarfish creature, he was reputed to possess supernatural powers. He had formed a quasireligious cult, with himself as its deity, and attracted thousands of black disciples. They would kneel before him at arcane rituals, carry him around in a curtained palanquin, and threaten his critics with hideous tortures. In 1928 Galmot suddenly died under mysterious circumstances, and, suspecting that he had been poisoned, his votaries rampaged through the streets of Cayenne. Brandishing spears, machetes and clubs, they pillaged shops and homes, and butchered everyone within reach. Galmot's adjutant, a deaf fisherman called Iquy, preferred to stone his victims to death, while an octogenarian named Mustafa skillfully wielded his umbrella as a sword. It was bruited about, though never proved, that the slaughter had been incited by a Madame Radical, the mother of four children and a local brothel owner. The judges leniently gave the women prison terms, sent seven of the men to the guillotine and condemned the others, ironically enough, to hard labor for life back in Guiana. In her report to *The New Yorker* at the time, Janet Flanner commented, "One can only regret that Conrad died too early to have written of their hearts of darkness."

Obsessed with escaping, convicts would sit up late at night, discussing schemes with trusted comrades. They traced evasion routes on crude maps, stashed away provisions and concealed dugouts for the trip. Most of them realized that fulfilling their dream would be difficult, if not impossible. They were infiltrated by informers and encircled by vigilant sentries. Even if they managed to get past the barbed-wire fences, they would be stumped by jungles, swamps and waters swarming with sharks. Nor could they anticipate a haven in the surrounding countries, which wanted nothing to do with fugitives. Adrien Rebut, whose four attempts had aborted, recalled to me during our chat in Bordeaux that he had been extradited by the British, the Dutch, the Brazilians and the Venezuelans. "The British treated me best," he said. "They gave me clean clothes, a good meal, a warm bed and, before I left, even apologized that they were obliged under a treaty with France to send me back."

Even leaving legally was tough. On condition that they pay their own passage—about two thousand francs—*libérés* were entitled to repatriation. But they earned no more than a few centimes daily at their servile jobs, and to achieve their goal meant saving every sou. They limited themselves to a single meal a day and renounced petty luxuries, like wine and cigarettes. If sickness prevented their working, their modest capital would evaporate and they would have to start all over again. Some of them made the mistake of confiding in companions and were murdered for their nest egg. Others devised clever gambits. One pair of characters, who had only two thousand francs between them, deposited the money with a warden, obtained a receipt, stole the money, were reimbursed the sum and, delirious with joy, sailed home shortly afterward. For one man, however, the strain was too much. He had been squirreling away the necessary amount for a ticket for five years, but when he saw his ship steaming into Cayenne harbor he went mad and was carted off to an asylum.

Until the turn of the century, when the bitter controversy over the Dreyfus affair focused their attention on Devil's Island, the French were undisturbed by the brutality of the penal settlement. Murderers and traitors, they felt, jeopardized society and deserved harsh punishment. Following World War I, however, a group of human rights militants began to advocate reforms. Prominent among them were Catholic liberals and the French branch of the Salvation Army. Their lobbying swayed Édouard Herriot, a leading Radical Socialist member of the Chambre des Députés and a paladin of progressive causes. Pledging himself to change, he induced several of his colleagues to back a bill aimed at alleviating the plight of the inmates. The campaign was further fueled in 1924 by Albert Londres, an ace reporter for *Le Petit Parisien,* who wrote a dramatic exposé on the horrors of the colony. Afterward the novelist Blaise Cendrars came out with *Rhum,* a fictionalized version of the savagery that had swept through Cayenne in 1928. The public was temporarily aroused, but then the crusade lost its momentum, and nothing happened.

The effort was resurrected in 1936 by the Popular Front government—and especially by Vincent Auriol, the minister of justice and later president of France. "The courts can sentence a man to death or life imprisonment," he declared, "but not to perpetual humiliation."

Under his auspices, magistrates, lawyers, priests and others convened meetings at which they lectured on the evils of the penal system. Auriol also persuaded shipping companies to lower their rates for returning *libérés*, and shortly afterward the first big contingent of them landed at the port of Saint-Nazaire. At the same time he delegated a parliamentary committee to study the penitentiary, and, within a year, it unanimously concluded: "The penal colony does not appear to discourage criminals nor does it furnish them with either redemption or rehabilitation. . . . Moreover, as France's only possession in South America it is an ugly blot on French prestige in the Western Hemisphere." The committee recommended that the institution be abolished "by extinction," and that Guiana's economy be modernized to eliminate its dependence on forced labor. The deportations gradually stopped while, in Guiana itself, the administration switched to enlightened policies. Convicts were moved from their crammed barracks into private shacks with shelves for souvenirs and photographs of their families, and urged to decorate the walls with pictures, borrow books from a library and even grow flowers.

When Germany defeated France in 1940, Guiana's governor and most of his staff sided with the Vichy regime. Several planters crossed into Dutch Guiana and rallied to the Free French. Many convicts joined them and went on to fight with de Gaulle's army in Africa, the Middle East and Europe, for which they were later pardoned. In a spasm of gratuitous vengeance, the Vichyites tyrannized those who remained behind, slashing their food rations to a minimum and intensifying their work schedule. Within less than a year, approximately eight hundred prisoners died. The despotic officials were never punished—or, as far as I know, even reprimanded.

The Liberation ushered in a new era for Guiana, and the beginning of the end of the *bagne*. In 1946 France was restructured and the region became an overseas *département*, with elected representatives in the National Assembly and the Senate. The closer link to Paris accelerated reforms—particularly an agreement by the government to assume the costs of bringing back the inmates. Returning in groups of ten, twenty or thirty, they landed at Le Havre, Cherbourg and Marseille and were sent to their hometowns in France—and even to Algiers, Abidjan and Beirut. The relics I had observed in Bordeaux were the last of them.

I did not usually follow up a story, but, a week after cabling my dispatch, curious to know how they were faring, I checked up on them. Those with unfinished terms, I learned, were undergoing "orientation courses" at the Fresnes prison to determine their future. Some of the others were being held in a hospital in Nanterre, a few miles outside Paris, and I drove there. Three or four of them, I noticed, wore bathrobes and slippers and sat alone in the cobblestoned courtyard, staring vacantly into space. I located Gaston Berthelot, whom I had encountered in Bordeaux. A frail, white-haired man in his seventies, he seemed to be cheered by my visit. It was a crystalline autumn day, and we shared a bench under the chestnut trees, smoking Gauloises and reminiscing on the past—his past. His experience fit the pattern I had heard repeatedly. From Rouen, he had been an employee in an insurance firm and had killed a colleague in a sordid squabble over a woman thirty-five years before. His wife had divorced him, remarried and was probably dead; he had no idea what had become of his children or whether he had grandchildren. I asked him if he had any plans, now that he was free—a dumb question. He laughed or—more exactly—cackled, "Free? What does freedom mean to an old, broken, worthless, rusty machine?"

10

Monsieur de Paris

Not many French could have identified Jules-Henri Desfourneaux, yet his death on October 1, 1951, made the front pages. Then seventy-four, he had operated the guillotine for twelve years as lord high executioner under the honorific title of Monsieur de Paris. By tradition the job was hereditary, but seventeen years earlier his only son, René, an adolescent with an appetite for nightclubs and brothels, had shot himself rather than follow in his father's grim footsteps. Nor did either of Desfourneaux's part-time assistants, one of them a butcher and the other a barber, covet the position; even if they had, their prospects of being chosen were remote. For centuries the function of *bourreau* had been the exclusive preserve of the same few families, and, like entrenched aristocrats, they jealously protected their turf. Reluctant to disrupt custom, the authorities secretly searched for weeks for a successor among their kin. Finally a terse communiqué announced the appointment of André Obrecht, who had periodically acted as Desforneaux's *valet*—jargon for an aide. They were, of course, cousins.

Though decapitation was probably no worse than hanging, electrocution or the firing squad, this uniquely Gallic phenomenon had long seemed to me to contain all the ingredients of a colorfully macabre story—an excursion into *humour noir.* Now, with a hook on which to fasten the narrative, I launched into my research. Had I been less squeamish, I would have sought to witness an actual execution; instead, I resorted to secondary sources. I dug into my files on the subject, rummaged through police dossiers and pored over the archives at the Bibliothèque Nationale. In addition I interviewed lawyers, magistrates and especially the crime reporters on the Paris newspapers, who were invariably generous about sharing their vivid recollections with *un confrère américain.* Some historic executioners had left behind wonderfully lurid if apocryphal memoirs, and I spent hours at the superb Musée Carnavalet, where a vintage guillotine was on exhibit. But Ministry of Justice officials refused me their cooperation; plainly, I was treading on taboo terrain. Perhaps it embarrassed them to acknowledge that France, the cradle of the Enlightenment and the lofty Declaration of the Rights of Man, still depended on such an anachronistic and horrendous method of punishment as beheading.

The executioner was similarly relegated to an anomalous and shadowy status. An independent contractor rather than a state employee, he received a fee per head—severance pay. He was expected to keep the guillotine in tiptop shape and cover his own expenses, including the salaries of his staff. References to his device were conspicuously absent from the penal code, which merely stipulated that "*le condamné aura la tête tranchée.*" Named for Dr. Joseph-Ignace Guillotin, its sire, the instrument acquired a variety of euphemistic sobriquets—among them "*l'appareil de la mort*"; "*la machine fatale*"; "*la louisette*" and "*la petite louison*" for its pioneer promoter, Antoine Louis; and, most descriptively, "*la veuve,*" conceived by a fin de siècle poet, Jules Jouy, who portrayed the apparatus as a sensuous widow luring men to their tombs:

Pale and shuddering he gasps his last death rattle
In hideous copulation.

For openers I focused on Desfourneaux, and there was nothing romantic about him. A gentle, taciturn, stooped figure with graying hair and a ragged gray mustache, he might have been a bank teller or a postal clerk. He and his wife, Georgette, resided in a small apartment in a typically petit bourgeois building on the rue de la Convention, in the drab Fifteenth Arrondissement. Their flat was furnished with an imitation antique armoire, heavy armchairs draped with antimacassars, faded engravings and a crucifix above the bed. Deeming Jules to be too prosaic a name, his wife called him Henri; to everybody else, he was "monsieur." One of his few diversions was to play dice over a glass of wine with the local grocer at a nearby café; for exercise he walked his poodle down the street to a park, where he fed bread crumbs to the pigeons. He had invested a modest sum in a bicycle repair shop around the corner from his building, and now and again he would drop in to see how it was faring. Obsessively frugal, he would stuff the cords that bound his victims into his pocket for future use. His work made him anxious; fearing that he might be assassinated or kidnapped, he often took circuitous routes to his dates.

Occasionally he pondered the notion of retirement, but as a freelancer he was ineligible for a pension and other benefits—and, on his monthly income of thirty thousand francs, roughly ninety dollars, he had saved little. As he aged, he grew so feeble that he could scarcely climb up to the guillotine platform. One day, following an abstemious lunch of an omelet, boiled potatoes and a lettuce salad, he complained of severe chest pains, and his wife, a former nurse, immediately recognized a coronary. At seven in the evening he passed away as quietly as he had lived.

Desfourneaux traced his pedigree back two centuries to Alsace-Lorraine, where his great-great-great-grandfather had been an itinerant executioner. The patriarch imparted his métier to his three sons, all of whom married the daughters of headsmen. Their progeny continued in the vocation until Desfourneaux's father, Nicholas, interrupted the line, took up carpentry and settled in Paris. There, after tinkering with a peculiar vehicle known as the automobile, Henri decided to become a garage mechanic. But he retained his links to his relatives. His uncle Léopold, a cabinetmaker, was an assistant to Anatole Deibler, then Monsieur de Paris. A car enthusiast, Deibler appreciated Henri's skills, liked him personally and began to invite him to his country estate for convivial weekend parties. Most of the guests at these parties belonged to the executioners' fraternity, and, at one of them, Henri met Madame Deibler's winsome niece Georgette, his future wife. By no coincidence her father, Louis, an engineer on a Seine river tourist boat, doubled as Deibler's senior *valet*. Deibler embraced Henri as his nephew, and coaxed him into accepting a place on his team. Thus, at the age of twenty-two, Henri returned to his ancestral orbit.

He started out by memorizing the guillotine in detail. Though it had been modernized over the years, its principle had not essentially changed. Suspended from the arch of its upright frame was a convex steel blade bolted to the *mouton*, an iron slab whose weight added force to the blade's descent. The blade, attached to a rope, slid along bearings into the *lunette*, the slot that held the condemned man's head. The executioner would trigger the mechanism by releasing a lever—and, ideally, a decapitation was supposed to take no more than five seconds. Success hinged on speed, precision and coordination, and, to achieve that combination, the *valets* were handed specific tasks.

To guarantee that it ran smoothly, they maintained the guillotine in flawless condition. They regularly oiled its lever, bearings, gears and springs; tightened its bolts and joints; and checked and double-checked the rope for snarls. The blade blunted easily, and they whetted it daily to razor sharpness. Frequently the machine was transported from town to town, which required them to dismantle and reassemble it overnight without destabilizing its chassis. They further administered *la toilette du condamné*, their victim's last haircut, then escorted him to the instrument, balanced him on the *bascule*, the tilting plank, and adjusted his head at exactly the proper angle in the *lunette* to enable the knife to slice his neck neatly. If he fought back, as sometimes occurred, it was their duty to overpower him. Later they would transfer the twitching corpse to a wicker basket and mop up the mess. Unless a family claimed the body, it was buried in an unmarked grave by a state agency or a charitable institution. Like film or drama reviewers, ghoulish crime reporters critiqued beheadings, and executioners endeavored to stage their decapitations swiftly and cleanly—not only because a mishap could blemish their reputation, but also because, in many cases, they were sensitive to the agony of the wretch about to be dispatched. Often it took repeated attempts to finish off the poor soul. Efficiency was also vital for the safety of the crews; they all knew about the assistant whose laxity had cost him three fingers.

Desfourneaux made his debut as a *valet* in January 1909 in Bethune, a town in the Pas-de-Calais *département*, where four bandits captioned "Le gang du Nord" had recently been convicted of marauding in the region. Deibler disposed of them in nine minutes—a virtuoso feat. Elated and relieved, the townsfolk regaled him and his crew with schooners of beer at a local café and, as a grisly memento, they left their bloody thumbprints on a table. The press acclaimed Deibler as *la vedette* of the season, and a satirical magazine featured his caricature on its cover under the banner: CAN YOU BE SURE THAT YOUR HEAD IS SECURE ON YOUR SHOULDERS? Over the next thirty years Henri helped Uncle Anatole in a string of major jobs. In February 1922, in the courtyard of the Versailles prison, they decapitated Henri-Désiré Landru, the notorious "Bluebeard," for strangling ten women by enticing them to his country house through matrimonial ads. Ambiguities clouded the case: the bodies of the women were never discovered and rumors spread that, at the last minute, someone substituted himself for Landru—as Sydney Carton had done for Charles Darnay in *A Tale of Two Cities*. A decade later, Deibler and his squad beheaded Paul Gorguloff, a mystical Russian poet and novelist who had assassinated France's president, Paul Doumer. At the trial in Paris, the prosecutor decried the Russian as "a mélange of dreamer, nihilist, fanatic Oriental and diabolical Asiatic." The execution nearly misfired when Gorguloff's thick neck would not fit into the *lunette*.

On the morning of February 2, 1939, Deibler suddenly dropped dead of a massive heart attack at the entrance to the Porte-de-Saint-Cloud Métro station. He was on his way to the Gare Montparnasse to board a train for Rennes to perform his four-hundred-and-first guillotining. Born and raised in the Breton town, where his grand-father and father had been headsmen, he was anticipating a nostalgic dinner with his old school comrades. He was then seventy-six and apparently robust, despite a lifetime of smoking Gauloises. His only son had died at the age of five, and Desfourneaux, his most trusted *valet,* was the logical heir.

*D*esfourneaux began his role as master in March 1939 in the same Versailles courtroom in which the Landru trial had been held. There Eugene Weidmann was sentenced to death for the murder of Jean de Koven, a beautiful young dancer from Brooklyn. She had come to Paris in hopes of landing a job and let herself be attracted by Weidmann, a German of thirty-one. Unbeknownst to her, he had done away with four or five other people. He was intelligent, glib and strikingly handsome, and the press consecrated pages to analyz-ing his behavior. Rifling through old newspapers, I ran across the voluminous accounts of *Le Journal*'s ace crime reporter, Georges London, who speculated on everything from Weidmann's family, education and psychological traits to the impact of his Teutonic background on his character. Noting that a female wig had been dis-covered among his possessions, Colette theorized in her eloquent essays in *Paris-Soir* that he must have been motivated by some arcane brand of erotic fetishism.

Weidmann's execution was slated for June 17, and throngs had been pouring in from Paris and elsewhere for days, lending a holiday mood to the town. Permitted to stay open all night, bistros over-flowed with customers as elated by the event as fans on the eve of a football match. The guillotine, which had normally done its deed in-side the jail, was moved to the street outside, and the proprietors of apartments above were cashing in by renting seats in their windows. From his cell Weidmann could hear loudspeakers blaring jazz inter-spersed with commentaries on his impending demise; worse still was the execution itself.

Scheduled to unfold at dawn, the customary hour, it was delayed by bureaucratic red tape. So it was broad daylight when Weidmann, flanked by a pair of *valets,* emerged from the prison. At first he winced at the sight of the guillotine, then recovered his composure and walked toward it stoically. Despite his years of experience, Des-fourneaux was slow and jittery. Only after three tries did he manage to squeeze Weidmann's neck into the *lunette,* and he also fumbled with the lever. The operation lasted twelve seconds—twice the nor-mal time. The crowd, which had been waiting with hushed anticipa-tion, stormed the police barrier as the blade fell. Men shouted anti-German epithets; elegant ladies, avid for souvenirs, rushed to dip their handkerchiefs into the blood; and, for the rest of the day and far into the night, revelers chanted songs and swilled wine. As a reporter wrote, "Amid it all, attired in a gray suit and gray fedora, Desfourneaux had seemed to be placid—apparently unable to grasp that he was responsible for the upheaval."

Perched on rooftops, photographers recorded the tumult, and their pictures quickly appeared in newspapers around the world and became a staple of postcards. The fiasco shocked even the most in-transigent proponents of capital punishment, and also cast doubt on the doctrine that public executions deterred crime. Fearing that future outbursts would damage France's image abroad, Premier Édouard Daladier decreed that guillotinings were henceforth to be conducted within prison enclosures. Nobody reproached Desfourneaux, who shortly entered another chapter of his career.

He perceived himself to be a technician, for whom one boss was the same as another and, after the Germans defeated France in 1940, had no compunctions about serving them. Traveling around the provinces, he executed run-of-the-mill criminals along with Resistance fighters and Jews—frequently at the behest of the Gestapo. He also represented the Vichy regime, which obliged him to expand his clientele. Since the last one was beheaded in 1893, women had automatically been pardoned as a gesture of compassion. But Marshal Pétain, consonant with his emphasis on the sanctity of the family, ruled against any distinction between the genders, and, from 1941 to 1943, Desfourneaux guillotined five females without a qualm. He was totally unruffled when Élisabeth Décourneau, convicted of poisoning her mother and husband, shrieked and clawed the floor as his assistants dragged her from the death chamber. Nor was he affected as Marie-Louise Giraud, a laundress condemned for violating Vichy's harsh anti-abortion laws, contended that she had merely been rendering a favor to girls in distress.

In contrast to the thousands of collaborators arrested following the Liberation, Desfourneaux escaped retribution—as though, like the guillotine itself, he were just an instrument. In May 1946, in his biggest job since the Weidmann affair, he decapitated Dr. Marcel Petiot—labeled "Le Docteur Satan" by the press—who had committed sixty-three homicides in twenty years. His insanity plea spurned, Petiot went to his death behind the walls of the Santé prison in Paris, after which Desfourneaux gradually reduced his tempo.

In his classic *L'Esprit des Lois*, first published in 1748, Montesquieu expressed alarm that the same cruel penalties inflicted during the

Middle Ages were still in force. Death was prescribed for a wide spectrum of crimes—from murder, treason, robbery and arson to forgery, perjury, bankruptcy, sorcery, slandering the throne and disseminating seditious literature. Peasants were routinely hanged for poaching game, children for stealing a loaf of bread, servants for filching a towel. Ecclesiastical judges regarded as capital offenses such "sins against nature" as adultery, incest and sodomy. As a result, executioners were constantly active. The majority of them, appropriately butchers by trade, were remarkably versatile. A fate reserved for the aristocracy was decapitation, and the *bourreaux* had to be expert at wielding huge axes and swords. They were also torturers, which entailed roasting, flaying and flogging felons, burning them at the stake, breaking them on the wheel, boiling them in oil or tearing them limb from limb. Their perquisites included the right to draw free food for themselves, their families and their horses at public markets and exemption from taxes and military service. Frequently, to supplement their earnings, they sold cadavers to medical students and apothecaries, who were said to dose their formulas with human fat.

A complex web of intertwined dynasties dominated the profession. The most famous of them, the Sansons, spawned eighteen executioners over a span of six generations. Their progenitor, Charles Sanson, operated in his native Normandy until 1688, when by royal edict he was licensed to function in Paris. To set an example, the doomed were paraded around the streets in shackles to the fanfare of trumpets and the prayers of priests, and compelled to kneel in repentance at shrines along the way. Attired in a black hood and leather apron, Sanson would march in the procession, reciting the sentence at each stop—a ceremony that inflated his ego. His wife, Marguerite, was a Jouënne; her family had been noted Norman headsmen since the thirteenth century. Their only son, Charles II, assisted his father and succeeded him in 1707. He prospered and bought a mansion in the Faubourg Montmartre. His elder son, Charles-Jean-Baptiste, was a chip off the old block. As a child he would gleefully cling to the ankles of squirming victims while Papa whacked away at their necks. He was seven when his father died, and the government, impressed by his verve, engaged a surrogate to pinch-hit for him until he became strong enough to swing an ax. Equally talented, his kid brother Charles-Nicolas was sent to Reims. Soon Sanson uncles, nephews, cousins and in-laws were presiding over scaffolds throughout the country. Under an ancient protocol, devised to shield their anonymity, they informally cloaked themselves in the names of the towns they served, such as Monsieur de Rouen or Monsieur de Bordeaux.

The pride of the Sanson tribe, Charles-Nicolas's son Charles-Henri, ascended to the office in 1778, at the age of thirty-nine. Like his forebears, he had learned the métier from his father, but his competence was dubious. Once, while helping his father, he botched the banal hanging of a woman convicted of theft and subsequently, as executioner himself, he was no better than adequate. Then, on July 14, 1789, a mob assaulted the Bastille, the Revolution began to gather momentum, and before long he was vaulted into the limelight as Le Grand Sanson—a title he owed to his extraordinary ability to manipulate the new and eponymous contraption that bestowed immortality on Dr. Guillotin.

a physician and philanthropist, Guillotin was born in 1738 in Saintes, a town in the Atlantic coast province of Vendée. He taught in a Jesuit seminary in Bordeaux before moving to Paris, where he thrived practicing medicine and, among his myriad activities, lobbied to improve the city's sewers and parks. Highly esteemed as an amateur scientist, he also sat with Benjamin Franklin, then American minister to France, on a committee to evaluate Franz Anton Mesmer's assertion that "animal magnetism" was a miracle cure. He got into politics and was elected to the National Assembly, which progressive elements of the nobility, clergy and bourgeoisie organized in June 1789 in an effort to induce Louis XVI to abolish the lingering vestiges of feudal privilege—an initiative that presaged the Revolution.

As the clamor for liberalization intensified, Guillotin devoted himself to the issue of capital punishment. It was grossly inequitable, he insisted, to submit common criminals to gratuitously barbaric tortures while granting upper-crust lawbreakers the dignity of death under the ax or the sword, and he suggested as an alternative that beheading be imposed as the single form of execution. His notion was consistent with the utopian vision of a classless society espoused by Jean-Jacques Rousseau and other Enlightenment thinkers. As the story goes, Guillotin saw a tiny decapitating device in a marionette show and concluded that a large-size version of the apparatus would be efficient and, above all, humane. In December 1789, during a debate in the assembly on penal reform, he graphically described the imaginary instrument: "The blade whistles, the head topples, blood spurts, the man ceases to exist. *Messieurs*, with my simple machine I will lop off your head in the blink of an eye, and you will feel only a slight twinge in the neck." His colleagues tittered nervously and switched to more urgent matters, and Guillotin abandoned his idea.

A year later, when the debate on penal reform resumed, Maximilien de Robespierre and his radical disciples denounced capital punishment as inimical to their egalitarian ideals. Swayed by Guillotin's arguments, the assembly compromised by voting to ban torture and rely solely on decapitation, but the problem was how to implement this decision. If he were limited to beheadings, Sanson objected, he could not begin to make a dent in the dozens of convicts on death row with just one ax and two swords in his arsenal. The assembly thereupon delegated Dr. Antoine Louis, the secretary of the Academy of Surgery, to explore the feasibility of converting Guillotin's concept into a practical device. An Alsatian by origin, Louis was an army surgeon, a distinguished professor of anatomy and the author of articles on electricity. He came up with a design and, according to legend, Louis XVI offered him advice. Addicted to fiddling with locks, the king recommended that the blade be curved like a scythe to maximize its effectiveness; and, to clarify his point, he sketched the contrivance he contemplated. True or not, the anecdote was to circulate for years to come, always with the ironic punch line: "Little did His Majesty realize then that nine months later . . ."

Precursors of the device had long been used in Europe. A sixteenth-century German machine known as the *diele*, the *hobel* or the *dorbola* was depicted in etchings by Heinrich Aldegrever and Lucas Cranach illustrating the martyrdom of saints. The Halifax gibbet, an English analogue, was also being employed at the time in the Yorkshire parish of that name. In 1572, when he was designated regent of Scotland, the Earl of Morton brought with him a replica of the Halifax model, rebaptized it the Maiden and installed it in Edinburgh. A decade later, it was used by his opponents to eliminate him. The Italian equivalent of the instrument, the *mannaia*, played a central part in one of the piteous tragedies of the Renaissance: the execution in Rome on September 11, 1599, of Beatrice Cenci, a sixteen-year-old girl beheaded for the murder of her sadistic father. Based on Italian chronicles of the period, the story of her ordeal was recalled by poets and novelists from Shelley and Stendhal to Alexandre Dumas *père*, and it continued to drive readers to tears well into the twentieth century.

At first Louis proposed the task of constructing the device to a carpenter called Guidon, a builder of scaffolds. But Guidon quoted an exorbitant estimate, and Louis gave the commission to Tobias Schmidt, a harpsichord maker and fellow Alsatian. Schmidt completed a prototype in two weeks; and in March 1792, with Guillotin, Louis and Sanson present, he tested it in a courtyard abutting his atelier in the passage du Commerce-Saint-André, a Left Bank alley. The next month, after a bit of fine-tuning, they astonished a group of dignitaries gathered at the Bicêtre hospital near Paris by beheading several live sheep and five cadavers. Word of the marvel swept through the city, and it was instantly named for Louis. Soon, however, a magazine tagged it "*la guillotine*" and the label stuck—to the dismay of the kindly doctor, who until his death in 1814 at the age of seventy-six, preferred to be remembered as a humanitarian. Louis also regretted having invented "*cette machine atroce,*" his term for it. On the other hand, Schmidt ceaselessly advertised his part in the innovation. A jovial bon vivant and accomplished pianist, he would go on binges with his cronies, and sing arias from German operas. He patented the guillotine and, when it was certified as the national apparatus, procured the concession to sell it to provincial towns. He amassed a fortune, which he squandered on a rapacious demimondaine, and succumbed to alcoholism during the Napoleonic era.

The guillotine was introduced to the Paris populace on April 25, 1792, in the Place de Grève, a bustling market square on the Right Bank opposite the Île-de-la-Cité. The condemned man, Nicolas-Jacques Pelletier, found guilty of robbery, had been languishing in jail for months while the bean counters haggled with Louis over the extravagant price of the device. Multitudes, lusting for a glimpse of the new doohickey, packed the area. Dreading an accident that might discredit both him and the instrument, Sanson proceeded cautiously until it was nearly dark, and only misty silhouettes could be discerned on the scaffold. Then, in a flash, the execution was over and the crowd, accustomed to bloody bouts with the ax and sword, thundered in disappointment, "Bring back the block!" But Sanson, happy with the machine, said of it, "*Elle est très simple et, surtout, pas de bruit.*"

By summer, the Austrian and Prussian armies had invaded France, and, warning that the hallowed *patrie* was in danger, the left-wing militants in control of the assembly created a police state. Vigilantes embarked on a roundup of real or suspected enemies of the new order and hauled them before improvised revolutionary tribunals. The guillotine in the Place de Grève had chiefly dealt with ordinary criminals; now, to accommodate the increasing numbers of political targets, a duplicate was erected in the Place du Carrousel, adjacent to the Jardin des Tuileries. Its location within sight of the Louvre was uncomfortably close for Louis XVI, who had been confined to the palace with his family since his capture while trying to flee the previous year. In September the assembly dissolved the monarchy and proclaimed the republic; and, three months later, reversing his earlier hostility to capital punishment, Robespierre demanded that the king die so that, as he put it, "the country may live." His motion won overwhelming support, and the execution was fixed for the morning of January 21, 1793.

In preparation for that exalted event, the guillotine was shifted to the Place de la Révolution, originally the Place Louis XV, subsequently to be renamed the Place de la Concorde. The site had been selected as an expedient. It was close to the Temple prison, where the king had been moved, and the direct route to the scaffold would be easier to guard should his sympathizers dare to rescue him. Even so, fifteen thousand troops had been mobilized for the cavalcade, cannon were strategically deployed along the way and citizens had been instructed to shut their windows. The weather was foggy, and the sovereign's carriage and retinue struggled for two hours to get through the streets before reaching the crammed square. Solicitous for his former master's welfare, Sanson had inserted a fresh blade into his apparatus and, rumor had it, apologized to him. Yet he had a job to do—and did it with his usual vigor. He rejected Louis's request to spare him the humiliation of having his hair trimmed and wrists tied. When the king attempted to protest his innocence, Sanson signaled the drums to smother his voice. But he politely steered Louis to the device, and the deposed monarch, though witless in life, went to his death with courageous resignation. Conforming to procedure, Sanson held up his dripping head and the crowd of twenty thousand bellowed, "*Vive la république! Vive la nation!*"

In October the imperious Marie-Antoinette followed her husband to the scaffold; Sanson, taking a brief respite from his grind, assigned her decapitation to Gabriel, his elder son and *dauphin*. By then the revolutionary tribunals were busily convicting anyone even faintly associated with the ancien régime. Many of the victims, in demonstrations of bravado, sang, danced pirouettes or joked as they confronted the guillotine. One of them, a Colonel Vaujour, sniffed to Sanson, "*Vous savez*, this is interfering with my supper. Oh well, I can afford to skip a meal." But Louis XV's former mistress, the lubricious Madame Jeanne du Barry, condemned for purportedly conspiring with émigré aristocrats in England, screamed in horror and struggled with Sanson's *valets* until, with considerable difficulty, they managed to subdue her.

As revolutionary fever gripped the provinces, citizens of virtually every stripe volunteered to serve as executioners. In the Loire Valley town of Chinon, encouraged by extremists from Paris, a clown set up a guillotine and began by beheading his impresario, with whom he had been quarreling. Eventually the inhabitants rebelled, garbed him in his funny costume and put him under the blade. Another such eccentric was Joseph Le Bon, a village priest in northern France. He defrocked himself, married, preached anticlerical sermons, took over the scaffold and, to gratify his weird libido, fornicated with women before decapitating them. Ultimately he too was consumed by his knife.

In Paris, meanwhile, executions had become the most popular form of entertainment. A carnival atmosphere pervaded the Place de la Révolution, where the best spots for viewing the spectacle were from the terraces at the border of the Tuileries overlooking the square. Regulars would sit there every day, and frequently entire families appeared to stare in awe as the heads rolled. Some of them brought picnic lunches or dropped in for a snack at the convenient Cabaret de la Guillotine, whose carte du jour listed, along with the dishes, a docket of forthcoming executions. An enterprising publisher put out a bulletin containing morbid sketches of severed

heads, and theaters produced slapstick vaudevilles in which the actors, impersonating Sanson and his prominent victims, would chorus sinister lyrics that promised troublemakers a merry farewell:

Celui qui mutinera,
On fera sa fête
En coupant sa tête.

A guillotine craze also sprang up. Hordes of hawkers wandered around the square, peddling miniature guillotines as souvenirs. Parents purchased toy guillotines for their children, who derived a perverse pleasure from decapitating birds, mice or squirrels. A profitable business developed in guillotine bread slicers, fruit cutters, nutcrackers and other geegaws. Voguish ladies wore guillotine earrings and pendants, while men had themselves tattooed with guillotine motifs. Nicknamed "the little window," "the cat's hole" or "the national razor," the guillotine inspired a religious cult as well. Passionate revolutionaries known as *sans-culottes,* for their coarse peasant trousers, adopted the guillotine as their altar. They would conduct "red masses" in which they genuflected to the scaffold, chanting, "*Sainte Guillotine, protectrice des patriotes.*"

Sanson shunned these absurdities, yet he flavored the pageantry by attiring himself in an olive redingote and a jaunty tricornered hat garnished with a cockade. After a hard day he would retreat to his spacious *hôtel particulier* in the Faubourg Saint-Denis, where he resided with his wife and sons. For relaxation he puttered around in his garden or played the cello; now a celebrity, he was fair game for inquisitive visitors. He admired England, spoke impeccable English and was especially cordial toward English tourists. They would interrogate him at length, and he always answered them courteously. He kept an extra guillotine in a workshop, and, on one occasion, a capricious Englishwoman begged him to put her through the experience of a victim. Too gallant to refuse, he bound her arms, strapped her to the balancing plank and put her neck into the *lunette*. At that juncture, to his relief, she declared herself satisfied. Later Sanson confided to a friend, "I was afraid that she might ask me to let the blade fall."

In the spring of 1794, under the emblem of republican virtue, Robespierre and his Jacobin faction in the assembly unleashed the Terror. Day after day for six weeks, tumbrels carried victims to the scaffold—the more prestigious of them from the Conciergerie, the dreary dungeon beneath the Palais de Justice. The first to go were Robespierre's rival Girondists, led by Georges-Jacques Danton; then came dukes, princes, counts, barons, bishops, marshals, admirals, their wives, their children and even their servants. Also on the roster were such illustrious figures as the poet André Chénier and Antoine-Laurent Lavoisier, the chemist. Thomas Paine had recently arrived in Paris, suffused with naive notions about the Revolution. Before long he antagonized Robespierre by floating the preposterous idea of banishing Louis XVI to the United States. He might have met his end as well had not Robespierre's own execution in late July finally halted the carnage. Sanson surpassed himself: in one hectic afternoon he lopped off fifty-four heads in twenty-four minutes.

Altogether more than three thousand victims, including three hundred and fifty women and forty children, lost their lives to the

Paris guillotine—relatively few compared to contemporary standards of genocide. But in the provinces, where a virtual civil war raged, at least half a million people were slaughtered on local guillotines or in battles between opposing forces.

By 1795 the Revolution had exhausted France, but Sanson, now fifty-six, remained as energetic as ever. One morning, however, his son Gabriel slipped on a patch of blood while triumphantly displaying a head, fell off the scaffold and was killed. The calamity shattered Sanson. He ceded his sinecure to his younger son, Henri, and died in 1806. Like his father, Henri was ideologically neutral and went on to serve Napoleon and the restored Bourbon monarchs until his death forty-five years later. He was succeeded by his son, Henri-Clément, who brought down the glorious Sanson dynasty.

Then in his early forties, Henri-Clément was stout and bald. He adored music and composed verses, which he read to Baudelaire, his neighbor in the rue des Marais. But he suffered from an inhibition that made his job difficult—an aversion to the sight of blood. Though he was married, he muffled his sorrows by prowling around homosexual bars in quest of partners. He also accumulated immense gambling debts, borrowed heavily and was thrown into prison. Dunned by his creditors following his release, he surreptitiously pawned the guillotine, and was exposed when he could not produce it for a decapitation. The Ministry of Justice, after bailing out the device for nearly four thousand francs, promptly fired him. Gossip had it that he emigrated to Philadelphia and found work as a butcher; in fact, he lived with a widowed daughter in Versailles until his death in 1889 at the age of eighty-two.

During the nineteenth century, as their empire grew, the French exported the guillotine to their African, Asian and South American colonies as part of their grandiose *mission civilisatrice*. In France itself, at the same time, the new railway system had begun to connect the provinces, making it redundant for every city to subsidize its own executioner. The government consolidated the structure by appointing a single national headsman who would bear the unofficial title of Monsieur de Paris. Louis-Antoine-Stanislas Deibler, then Monsieur de Rennes and a scion of a long line of German hatchet men, was elevated to the prestigious position in 1879—and, on his death two decades later, it passed on to his son, the aforementioned Anatole.

There was a debonair belle époque quality to Anatole. As a youth he had worked under a pseudonym in a chic Paris department store, which had acquainted him with the world beyond the coterie of executioners. He sported a Vandyke beard and a waxed mustache, and dressed fastidiously in a black swallowtail coat and a silk top hat. Among his hobbies he dabbled in pottery, cultivated roses, cycled, tooled around in his spiffy Darracq limousine and seldom missed a horse race. He was brilliant with the guillotine—though some connoisseurs felt, as Jean Lorrain niggled in *Le Journal,* that "his brisk rhythm tends to deprive the decapitation of the solemnity that is, after all, its raison d'être." His protégé, Desfourneaux, never measured up to him.

When Desfourneaux died, I attended his funeral service at an ugly district church. The pews were filled with his neighbors, many of whom had undoubtedly snickered about him during his lifetime. They dozed as first the priest droned on; then a faceless bureaucrat in a ritual red, white and blue sash delivered a boilerplate eulogy. I accompanied the cortege to the Montparnasse cemetery, where a local tailor extolled Desfourneaux to a cluster of reporters: "As long as murderers threaten us, we will need men like him. He was an honest and dedicated civil servant." The next morning a newspaper ran a headline that could have applied to every executioner: *ENFIN,* MONSIEUR DE PARIS JOINS HIS VICTIMS.

11

Massacre at Le Mans

o sooner did they climb into their automobiles than the
French underwent a dramatic transformation. They might
normally be courteous, calm, even docile, but once behind the wheel they became daredevils. At intersections they would
gun their engines while waiting nervously for the light to turn green;
then, disregarding pedestrians in their path, charge forward lest they
lose a second. Flouting a Paris ordinance forbidding the use of horns,
they berated laggards with strident honks and earthy epithets. Policemen, bent on keeping the traffic flowing briskly, would wave their
batons and bellow at motorists, *"Vite, vite, messieurs, dépêchez-vous!"*
Presuming that life was less important than liberty and the pursuit of
happiness, the government refused to establish a speed limit—thus
emancipating drivers to hurtle headlong through the countryside, one
eye on the road and the other on the speedometer as they clocked
their *moyenne de vitesse.* To be overtaken was a disgrace; and, risking the
lives of their passengers and themselves, they would press their accel-
erators down to the floor. A perceptive student of French singularities,
Pierre Daninos, noted that while Americans "are convinced that a car

travels more slowly than an airplane, the French seem to be intent on proving the contrary." For all their ferocity, however, the French were astoundingly competent. Obeying an apparently implausible though eminently logical code known as *priorité à droite*, they would blithely zigzag in and out of the swirl around the Étoile or the Place de la Concorde with scarcely a crinkled fender.

The French romance with the automobile dated back to 1769, when Nicolas-Joseph Cugnot invented a steam-propelled tricycle that inched along at two miles an hour. Alphonse Beau de Rochas discovered the principle of the four-stroke engine in 1862, and twenty years later Léon-Paul-Charles Malandin pioneered the internal combustion engine. In 1891 René Panhard and Émile Levassor began to manufacture gasoline vehicles commercially, using a motor developed in Germany by Carl Benz and Gottlieb Daimler, the fathers of the Mercedes. Around the turn of the century, France was producing expensive models like the Clément-Bayard, Darracq, Delage, Delahaye, Delauney-Belleville, Dietrich-Lorraine and Hotchkiss; the Bugatti, handcrafted in his Alsace atelier by Ettore Bugatti, an imaginative Italian, fetched as much as forty thousand dollars. Shortly afterward André Citroën and Louis Renault shifted from high-priced to assembly-line cars that were within reach of the public.

In 1909, to accommodate the rising number of motorists, Michelin, the French tire company, launched its famous guide, an annual compendium of maps and garages as well as restaurants and hotels scrupulously rated by covert inspectors. Car clubs proliferated throughout the country—the swankiest of them, the Automobile Club de France, perched above the Place de la Concorde, abutting the majestic Hôtel Crillon. Detroit may have been the world's car manufacturing center, but the most prestigious showcase for the latest models was the Salon de l'Automobile, which had been inaugurated in Paris in 1913. Housed in the elaborate Grand Palais, designed for the Paris Exposition of 1900, it rapidly became a fashionable social occasion, attracting more than a million visitors a year, to the delight of shopkeepers, restaurants, hotels, nightclubs and prostitutes. In 1950 I had splurged on a minuscule Renault with a four-horsepower rear engine that sounded like a sewing machine. And, as a proud car owner, I would browse around the huge palace, its intricate glass-and-steel ceiling and allegorical statues reminiscent of a fin de siècle railroad station. Flanking the French, Dutch, Czechoslovakian and Swedish vehicles on display were Germany's dynamic Mercedes, the potent British Jaguar and the sophisticated Ferrari from Italy—testimony to Europe's astonishing economic recovery scarcely a decade after the ravages of World War II. The Americans were there primarily for public relations; as the Chrysler representative told me, "We're flying the Stars and Stripes."

Another vintage French institution, automobile racing, blossomed toward the end of the nineteenth century as a way for connoisseurs to evaluate the reliability of their crude contraptions. Clattering along country lanes, they would kick up dust, frighten peasants, scatter dogs and chickens, and frequently break down. In June 1895 the first formal competition ran from Paris to Bordeaux, a distance of six hundred miles. The winner was a Panhard, which averaged fifteen miles an hour—a feat that lent credibility to the newfangled horseless carriage. The sport quickly spread across Europe and to the United States, where in 1909 it spawned the Indianapolis Speedway. As a device to promote their vehicles, manufacturers sank enormous sums into races; the American press lord James Gordon Bennett created a trophy to publicize himself. Throngs out for vicarious thrills lined roadsides, often with calamitous consequences. In 1903 several drivers and spectators were killed in the race between Paris and Madrid, prompting the authorities to ban "point-to-point" contests.

Eventually I graduated from my Renault to a slightly larger Peugeot and, imitating the French, became a maniac about bettering my speed record. I also started to report the auto races—a plum beat that took me every year from the Rallye de Monte Carlo on the Côte d'Azur to the Grand Prix de Reims in the Champagne region and finally to the formidable Vingt-quatre Heures du Mans.

Over lunch one day in Paris in October 1922, a few French car devotees got to ruminating on the future of the adolescent automobile. No longer the exclusive playthings of the rich, cars were increasingly being acquired by the middle classes; yet even costly custom models had untrustworthy brakes, weak suspension systems and engines too powerful for their frail bodies. They also lacked such elementary accessories as headlights and windshield wipers, thereby jeopardizing a motorist out on a dark, rainy night. So, the aficionados concluded, a practical laboratory was needed to simulate all the problems that might bedevil Monsieur Dupont on a Sunday jaunt in the country. Before they had finished their coffee, cognac and cigars, they had hit on the idea of a tough round-the-clock competition to test not just speed but endurance; or as one of them, quoting an English axiom, said, "Racing improves the breed." The marathon would be restricted to factory vehicles of various horsepowers carrying standard equipment like fenders, mirrors, running boards, toolboxes and spare tires and, to replicate actual conditions, be conducted on a closed span of paved public road. Anticipating a bonanza in commerce, the Automobile Club de l'Ouest volunteered to donate an eight-mile stretch outside Le Mans, a town about one hundred and twenty miles southwest of Paris. It had been used since 1906 for the French Grand Prix, whose winner in 1921 was an American car hitherto unknown in France, the Duesenberg.

On a cold, drizzly Saturday afternoon in May 1923, an array of cars with since-forgotten names like Bignan and Rolland-Pillain, their hoods belted down, were pushed into place by mechanics. At four o'clock, an official waved the flag and the drivers, in goggles and dusters, sprinted to their vehicles and sputtered off. Completing the grind at an average of fifty-five miles an hour, a Chenard-Walcker captured the laurels. Before long elegant British Bentleys and spiffy Alfa Romeos from Italy were earning prizes. The Americans entered Chryslers, Stutz Bearcats and, one year, a Duesenberg piloted by Prince Nicholas of Romania—but they failed to click.

The giants that emerged following World War II brought phenomenal velocities to the race. During the early 1950s, Ferraris and Jaguars were regularly fracturing records with averages as high as one hundred and four miles an hour. To attain such speeds required them to zoom down straightaways at more than one hundred and eighty and to slow up at curves to ninety-five or one hundred. Success translated into fat profits for manufacturers. Its victories in 1951 and 1953 swamped Jaguar with orders; a Panhard official, whose little two-cylinder cars consistently led their class, explained to me, "Winning *les vingt-quatres* means big sales." A French journalist put it more bluntly: "There's a lot of hyperbole about glory and honor, but it's strictly money."

By then, to the disappointment of many automobile mavens, the original concept of the race had disappeared. Once similar, the cars were now a hodgepodge of horsepowers, all of them out to achieve the best speeds and mileage for their size. So on a track only thirty-five feet wide, a tiny Triumph could be pulverized by a mammoth Maserati thundering down the adjacent lane. More hazardous still was the narrow corridor in front of the pits, where vehicles pulling in for servicing faced the tricky task of jockeying for position. After a near miss, one driver confided to a friend, "We're going too fast. Unless we work out a system of signaling, there'll be trouble." It was a prescient admonition that, at the time, nobody heeded.

Moreover, production models available to the ordinary consumer had almost entirely been supplanted by vehicles expressly built for competition. Because their finely tuned engines performed poorly at low speeds, and also to preserve their delicate motors, the majority of them had to be towed to the course. "We are at a critical phase in history," warned Roger Coudrec, the editor of *Auto-Journal*. "With the industry chiefly dedicated to winning races, pure sport is being sacrificed more and more to commercialism." Fearful that their image might be tarnished by a defeat, two of the top contenders, Mercedes and Lancia, recused themselves from the 1954 lineup. But that year I went to Le Mans anyway to see Stirling Moss, the twenty-four-year-old son of a London dentist, pilot his green Jaguar against Juan Manuel Fangio, a former Buenos Aires mechanic, in a red Ferrari equipped with three carburetors. Steady and patient, Fangio did some twenty-four hundred miles at an average of nearly one hundred and seven miles an hour, nosing out Moss by a lap. For cosmetics, Ferrari's crew of drivers included the suave Dominican diplomat and playboy Porfirio Rubirosa, who was accompanied by Zsa Zsa Gabor, the latest in his multitude of girlfriends. A French mechanic, ogling her as she strutted her stuff in a skimpy bolero and contoured slacks, quipped, "*Et voilà un châssis!*"

With the big cars slated to come back in 1955, I returned to Le Mans. The drab, sleepy town's ninety thousand citizens went about their habitual business for eleven months of the year; then, in the weeks prior to the contest, they braced themselves to receive the two hundred thousand fans expected to arrive by airplane, excursion train, chartered bus, car, truck and motorcycle. An outdoor chapel erected near the track would celebrate Sunday mass; the post office was issuing a special commemorative stamp. Entrepreneurs carved out a campsite, a trailer park and an enclave called the Village des Vingt-quatre Heures, which featured cafés and food stalls, dance floors, carousels and sideshows to amuse bored mothers and children. Swarms of peddlers poured into the compound to hawk souvenir pennants, key rings, plastic helmets and other gimcrackery. Car fever even infected French intellectuals, who invariably denigrated such mass events. The highbrow Paris literary weeklies reviewed a spate of new novels with racing themes; gripped by nostalgia, the distinguished sociologist André Siegfried commented in *Le Figaro*:

"Once again France is experiencing the golden age of the automobile."

Hotel rooms were usually booked a year in advance, but I had reserved one at the venerable Concorde. Drifting into the bar, I encountered a gang of car zealots—French, British, German, Italian, American—babbling away in their disparate languages about overhead camshafts, disc brakes, fuel-injection engines and other baffling automobile anatomy. For the next couple of days I cruised around the nearby countryside, poking into rented barns and châteaux, where mechanics were grooming vehicles to function flawlessly for more than two thousand miles. They were also rehearsing their routines: refueling a car, changing its wheels, wiping its windshield, cleaning the driver's goggles and giving him a fast drink and a puff on a cigarette—all in thirty seconds or less. "The secret to winning," a mechanic explained to me, "is ninety-five percent preparation and five percent luck."

For efficiency, no squadron matched the Mercedes staff, managed by Alfred Neubauer and Rudolf Uhlenhaut, his deputy. A technical genius, Uhlenhaut had conceived a hydraulic air brake that minimized the immense pressure on a car's gears, which drivers habitually use to slow down. Solicitous for their comfort, he also remolded the seats to fit their derrieres. The most recent Mercedes, an eight-cylinder, three-hundred-horsepower model, had an innovative magnesium alloy body that reduced its weight without diminishing its strength. Imbued with Teutonic discipline, the company's engineers and mechanics had been in Le Mans since early May, stripping, reassembling and tuning up vehicles. Neubauer, though ostensibly the boss, checked every step with the head office in Stuttgart.

Lionized by the press and the public as though they were movie stars, some of the drivers could not resist the temptation to pose for photographers, grant interviews and sign autographs. The Jaguar team, which starred Duncan Hamilton and the intrepid Mike Hawthorn, was all British. But the regulations permitted pilots to work for whomever they wished, and, lured by lucrative contracts, many of them were flying under the banners of countries other than their own. The Ferrari contingent included Maurice Trintignant, a Bordeaux winegrower, and Phil Hill, an American expatriate. Jean Behra, a Frenchman and perhaps the steadiest driver in Europe, had been hired by Maserati, while Mercedes had wooed Moss away from Jaguar and Fangio from Ferrari. Mercedes had also recruited Pierre Levegh, a former antique dealer whose real name was Bouillon. A graying veteran of fifty, he had made his debut at Le Mans seventeen years earlier and nearly won in his private Talbot in 1952. To prevent a battle between them, Moss and Fangio were assigned to alternate in the same car. As a Mercedes employee told me: "Everything hinges on the drivers. No matter how well we've trained them, in the fury of a race they are beyond your reach. Human behavior is one thing you can't adjust with a wrench."

Most of the sixty entries belonged to companies, though a few were owned by amateurs who did their own driving. The largest number—twenty-seven—were British: mighty Jaguars and Aston-Martins, midsize Austin-Healeys, compact MGs and Coopers. The French cars ranged from Salmsons and Talbots to Panhards, Peugeots and Renaults; among the Italians were Ferraris, Maseratis, Morettis and a Stranguellini, a small, streamlined vehicle confected from Fiat parts. In addition to Mercedes, the German roster included a couple of Porsches. A Swiss stable was running a Porsche, and a Belgian firm a Jaguar. The multimillionaire New York socialite and yachtsman Briggs Cunningham never came even close to winning, but he showed up as he did every year with his gas-guzzling Cunningham and a regiment of assistants—only to be scratched because of a new curb on fuel consumption. The same regulation deterred General Motors from enrolling the Chevrolet Corvette.

The race was scheduled to start on the afternoon of June 11, a Saturday, and I spent the evening before at the Concorde bar, exchanging drinks with the pros and listening to them speculating on the outcome. The odds overwhelmingly favored Ferrari, Jaguar or Mercedes—depending, of course, on this, that or the other circumstance.

Dufy might have painted the scene at the track the next day. Wispy clouds wafted across the blue sky, and the flags of the participating nations fluttered in the faint breeze. Climbing into the grandstand, I located my seat in the press box. It was jammed with racing journalists armed with the tools of their trade: binoculars, chronometers, portable typewriters, time charts, stud books, manuals, sandwiches, coffee and, in some cases, flasks of booze. My neighbor, a writer for a California car magazine, wore a visored cap, necktie and navy blue blazer inscribed with the insignia of his automobile club. When I inquired how he intended to cover the contest, he earnestly described his plan to maintain an hour-by-hour, lap-by-lap ledger that would, he boasted, be a lasting contribution to the annals of the sport. I shuddered at the thought of him nailed there for the grueling twenty-four hours.

By contrast I decided to focus on color, and wandered around collecting material. A festive holiday atmosphere pervaded the crowd. The grandstand was crammed to capacity, and people spilled across the section in front. Wielding cardboard periscopes, some of them stood giddily on chairs, crates, ladders and whatever else would afford them a view; others pressed against the picket fence at the edge of the track, which for the sake of security had been bulwarked by a six-foot-high earthen barricade. In typical French style, families were savoring lavish lunches, including wine, at folding tables fastidiously laid with napkins, cloths and silverware. Uninhibited couples smooched on the grass. As usual, the drivers and mechanics had invited along their lady friends, a practice forbidden in prudish America. The popsies slunk around the pits in tight shorts or clinging leotards, and I made a note to remind myself to explore the intimate connection between sex and automobile racing.

The sweet and pungent smells of castor oil and exhaust fumes filled the air as mechanics revved their car engines. On the dot of four o'clock—the traditional starting time—an official waved the flag. The drivers sprinted to their vehicles and roared away.

Just as my buddies at the Concorde bar had forecast, Ferrari, Jaguar and Mercedes instantly dominated the race. Record after record fell as Hawthorn in the Jag and Fangio in the Mercedes escalated to one hundred and fifty an hour, then one hundred and seventy-five, then nearly one hundred and eighty. The spectators went berserk, craning their necks and shouting deliriously as the rivals tore past in what promised to be a two-man duel. I briefly shared the excitement until, realizing that the struggle was going to be monotonous, I ambled off to gather nuggets for my piece. At roughly six-thirty, I suddenly heard a deafening noise and spotted black smoke billowing over the grandstand—and witnessed the worst accident in auto-racing history.

As I subsequently reconstructed the episode, Hawthorn had lapped Levegh and, due to refuel, was barreling toward the Jaguar pit. He was slaloming through a pack of slower cars, including an Austin-Healey piloted by Lance Macklin. To gain a precious minute as he made his approach, Hawthorn swerved around the Healey, scraping its left side. Macklin slammed on his brakes, which locked. He lost a wheel, spun out of control, mowed down a gendarme and crashed into a wall along the pits. At that point Levegh, coming from behind at top speed in his Mercedes, hit the rear of Macklin's pirouetting Healey, ricocheted across the track, vaulted over the fence in front of the grandstand and plunged into the crowd. The car's inflammable magnesium body exploded, its hood ripped loose, and engine parts, like bomb pellets, riddled the spectators. Running into the road, officials, mechanics and policemen frenetically waved to the other drivers to slow down. By some miracle Macklin escaped with only bruises. Levegh's brains had to be washed out of his helmet before a Mercedes executive could deliver it to his widow as a memento. His ultimate gesture had been to signal to the cars trailing him to the danger ahead, among them Fangio in another Mercedes. Trembling like a leaf after he pulled into his pit two laps later, Fangio said, "I owe him my life."

Instinctively I had rushed toward the section in front of the stadium. It was a battlefield. Bodies were sprawled across the ground, some dead, others writhing in agony, many of them mangled beyond recognition. Virtually all the railbirds had been decapitated, probably by the Mercedes's hood. A sobbing father clutched a headless infant to his chest; one of her arms severed at the elbow, a woman was screaming for help. Threading through the carnage, I saw a man, his shattered face soaked in blood, a cigarette still between his lips. "I was going to the toilet," a stunned teenage girl told me, "when out of nowhere a foot fell on me." Drenched in sweat, their clothes in tatters, people staggered around in shock, not knowing what had happened, not knowing where to turn. Wives were frantically searching for husbands, parents for children, friends for friends. Those who found each other embraced and burst into tears; others went on looking.

The cataclysm degenerated into unbridled pandemonium as the survivors, howling and shoving in a desperate effort to flee the enclosure, collided with ghoulish mobs surging in from the opposite direction to gawk at the massacre—and possibly pick up gruesome souvenirs. The stampede snarled traffic; thousands, anxious to reassure relatives that they were unharmed, paralyzed the telephones.

Themselves dazed, gendarmes stumbled around, unable to cope with the mayhem.

Soldiers removed the corpses to an improvised morgue as a few doctors and first-aid attendants, overwhelmed by the massive number of casualties, treated them either where they lay or in tents hastily set up by Boy Scouts. A group of GIs stationed at a nearby American military base had been watching the race, and they pitched in. A priest from the outdoor chapel appeared to administer last rites. Despite my iron stomach, I almost vomited. The final toll turned out to be eighty-three dead and nearly one hundred injured, several of whom would be hospitalized for years.

To my amazement, at least twenty minutes elapsed before the arrival of the initial ambulance, which had been forced to take a circuitous route through bumpy fields and winding back lanes. The French organizers were responsible for the detour: they rejected appeals to halt the race and open the main roads into the ravaged area, and balked at announcing the disaster or even broadcasting the names of the victims. Justifying their decision, they contended that they wanted to prevent panic, but insiders claimed that their real motive was to avoid reimbursing the ticket holders. So the contest went on and on at its increasingly dizzy pace as the track announcer spouted statistics and, in a voice vibrating with contrived emotion, repeated over the loudspeaker, "*La bataille continue, la bataille continue!*"

Kept in the dark, spectators who had been a mere sixty or seventy yards from the site of the tragedy had no inkling of what had occurred. All he first heard, a man who had been seated at the extreme of the grandstand later told me, was that seven or eight people had been hurt in some sort of mishap. Returning to the press box to retrieve my belongings, I was flabbergasted to see reporters still concentrating on the race. My neighbor from California was solemnly hunched over his charts, his stopwatch in hand, oblivious to the extent of the accident. "Don't interrupt me," he said peevishly when I tried to describe the havoc to him. "You're fucking up my tabulations." I found it equally bewildering that the revelers at the Village des Vingt-quatre Heures, less than a mile away, had not been disturbed. The cafés, dance floor, shooting gallery and other carnival entertainment had gone on throughout the night, and they learned the news only from radio or the morning papers.

Alfred Neubauer, the Mercedes chief, was determined to stay in the contest; and the French organizers, concerned that his team's withdrawal would blemish the reputation of the race and damage its future, supported him. But most of his associates disagreed. After hours of acrimonious debate, Fritz Koenecke, the Mercedes general manager in Stuttgart, chose to retire. "Even if we had triumphed," he said, "I would not have accepted the victory." Reluctantly ordering his mechanics to flag in the company's two remaining cars, Neubauer muttered, "Too many dead. It's finished. *Finito.*"

Hawthorn won in the big-car category, having completed approximately twenty-six hundred miles at an average speed of more than one hundred and six miles an hour. But controversies over the race dragged on for weeks, frazzling national nerves. Some German newspapers blamed Hawthorn's maneuver for the upheaval, and the British press denounced them for attacking him. Criticizing the French organizers for failing to suspend the contest, several commentators suggested that the event ought to be canceled forever—to which a French automobile expert, Raymond Marcillac, replied with faultless Cartesian logic: "Just because we have train catastrophes, should we dismantle the railway system?"

My dispatch earned three columns in *Time* and a page in *Sports Illustrated.* I never went to a car race again.

12

The Good Samaritan

Paris winters could be marrow-chilling. The climate was clammy, leaden clouds curtained the sky for months and the leafless trees in the squares and parks resembled rows of skeletons. The *chauffage central* in their apartments a fiction, people would spend their evenings huddled around potbellied stoves in their neighborhood cafés, bracing themselves with alcohol and grumbling more than the French habitually did. But the atmosphere, if dark and depressing, was at least tolerable. Then, in early February 1954, the worst cold wave in memory struck the city, awakening its residents to a grim reality: despite their conviction that they had the best welfare system in the world, the situation was abysmal for thousands.

Over the course of a week, the severe weather claimed the lives of approximately one hundred citizens, among them infants and elderly folk trapped in ramshackle, unheated tenements. The police found a woman sprawled dead on the Boulevard de Sébastopol, an eviction notice from her landlord clutched in her fist; the morgue was crammed with the frozen bodies of *clochards,* the bums who camped under the bridges along the Seine. Countless others were

sick and shivering, and the authorities seemed to be unable to cope until a remarkable Jesuit priest emerged. Calling himself Abbé Pierre, he was a tiny figure of forty-one, with a craggy face, crooked teeth, dewy eyes and an unkempt beard. He wore a black, threadbare, ankle-length soutane, a tattered beret and thonged sandals, and carried a gnarled cane as though he were a medieval monk. But his quaint guise concealed a prodigious organizer and showman with a shrewd sense of the dramatic—talents he orchestrated to launch a remarkable relief operation.

A tireless promoter, he spoke from church pulpits, in the streets, over the radio, during theater intermissions, even in nightclubs. One evening he brazenly climbed onto the stage at the Gaumont Palace, an enormous Paris cinema, interrupted the film and, with a spotlight silhouetting his profile against the white screen, confronted the audience. "*Mes amis, aidez-nous,*" he pleaded in a gentle voice. "Dig into your attics and cellars. They may contain valuables you cherish and want to keep forever, but nothing is more valuable than saving our babies."

The French were not particularly philanthropic. They traditionally confined their benevolence to their families and tended to spurn charity as degrading to the donor and humiliating to the recipient.

The fiscal system, which lacked provisions for tax deductions, also deterred their altruism. But they responded to Pierre's entreaties with unprecedented generosity. Within two weeks more than one billion francs—nearly half a million dollars—had poured into his coffers from actors, writers, artists, politicians, businessmen, sentimental prostitutes and habitually tightwad peasants. Schoolchildren pooled their pocket money. To set an example, Vincent Auriol, the amiable former president of the Republic, donned his swallowtail coat, top hat, tricolor sash and rows of medals, and posed for photographers signing a personal check. The Red Cross offered its services. News of the crisis spread abroad, eliciting funds from Britain, Belgium, Switzerland, Holland, West Germany and Scandinavia; a club of Francophiles in the United States pledged to send over the equivalent of CARE packages.

Caught up in the campaign, the directors of the Métro converted three unused stations into a dormitory for the homeless, and the French railways reopened a closed wing of the gingerbread Gare d'Orsay as storage space for supplies of food, clothing and medicines. With the unanimous approval of his guests, the proprietor of a pricey hotel near the Place de l'Opéra turned his lobby over to Pierre as a distribution center. A movie company announced plans to produce a picture about him titled *The Ragpicker Priest*. Day after day the popular press featured his efforts, and helping him became one of those fashionable diversions that periodically enchanted Parisians. Society ladies and aristocrats who would normally flinch at sullying their fingers volunteered to run makeshift refuges, while Sorbonne professors and students deserted their lecture halls and cafés to serve meals and wash dishes at hastily constructed canteens.

"The Abbé Pierre's courageous battle against distress deserves high praise," editorialized *La Croix,* the Catholic daily. The comment was privately echoed by Cardinal Achille Liénart, the archbishop of Lille, and other Church dignitaries, who welcomed any publicity that countered the anticlerical sentiments that pervaded much of France. But, reluctant to lionize an individual priest, the Church hierarchy balked at endorsing Pierre officially—especially after a fanciful newspaper columnist touted him as a candidate for sainthood. The Communist Party was ambivalent. Predictably condemning charity as an artifice contrived by the bourgeoisie to hoodwink the downtrodden masses, its propagandists asserted that the only solution for poverty was the Marxist revolution—while members of its satellite labor union, the Confédération Générale du Travail, straying from party doctrine, enthusiastically applauded Pierre's endeavors as preferable to allowing the indigent to suffer.

The zealous little friar striving against overwhelming odds to achieve good was a story that perfectly fit *Time*'s moralistic formula. Covering him also promised me a glimpse into the squalid side of Paris—an aspect of the city that differed drastically from its romantic stereotype. One icy night I accompanied Pierre as he toured his installations, and it was a frenetic experience.

Crouched behind the wheel of his green Renault, he tore back and forth across town, careering around corners, ignoring traffic lights, disregarding pedestrians. He would suddenly stop at an improvised warehouse for a fleeting look, then, his cassock flapping behind him, sprint off to another destination. At seven we visited a Left Bank lycée, where he checked a mound of shirts and trousers, and cautioned an assistant to guard against thieves: "*Fais gaffe aux voleurs.*" Less than hour later, at a similar depot, he examined piles of sheets and blankets before proceeding to the auditorium of a local *mairie* to dun a crowd for money. After leaving there he pulled up with a screech of his brakes at a cluster of tents on the grounds of Saint-Étienne-du-Mont, the magnificent Romanesque and Gothic church near the Panthéon. "Don't worry about the gendarmes," he assured the unemployed plumber in charge. "I consulted the commissioner, and he guaranteed me that they won't bother you." Toward midnight, his pace undiminished, he dashed over to the Seventeenth Arrondissement to investigate an office building that had been emptied of its bureaucratic paraphernalia to accommodate the needy. He requested a list of their names, explaining, "We'll aid anyone who requires assistance after this cold snap is finished." It was past three as he headed for his seedy hotel off the boulevard des Italiens. He was exhausted, as indeed I was, but he could not resist the temptation to ask the police patrolling the streets if any people were sleeping on the sidewalks.

I caught up with him at six-thirty the next morning at Saint-Philippe-du-Roule, a church tucked away among the chic boutiques of the rue du Faubourg Saint-Honoré, where he had been invited to celebrate mass. Then he hurtled off to an appointment in the suburbs to discuss emergency housing; by eleven he was back in Paris to recommend to the municipal council that a select number of restaurants be subsidized to provide the destitute with free lunches. A couple of hours later he met at a theater with a group of entertainers who visualized a project for putting on a benefit on his behalf. I stuck to him for the remainder of the day and into the night as he continued to make the rounds of his shelters—patiently listening to tales of woe, dispensing advice, issuing instructions to his adjutants, fretting about details. At one point an upper-crust matron in a leopard coat and matching busby stepped out of a chauffeur-driven limousine and handed him an envelope filled with banknotes. "*Monsieur l'Abbé*," she gushed, "only now do I appreciate the agony of others. You have opened my eyes."

Long before the frigid winter thrust him into the headlines, Pierre had been concerned by the plight of the poor—and, as we zigzagged around Paris, he recalled his past. The fifth of eight children of a rich Lyon silk manufacturer, he was baptized Henri-Antoine Groues. He grew up in comfort, attended Jesuit schools and was scheduled to follow in his father's footsteps. "But deep in my soul I felt unfit for the bourgeois life," he told me. In 1931, at the age of eighteen, with his family's blessing, he entered a Capuchin monastery in northern France. The routine was rigorous, he contracted tuberculosis, and his superiors transferred him to the city of Grenoble, whose invigorating mountain air soon restored his health. Along with his other duties, he dedicated himself to proselytizing among youth groups and factory workers, and was eventually appointed vicar of the cathedral—a position he held until late 1942, when the Germans occupied the whole of France.

Joining the Resistance, he took advantage of his status as a priest to camouflage his covert activities. He helped Jews to flee the country, forged official documents, printed secret leaflets and, writing for clandestine publications, maintained that it was ethically justified to kill Nazis. Threatened with arrest, he enlisted in the legendary Vercors maquis and engaged in guerrilla attacks against the German forces. Once, when General de Gaulle's brother, Jacques, ill and disabled, was being pursued by the Gestapo, he lugged him in his arms through the Alps to safety in Switzerland. Captured and imprisoned by the enemy, he escaped, crossed the Pyrénées into Spain and finally reached Algiers, the headquarters of the Free French government, which awarded him six decorations for valor. It was during this hegira that he adopted the nom de guerre of Pierre, after St. Peter, to whom he attributed his salvation.

After the excitement of war, like many another hero, he had trouble adjusting to the humdrum of peace. But unless he carved out a mission for himself, his only alternative was to become a simple parish priest, a prospect that alarmed him. One day over drinks an Underground comrade suggested that he explore politics, and the notion sounded attractive. Several distinguished veterans of the Resistance, notably Georges Bidault and Pierre-Henri Teitgen, had just mobilized the Mouvement Républicain Populaire, a Christian Democratic party that, in contrast to the reactionary Catholics of the prewar era, was committed to a progressive platform. Aware of his record, they gave Pierre a slot on their ticket and, in 1946, he was elected to the National Assembly.

Initially, eager to educate himself in the complexities of politics, he fastened on parliamentary matters. He was also intrigued by the World Federalists, who preached the vision of global government, and, in 1948, he traveled to their convention in Minneapolis. The vitality of the United States astounded him but, Pierre said to me, "I was appalled by its materialism. For Americans, acquiring goods is an end in itself."

Back in Paris, he resumed his legislative functions, but politics increasingly disillusioned him. To marshal a ruling majority, the disparate factions in the chamber were constantly cobbling together coalitions, often with partners whose principles they abhorred. In 1950, as an expedient, the Christian Democrats and Radical Socialists created a cabinet that offended Pierre's naive idealism. To him the Radicals represented the avaricious bourgeoisie—and, in addition, they were anticlerical. In protest he quit his party and formed his own movement, which he labeled the Centre de la Gauche Indépendante. Running for office from a constituency in Alsace, he was badly defeated. The loss of his seat in the National Assembly cost him his slender wage. Presently, down to his last sou, he was actually reduced to panhandling to make ends meet. "There I was, without the slightest idea what to do," he confided to me. "I was desperate."

By chance a dilemma propelled him into a new vocation. Evicted from his apartment, he located a seamy house in an industrial district on the fringe of Paris and repainted its interior, repaired its shattered windows, rehinged its shaky doors and shingled its roof. Shortly afterward he encountered a young couple and their two small children, who had been expelled from their cheap hotel room. He took them in, and word immediately circulated that "*le petit prêtre à barbe*" was a soft touch. Before long he was besieged by swarms of invalids, widows, orphans, drunks and assorted other outcasts, clamoring for lodging, clothing, medicine and money. Beggars would show up out of nowhere to share his meager dinner. He wrestled with their problems as best he could, frequently sacrificing himself in the process. One family of six, whom he allowed to stay for a month, squatted for a year. Now, he resolved, he had been ordained by God to care for the impoverished and embarked on fulfilling the role of Good Samaritan.

*H*earing that an abandoned army barracks was on the market for four hundred thousand francs, Pierre floated a loan to buy it, then persuaded some political cronies to underwrite the debt. He salvaged decrepit furniture from dumps and, in 1951, charging fifty francs a night, sheltered a total of three thousand men, women and children. But if he expected to cater to the deprived masses, he would have to accumulate far more capital. Contemplating the challenge, he concluded that the junk trade, efficiently run, might yield enough to finance a larger venture. He decided to title it Emmaus, from the Gospel of Luke: "And behold, two of them went that very day to the village called Emmaus, which was from Jerusalem about three-score furlongs."

To start out, he wangled a spot on a radio quiz show, *Quitte ou Double,* breezed through a series of questions on international affairs and won three hundred thousand francs. Exploiting every opportunity to generate funds, he delivered the eulogy at the burial of a six-month-old who had died of exposure, and shamelessly passed a plate among the mourners. He sank the money into two secondhand trucks, and by hook or by crook acquired other articles. Contacting a dealer in American military surplus, for example, Pierre propositioned him, "*Écoutez, mon ami,* you're Jewish and I'm Catholic, but we both worship the same God. Find me tables, chairs, pots, pans, whatever you have, and I will pay you when I can." A congenial real estate agent steered him to three vacant lots on the dreary outskirts of Paris, and he induced the man to extend him credit to purchase them. Scores of jobless mechanics, carpenters, electricians, masons and other craftsmen drifted in, many of them with their wives and children, and, under Pierre's guidance, they began to build shanty-towns.

On a damp, nippy afternoon a couple of years later, he guided me around one of the sites. Its roughly two hundred inhabitants lived in sleazy shacks, derelict trailers, buses and freight cars, without gas, electricity or running water. Filthy children darted about and, hunched over tubs, women were doing laundry. As we slogged through mud and skirted brackish puddles, Pierre said, "I admit that it is not a very pretty sight, but better than sleeping in the cold streets, *n'est-ce pas?*" He introduced me to some of his protégés, whose diverse backgrounds were a reminder that poverty spared no-body—including the privileged classes. One of them, Comte Ferdinand d'Oullenbourg, was descended from forebears ennobled by Napoleon and, Pierre intimated, had squandered his inheritance gambling. Raymond Delfau, a graduate of the Saint-Cyr military academy, was a veteran of North Africa and Indochina, and André Loubet had been a stockbroker. Unskilled, they sorted out junk. Hippolyte Bragard, a former garage owner, kept the vehicles tuned up, and François Wetzel, an engineer, drove trucks. Louis Trahan, a professional chef, commanded the soup kitchen.

Every morning they fanned out to cull rubbish heaps and garbage cans for anything that might fetch a few francs—a piece of copper pipe, a cracked bathroom sink, a sheet of corrugated tin, a rusty automobile motor—which they towed back by truck, cart or hand. Alexandre Simonet, a onetime shopkeeper and reformed alcoholic, would telephone wholesalers, who hauled the scrap away. "We are just about breaking even," Pierre explained to me, "but our essential objective is to boost the morale of these men and develop their confidence in themselves—and in that respect we're making headway."

Originally he pondered the possibility of founding a utopian Christian community but soon discarded the concept as too sectarian. "I didn't want to insist on religion," he stressed. "Our gates are open to all, including agnostics and even atheists. You're given your daily bread whatever your creed." Almost nobody went to morning mass in his little cinder-block chapel; some showed up on Sunday and the others stayed in bed. Still, he counted three priests and seven novices among his staff. I also noticed that crosses dotted the terrain, and rising from a hillock was an ugly cement statue of the Virgin Mary. His settlers, Pierre mentioned, jokingly styled the haven Notre-Dame-des-Sans-Logis—Our Lady of the Homeless. "For me that symbolizes our spiritual success," he observed. "We're no longer in the Middle Ages, when the Church depended on the fear of hell to recruit believers. My approach is practical. Give people warmth, food, a roof over their heads—and, above all, hope—and perhaps they'll embrace the faith. I can't be certain, however. Come back in a century or two, and we will see."

The workers in and around his colonies were invariably Communists or sympathizers who participated in such rituals as the Fête de l'Humanité and the annual May Day procession from the Place de la Bastille to the Place de la République. To display his solidarity with them, Pierre regularly appeared in the parade, carrying a placard, clenching his fist and chanting anti-American and pro-Soviet slogans. He also marched in demonstrations denouncing the Marshall Plan, the North Atlantic Treaty Organization, even Coca-Cola. As a result, conservatives assailed him either as a Communist or a dupe. One evening, as we chatted about the allegations, he said indignantly, "*Vous savez*, I am first and foremost a priest. It is insidious to suppose that I could subscribe to an ideology that denies the existence of God. At the same time, however, I cannot alienate my proletarian friends—partly out of loyalty and also because, without them, it would be impossible for me to discharge my responsibilities."

Pierre repeated again and again to me—and to anyone else who would listen—that his goals were limited. "The aim of our modest agitation is to alert our compatriots; unless urgent measures are taken to meet the mounting demand for social justice, a violent insurrection could convulse the nation. Only the administration has the resources to avert that peril, but it must act now." But the politicians were too involved in their own struggle for survival to heed his message.

Since the end of World War I, France had lagged behind the rest of Western Europe in the construction of dwellings. Stiff rent controls, imposed by the government to ease the burden on millions of veterans and war widows, made new building unprofitable; and the chronically stagnant economy further discouraged investment. But no sector was more neglected than public housing, which principally affected the poor. To punctuate the deficiency, Pierre haunted the corridors of the National Assembly, collaring members and exhorting them to vote for appropriations. One day, after a baby succumbed to the cold in a slum, he addressed a caustic letter to the minister of housing, Maurice Lemaire, and leaked a copy to the newspapers. In it he virtually blamed Lemaire for the death, and defied him to attend the child's funeral. His reputation at stake, the minister agreed, and together they drove to a shabby Paris cemetery, where Pierre conducted the ceremony. Lemaire wept and, as they strolled away from the grave, apologized to the priest: "It never occurred to me that we have such misery in France." The next morning, in a note to Pierre, he vowed to sponsor a liberal housing bill, affirming, "I intend to make it my priority." A legislative wrangle over the budget delayed the motion, however, and Lemaire lamely announced a week later that work would start on two hundred emergency dwellings in May—three months hence. Furious, Pierre barged past the *huissiers* guarding the minister's office and, brandishing his cane, shouted, "*Trop peu, trop tard!* There are no fewer than a thousand homeless in Paris alone, and thousands more elsewhere! Children are dying daily! They can't wait while politicians squabble! For them a week, a month or a year is a century!"

Stunned by Pierre's outburst, Lemaire initiated a new measure to spend ten billion francs on public housing over the coming year. It languished in committee, yet another reshuffle of the turnstile government compelled the cabinet to resign, he lost his portfolio—and nothing was done.

Disappointed, Pierre forged ahead on his own. Relying on junk sales, contributions and other revenue, he expanded Emmaus to thirty shelters capable of caring for more than two thousand homeless a night. He also compiled a register of volunteers that he termed his *fraternité*. But soon spring arrived, and the needy faded from the minds of Parisians. Basically, though, their conditions had not improved, and I wondered whether Pierre could again muster support for them when winter, as it inevitably would, returned.

13

Le Strip-Tease

~~~

rench chauvinists were constantly cautioning against the sinister influence of American pop culture, contending that it
threatened to subvert the nation's glorious patrimony. But, as
far as I could judge, the overwhelming majority of French citizens
disregarded such warnings. They were already addicted to *les westerns,*
and the younger generation had long been captivated by *le jazz hot;*
now, during the 1950s, they began to embrace yet another Yankee
import—a perambulant art form that, for lack of a term of their own,
they called *le strip-tease.*

At scores of Paris nightclubs and theaters, ecdysiasts with such
suitable noms de guerre as Kira Takitoff, Lilli La Pudeur and Coco
Minette were peeling down to the irreducible *cache-sexe,* or G-string,
a phrase recently validated by the editors of the authoritative *Diction-
naire Larousse.* Nearly every *boîte* in town was touting *"les merveilles du
strip,"* *"les champions du strip"* or *"l'élite du strip."* One of them had concocted *"le strip-quiz,"* which entitled a customer with the correct answer to remove an article of clothing from the girl in the spotlight; at
others, dancers were disrobing to appropriate Bizet arias or verses by

Baudelaire. The craze was also sweeping the provinces as typists, seamstresses and shop clerks wiggled their *poitrines* and *derrières* in amateur striptease contests at carnivals or country fairs.

The phenomenon kindled a passionate debate among the French, who as usual rejoiced in controversy. Conservative Catholics denounced it as a deplorable symptom of mounting immorality, and Communists decried it as another example of France's pusillanimous surrender to American imperialism. The intelligentsia welcomed it as a blow for aesthetic liberty, while the theater milieu applauded it as a boon to business. One impresario, Robert Baze, carried away by the sound of his own hyperbole, hailed the trend as a progressive step forward in Franco-American relations: "I am profoundly gratified," he proclaimed, "to witness this new and fruitful exchange between two great countries and traditional allies—France and the United States. It is my dream that someday, when we have perfected an authentic French version of *le strip-tease,* one of our companies will, like the Comédie Française, undertake a state visit to America."

The juicy subject charmed *Time*'s editors and appealed to my own prurient tastes, and I enthusiastically dug into it. Combing through archives and old periodicals, I found that *le strip-tease* had inadvertently originated one night in February 1893 at the Moulin Rouge, the Montmartre cabaret immortalized in Toulouse-Lautrec's posters. Students had leased the hall for their annual Bal des Quat'z Arts, which invariably degenerated into a drunken bash. Encouraged by the delirious youths, a zaftig model named Mona jumped onto a table and discarded her clothes in a flamboyant fandango. Accounts of her indecent exposure incurred the righteous wrath of a certain Senator Béranger, a vehement puritan. He engineered her arrest, and the Latin Quarter exploded. Students burned him in effigy, then paraded up and down the boulevard Saint-Michel, carrying placards and thundering slogans vowing to struggle for "artistic nudity." Gendarmes attacked the marchers, and, in the ensuing fracas, an innocent bystander was fatally wounded. A mob besieged the police station, and troops had to be summoned to restore order. The government, embarrassed at having lost control, apologized to the protesters, acknowledging indirectly that Mona and other women had every right to shake off the shackles of convention.

The publicity caused by the tumult persuaded the owner of Le Divan Fayouau, a dinky Montmartre cabaret, that there was money in nudity—or at least the illusion of nudity. To circumvent censorship he contrived a sketch called *"Le Coucher d'Yvette,"* whose leading lady prepared for bed, yet never actually disrobed, leaving the spectators to envision her in the buff as the lights dimmed. Fayouau packed the house night after night, the vogue spread, and soon his rivals were advertising similarly risqué skits, like *"Le Bain de Suzanne"* and *"Nicole Chez le Médecin."* One of them, titled *"La Puce,"* in which the ingenue went through the motions of examining herself for a fleabite, toured Europe to rave reviews, encountering different statutes in different cities: she could provocatively bend over to scratch her ankle in Munich, though not in Budapest. Another way to evade the blue laws was to mount *tableaux vivants,* renditions of classical paintings of scantily clad goddesses and nymphs suggestively gamboling with lecherous gods and satyrs in sylvan settings.

Paris music halls evolved from the *café-concert,* whose customers, most of them workers and small shopkeepers, could nurse a cheap beer or a cup of coffee as a chanteuse performed to the strains of a string ensemble. Inaugurated in 1869, the Folies-Bergères immediately became famous for its eclectic repertory of singers, dancers, jugglers, wrestlers, magicians, women weight lifters and one-legged tightrope walkers. One of its early sensations was *"Buffalo Bill et Ses Peaux-Rouges"* in a breathtaking display of horsemanship and sharpshooting. Crowds streamed in merely to stare at its exotic decors—Moroccan gardens, Algerian bazaars, Egyptian temples, Turkish harems, Japanese pagodas. Despite complaints by reformers, the director allowed selected prostitutes to ply their trade in the semicircular *promenoir* behind the auditorium, where interpreters were also on hand to assist foreigners unable to speak French. Little hotels nearby, known as *maisons de passe,* discreetly rented rooms by the hour.

A grievous setback befell the Folies in 1880, after its boss, Léon Sari, inexplicably experienced a religious conversion and, along with other drastic revisions of the program, commissioned a choir to sing hymns. Its clientele swiftly switched to livelier spots, notably Le Chat Noir, a Montmartre cabaret whose *compère,* Aristide Bruant, shocked and titillated his fans by ridiculing the authorities in gutter argot. Garbed exactly as Toulouse-Lautrec portrayed him, in a flowing crimson scarf, broad-brimmed hat and black velvet cape, he presaged the *chansonniers* of later years, who delighted the starchy bourgeoisie by satirizing their foibles.

Now under new management, the Folies recouped with the daring cancan, whose high-kickers tantalizingly revealed a trace of skin between their silk stockings and their fluffy drawers. In 1907, inspired by the permissive ambience of the belle époque, the theater boldly presented bare breasts for the first time on a Paris stage in a pantomime in which a cuckolded husband, in a fit of jealousy, angrily tears off his wife's negligée. The abused spouse, Colette, would retire between scenes to her dressing room to write the lyrical novels and short stories that subsequently made her one of France's foremost authors, a *grand officier* of the Légion d'Honneur and the first woman to be elevated to the Académie Française. Earlier she had scandalized Paris by appearing in a lesbian playlet at the Moulin Rouge with her lover, the Marquise de Belbeuf. Colette enchanted Maurice Chevalier, then a soaring young Folies star, who was to recall that she had the "most luscious *tétons* in the world."

For years nudes were standard fare at the Folies and other Paris music halls—though regulations required them to remain immobile lest they divulge too much flesh. The ordinances became increasingly lax and by the 1920s, the unchallenged *vedette* at the Folies,

Josephine Baker, was prancing around in nothing except banana leaves. Shortly afterward another innovation came to the Folies—a male nude from Vienna whose act consisted of flexing his muscles.

By comparison, Broadway lagged behind under stringent obscenity codes, which prohibited even uncovered navels. Not until in 1918 did its preeminent impresario, Florenz Ziegfeld, reluctantly include a nude in a revue, concealing her among the frills and foliage of his fabulous scenery. He made the move only to keep up with his competitors, and condemned the practice as outrageously lewd: "These orgies of nakedness are disgusting, worse than one can find in the dives of Europe."

Pursuing my research, I wandered the Montmartre area around the Place Pigalle—"Pig Alley," in GI parlance. Once a magnet for such creative titans as Berlioz, George Sand, Zola, Turgenev, Manet, Degas, Toulouse-Lautrec, Utrillo and Picasso, it had deteriorated into a tenderloin of scruffy joints, whose hostesses and dancers often doubled as hookers. Hustlers lined its narrow streets, proposing porno films and live *exhibitions* that offered a staggering array of sexual permutation. It was this sort of sleaze that represented *"Gai Paris la Nuit"* to much of the world.

At the opposite extreme of the social spectrum was the Crazy Horse Saloon, a cellar boîte located across from the American Cathedral on the posh avenue George V, which featured the most elegant strip show in Paris. Popularly known as Le Crazy, it was a facsimile cowboy bar furnished in quaint Americana, with swinging doors and signs reading "Ask for Credit and Drop Dead" and "Check Your Guns Here." The waiters wore tattersall vests, candy-striped shirts, red suspenders and sleeve garters. One night, as I entered, a banjo player was strumming Western tunes as the master of ceremonies rattled on in an approximation of twangy English, "Howdy, friends and neighbors. Pull up a stool and make yourselves at home."

The clientele was chiefly composed of chic Parisian couples—the men in black tie, the women in fashionable gowns. During the two-hour spectacle, I noticed, they were almost reverently silent; and knowing the French penchant for intellectualizing, I wondered whether they intended to analyze it afterward, as though they had been to a Giraudoux drama, a Renoir film or an Erik Satie ballet. It also occurred to me how remote this all was from my high school days, when I cut classes to spend an afternoon at Minsky's in Times Square to ogle Ann Corio, Margie Hart, Georgia Sothern or Gypsy Rose Lee as she swiveled down the runway, bumping and grinding to raucous chants of "Take it off!" from the rows of bald heads.

In contrast to those veterans, some of whom tended to be Ruben-esque, the deciduous girls at Le Crazy were lithe and nubile. And, unlike the crude ribaldry at Minsky's, their routines were erotic fantasies. In one, a tall brunette billed as Miss Candida languorously undressed, slipped into a bath and meticulously lathered her slender body. She was followed by Pussy Deluxe, who squirmed on a divan by candlelight as she awaited her lover. In another act, African savages stripped Didi Fortunia to the throb of a tom-tom. For kinkier appetites there was a Teutonic blonde labeled Dodo d'Hambourg, shedding her leather miniskirt and cracking a whip in a simulated sadomasochistic tryst. The finale, which was supposed to be a political pastiche, fell flat after France's humiliation during the German occupation: Bertha Von Paraboum, appareled only in boots and a spiked helmet, with a swastika for a fig leaf, swaggering around like a Nazi gauleiter.

But whatever its flaws, Le Crazy was booming, and, to learn the key to his success, I returned a few days later for a chat with its proprietor, Alain Bernardin. A sinewy, balding athletic former antique dealer of about forty, he ruminated on the obstacles that had confronted him back in 1951, when he first contemplated the idea of opening a club. "Nudes are de rigueur, and I knew that I would have to employ them—though how? In most Paris boîtes they just stand on the stage with a stupid expression on their faces; if I hoped to be distinctive, I had to conceive a more imaginative angle. An imitation of the American striptease, which conforms to a folkloric pattern, would never click here. Americans, for instance, prefer mature strippers; the French like theirs to be as young as possible. I needed a fresh angle to attract blasé, sophisticated and, above all, pretentious upper-crust Parisians—in short, *le strip-tease à la française,* not a prosaic *déshabillage* to a pounding bolero beat. They want something cerebral, with a credible theme, that gives them the impression that they are being uplifted—an event, you might say, that they can peer at through their monocles."

Bernardin pinned seductive sobriquets on his girls and taught them the art of stripping. To illustrate the various techniques, he made a training movie, *L'École du Strip-Tease,* and translated American burlesque patois into French: *le coup de cul* for "bump," *moulin à café* for "grind." When I mentioned that his sketches were rather raunchy, he replied, "This is Paris, not Boston; the vice squad leaves us alone, and we can do what we please." As a promotional gimmick, and also to cloak himself in institutional respectability, he founded the Académie du Strip-Tease, borrowing, as its pertinent motto, *"Honi soit qui mal y pense,"* from the Order of the Garter. Its directors included Jean Baylet, the former Paris prefect of police; the actress Martine Carol; and Edmond Heuse, a professor at the École des Beaux-Arts and a member of the distinguished Institut de France. Their initial gesture was to elect *"la reine du strip-tease"*—who by no coincidence turned out to be Miss Candida, one of Bernardin's protégées.

Intrigued that the august professor would lend himself to such an obvious publicity stunt, I arranged for a rendezvous and took the Métro to the Left Bank, where he occupied a vast, sunny atelier atop a medieval building overlooking the Seine. A gaunt, garrulous eccentric nearing eighty, with stooped shoulders and a shaggy gray mane, he waved me to an armchair and mused on his life, recollecting that he had been a professional cyclist, a circus clown and a

cabaret dancer before becoming an academic. Then, launching into a long-winded discourse, he said: "I worship beauty, hence I defend *le strip-tease* out of admiration for feminine beauty and loveliness, and respect for human dignity. To call it immoral is absolutely ludicrous; you have only to observe our Romanesque churches, with their subtle symbiosis of the profane and the sacred. Speaking as an art expert, I would add that these girls are splendid animals. They demonstrate that nudes can be as gorgeous as anything on earth. With homosexuality on the rise, they are also rendering a service to our youth. But, I must concede, they are frequently filthy, even pornographic. Unless we limit the practice to the most skilled among them, we are in danger of disgracing France."

While the Paris smart set patronized Le Crazy, the French petite bourgeoisie and foreign tourists favored such big nightclubs as Le Bal Tabarin, La Nouvelle Ève, the modernized Moulin Rouge and particularly the brassy Lido, which was situated beneath a shopping arcade on the Champs-Élysées. I caught the revue one night, and it was straight out of Las Vegas. As the orchestra struck up a schmaltzy melody, eighteen statuesque girls in elaborate costumes floated across the floor. Then, in rapid sequence, followed crooners and torch singers, gymnasts, puppeteers, a ventriloquist, a female impersonator, slapstick comedians and a relic of the golden age of vaudeville, Borah Minevitch and his Harmonica Rascals. But nothing dazzled me more than the multitude of nudes. Minimally attired in multicolored *caches-sexe* and embellished with bouffant wigs, ostrich plumes and rhinestone tiaras, they were poised on pedestals, under illuminated fountains, suspended from ceiling contraptions, reflected in gigantic mirrors. My pal Art Buchwald of the Paris *Herald Tribune,* who knew nightclubs as well as anyone, rated the Lido "the finest in the world today."

Next morning I went back to see its owner, Pierre-Louis Guérin, a stout, amicable figure in his early fifties. We sat in his spacious office amid signed portraits and other showbiz mementos as he rambled on in a potpourri of French and English, much of it slang. He had studied the cello as a boy but was rejected by the Paris Conservatory and stumbled into various jobs, like running a restaurant and a ski resort in the Alps. After a stint in the army during World War II, he bought into a boîte near the Champs-Élysées. The city was then swarming with GIs, their pockets bulging with cash, and Guérin flourished. Later, in partnership with a couple of wealthy Italians, he took over the Lido, which had fallen into disrepair. They decorated it to resemble a Venetian palazzo and spared no expense to stage the most glittering revues in Paris. "The French are hard to budge in the evening," Guérin explained to me. "All they want to do is hang out in their cafés, go to the cinema or listen to the radio at home. My ambition was to lure them out with a disciplined, fast-paced *spectacle à l'américaine* that would also draw the tourist trade."

Convinced that top talent was available only abroad, Guérin recruited English chorus girls, Belgian acrobats, Gypsy violinists and a German marksman who emulated William Tell. Twice a year he scoured the United States, bringing back designers, choreographers and legends like Danny Kaye and Lena Horne, who willingly accepted a small fraction of what they made in America for the prestige of performing in Paris. Reaching for new ventures, he sent Lido troupes on global tours, sank his profits into other nightclubs and invested in Holiday on Ice and the Harlem Globetrotters. In 1954 his empire earned some five million dollars, and he was crowned "*Le Napoléon des Cabarets.*" He was not infallible; in 1952 he dropped a bundle on an extravaganza starring Maurice Chevalier, who was then sixty-four and well past his prime. I was curious to know how Guérin managed to mobilize his many nudes. "*N'y a pas la fesse qui manque ici,*" he said breezily: "We've got no shortage of ass here." When I asked him why the striptease was conspicuously absent from his shows, he explained, "There's a distinction between sex and nudity. We provide wholesome family entertainment."

*A*s the market for strippers expanded, it spawned dozens of agents, among them Roger Diaz. A swarthy character with a pencil-thin mustache, he operated out of Le Strip-Tease Club, a *boîte* near the boulevard des Italiens, and we met there one day to discuss his business. He discovered most of his girls by organizing amateur striptease contests. "I put up posters and run ads in the newspapers, and you would be surprised by the response—schoolteachers, hairdressers, stenographers, waitresses, nurses. Daughters arrive with their fathers, wives with their husbands, sisters with their brothers, nieces with their uncles. Once I walked into a bakery for a baguette and signed up the salesgirl. Their main motive is money; they can earn as much in three hours as they do in a week at an ordinary job. Some of them think that they can build a career—and many do. More than thirty of my girls are now professionals."

Hiring novices, Diaz continued, had clear advantages: "A woman who has never disrobed in public before is apt to be shy, nervous and awkward, but that's precisely what gives the performance a dash of pimiento and makes it *encore plus intéressant*—or, as you would say in English, more exciting. *Après tout,* the clients are essentially voyeurs with filthy minds who secretly lust after virgins."

Presuming that Diaz rigged these "amateur" contests, I asked if I might attend a rehearsal, and he kindly agreed. Later in the week I climbed the stairs to a drafty studio above Le Strip-Tease Club. He wore a charcoal turtleneck sweater and tennis shoes, and was reassuring three pretty girls in flowered frocks that stripping could be naughty without being dirty. "If you are modest, don't worry," he said. "Remember that the lights will go out as soon as you are naked. But to capture and retain the attention of the audience, you must emphasize your sensuality. Make believe that you have bought new underwear to arouse your boyfriend. You undress and try it on, doing your best to stimulate him. Or primitive tribesmen are holding you on a desert island, and to gain your release you offer up your clothes as a sacrifice to their idols. And never forget, it's only theater."

Diaz followed up the skull session by putting a sultry Piaf ballad on the record player, and, one by one, his pupils timorously stripped. Contrary to his theory that their clumsiness would be beguiling, they were dreadful. They fumbled with zippers, catches and straps until they were stark naked, and looked more like plucked geese than sex objects. Diaz concurred. Shrugging, he said to me, "I guarantee you that, under my guidance, they will improve."

He introduced me to Désirée Masson, a buxom redhead of twenty-one who worked as an assistant bank teller. She had read about his contest in a magazine and joined up without informing her parents. "At first, naturally, I felt a bit inhibited," she told me, "but I quickly lost my timidity after watching the other girls undress. Perhaps, with practice, I can become a full-time *strip-teaseuse*. It would certainly be better than being cooped up in an office all day."

14

Ce Petit Annamite

⟋⟍

 t daybreak on May 7, 1954, after six months of bitter fighting, the Communist-led Vietminh overran the last belea-
guered French garrison at Dienbienphu, a remote valley in
northwestern Vietnam. Thus ended France's six-year war to retrieve
its empire in Indochina, which reached back nearly a century. At
home the French had grown increasingly disgusted with what they
called "*la sale guerre.*" The mounting costs of the conflict had depleted their treasury, poisoned their political system and punctured
their dreams of glory. They had long realized that they were trapped
in a futile venture, yet the defeat, when it came, dealt a devastating
blow to their pride. Fresh in their minds was the disgrace of June
1940, when the Germans had marched into Paris; now their finest
soldiers had been routed, not by panzer divisions but by a ragtag
army headed by an emaciated, goateed figure in a worn topee, frayed
bush jacket and rubber sandals: Ho Chi Minh.

A French acquaintance of mine, peering at Ho's face in the newspapers, could not conceal his shock and dismay. Using the old

French term for the Vietnamese, he lamented, "Conquered by *ce petit Annamite*! What a humiliation!"

Mobilizing its immense staff, *Time* planned one of its blockbuster stories on the event. Correspondents around the world were alerted to pour out reams of words describing and analyzing France's foreign and domestic policies, the rise of communism in Asia and its implications for America's global strategy—all of which would be, as usual, homogenized by the editors in New York. Ho was to be featured on the cover; as a junior reporter presumably unqualified to handle heavyweight stuff, I drew the relatively minor task of retracing his footsteps through Paris, where he had lived from 1917 to 1923. It was like doing a jigsaw puzzle whose pieces did not quite fit.

Predictably mirroring their own political views, my sources variously depicted Ho as cruel, humane, dogmatic, flexible, duplicitous or honest. Nor could I rely on much that Ho had divulged about himself. He produced numbers of tracts and pamphlets but seldom wrote letters and never kept a journal or confided in a biographer, as Mao Tse-tung did to Edgar Snow, the American journalist. When queried about his personal background, Ho would respond with the contrived or genuine air of humility that became his signature, "My past holds no interest. Only the future is important."

I dug into dusty archives, excavated faded newspapers and interviewed Parisians who recalled him—or claimed that they did. My landlord, Robert-Jean Longuet, the grandson of Karl Marx and son of Jean Longuet, a Socialist leader who had known Ho during the early 1920s, provided me with his father's notes. From it all I managed to unravel at least part of the Ho enigma.

Like many educated Vietnamese of his generation, Ho had been captivated by the French ideals of *liberté, égalité et fraternité*. He first heard of those precepts as a teenager and, he later remembered, "immediately yearned to understand their significance." But he was to learn that they did not extend to the colonies and, out of frustration, gravitated toward communism.

Until 1940, when he adopted his final nom de guerre, Ho Chi Minh, roughly "Bringer of Light," he operated under a baffling assortment of aliases, among them Nguyen That Thanh, Van Ba, Vuong, Thuy, Khach, Wang, Victor le Bon, Nilovsky, Linov, Wargon and Lou Rosta. Before Ho, his most durable pseudonym was Nguyen Ai Quoc–"Nguyen the Patriot."

He was born Nguyen Sinh Cung in May 1890 in a village in Nghe Anh province, in central Vietnam. Titled the Kingdom of Annam, the region was ruled indirectly as a protectorate by France through a pliable emperor. But the French never fully subdued its destitute peasants, and the ambience of chronic dissidence that permeated the area molded Ho during his formative years.

His parents were impoverished though respectable rural gentry. The youngest of three children, Ho was ten when his mother died. His father's potential had been recognized by a local scholar, under whose tutelage he passed the ritual examinations for the mandarinate and was assigned to a post at Hue, the royal capital. But, convinced that the emperor and his court were nothing more than French tools, he quit to become an itinerant teacher and herb doctor. Inheriting his father's rebellious bent, Ho started to participate in local tax revolts and, even at a tender age, gained a reputation as a troublemaker. His brother and sister, also agitators, were later jailed by the French on charges of sedition.

$\mathcal{J}$n 1904 the Japanese vanquished czarist Russia–the first time since Genghis Khan's cavalry swept across Europe in the thirteenth century that Asians had crushed a Western power. The victory reverberated through the Far East as proof that white men were not invincible. Numbers of young Vietnamese rushed to embrace Japan as their model, but Ho, despite his hostility to French colonialism, clung to the notion that France's liberal traditions were superior. After graduating from his village school, he went to Hue and, assuming the name Nguyen That Thanh, enrolled in a French-run lycée. He could not endure its headmaster, a French Foreign Legion veteran who had been harassed by Vietnamese insurgents and, out of revenge, tyrannized his Vietnamese students. Eventually Ho escaped and made his way to the coastal town of Phan Thiet, where he taught briefly at a private college patterned along French lines. Then he drifted south to Saigon under still another name, Van Ba—*ba* meaning "third child." The port was the hub of Vietnam's foreign trade, and its bustling cosmopolitan atmosphere fascinated him. In July 1911, eager to see the world, he signed on as a galley boy and stoker aboard the *Amiral Latouche Tréville* of the Compagnie des Chargeurs Réunis, which regularly carried passengers and cargo between the Orient and Europe. Thirty years were to elapse before he again saw Vietnam.

Bursting with curiosity, he soaked up the sights as the ship crossed the Indian Ocean and threaded through the Suez Canal into the Mediterranean. At Marseille, the end of the line, he applied for admission to a new academy that prepared native auxiliaries for the French colonial administration. "I wish to serve France among my compatriots and also to improve myself," he wrote. When the document emerged years later, his nationalist rivals seized on it to contend that Ho had aspired to become a French collaborator. But his goal was unclear. He may have been seeking permanent employment in the French bureaucracy in Vietnam or simply striving to further his education. In any case he was rebuffed, perhaps because of his record of dissent. He had already earned a dossier in the Colonial Ministry's voluminous intelligence files on dubious persons. Its description of him was not especially flattering: "General appearance arched and awkward, mouth constantly half-open in a rather ingenuous smile."

Disappointed by the rejection, Ho roamed around France, toiling at assorted menial jobs before returning to sea as a cook aboard a French tramp steamer. The freighter plied the coast of Africa for about a year, then crossed the Atlantic to Boston. Ho may have been the first Vietnamese ever to set foot in the United States. I gleaned the scant details on his sojourn there almost entirely from his conversations with American agents of the Office of Strategic Services, who parachuted into the jungles of northern Vietnam during World War II to train his guerrillas to fight the Japanese. But Ho was typically secretive, and his recollections tended to be a blur of fact and fiction.

After disembarking in Boston, he traveled by train to New York and settled in Brooklyn for several months as a laborer. He explored nearly every inch of the metropolis, riding the ferry to Hoboken, the subway to the Battery and the trolley to Harlem. Manhattan's skyscrapers and bridges awed him as emblems of America's phenomenal industrial progress. In Chinatown he chatted with Chinese immigrants in their Cantonese dialect, and, to his surprise, discovered that, even though they were barred from citizenship, they enjoyed more legal benefits than did the Vietnamese in their homeland. Picking up some English, he memorized the first lines of the Declaration of Independence, and was to quote them in his own proclamation of Vietnamese independence in 1945. The Statue of Liberty and all that it symbolized electrified him, but he argued that it had been wrong for the United States to have accepted the gift from the French as long as they violated its tenets in their overseas possessions.

Late in 1914, now calling himself either Ba or Thanh, he popped up in England. World War I had erupted the summer before, and he sought to enlist in the British Army but was diagnosed as tuberculous. He eked out a living by shoveling coal, washing dishes and sweeping snow until, through a Soho employment agency, he was hired as a kitchen hand by Georges-Auguste Escoffier, the celebrated chef at London's elegant Carlton Hotel. Impressed by his fluent

French, courteous manners and nimble fingers, Escoffier soon elevated him to assistant pastry cook. As his English became increasingly proficient, Ho mingled with the Irish, Chinese and Indian nationalists who congregated in London—though, for some reason, he avoided British leftists. There was no evidence that he genuflected to Karl Marx's tomb at Highgate Cemetery, nor that he had even read Marx.

*D*esperately in need of manpower as the war dragged on, the French were compelled to import troops and factory workers from their colonies. They recruited more than one hundred thousand Vietnamese, and Ho, by then a militant, envisioned them as candidates for the nationalist ranks. Late in 1917, now known as Nguyen Ai Quoc, he shifted to Paris, where he installed himself in a squalid hotel on a dead-end Left Bank street. His tiny room was sparsely furnished with a small armoire and a table stacked with newspapers and magazines; there was also a narrow iron cot, but he slept on the floor with a book or two for a pillow. An accomplished Chinese calligrapher, he made ends meet by decorating counterfeit Chinese antiques and, using the same delicate brush strokes, supplemented his meager income by retouching photographs. He advertised in *La Vie Ouvrière*, a left-wing periodical: "Should you desire a lifelong souvenir for your family or friends, have your photographs enlarged by Nguyen-Ai-Quoc, 9, Impasse Compoint. A beautiful portrait in a beautiful frame from 45 francs." As an exotic extra, he would stamp his chop in the corner in big red Chinese ideographs.

The many hedonistic pleasures of Paris were beyond Ho's means. He could not afford fancy restaurants or romps with prostitutes, hordes of whom were available everywhere. His only visible indulgence was chain-smoking American cigarettes, preferably Camels or Lucky Strikes. It may have been during that period that, out of necessity rather than virtue, he started to shape the ascetic image that subsequently personified him.

By contrast, he was overwhelmed by the city's cultural brilliance. A voracious reader, he always had a book under his arm—mostly such French and English authors as Hugo, Zola, Romain Rolland, Anatole France, Shakespeare, Dickens, H. G. Wells, even Conan Doyle. He haunted the Bibliothèque Nationale, accumulating material for his articles. Adding to his repertory of languages, he studied Spanish and Italian. He also acquired a taste for art, and would browse through museums and galleries, sharing his comments on the paintings and sculptures with the other aesthetes, who prized his opinions. One of his favorite pastimes was to stroll the boulevards, mixing with the crowds and perhaps dropping into a music hall to catch a performance by Maurice Chevalier or Mistinguett—whose enchanting songs he would never forget. For a while he belonged to a Masonic lodge. A fashionable diversion for Parisians with intellectual pretensions was genteel literary and debating societies, like La Muse Rose and La Gorge Rouge. Ho tried several, then began to frequent one of them, Le Club du Faubourg.

After much effort I located the club's former president, Léo Poldès, who ushered me into his large apartment overlooking the boulevard Montparnasse. He poured me a cognac, and we sank into comfortable armchairs in his den, which was piled high with books and bibelots. A congenial, perceptive, occasionally pompous man in his seventies, Poldès plainly relished nostalgia, and rambled on about Ho: "It was at one of our weekly gatherings that I noticed this thin, almost anemic *indigène* in the rear. He had a Chaplinesque aura about him—simultaneously sad and comic, *vous savez*. I was instantly struck by his piercing dark eyes. He posed a provocative question; it eludes me now. I encouraged him to return. He did, and I grew more and more affectionate toward him. He was *très sympathique*—reserved but not shy, intense but not fanatic, and extremely clever. I especially liked his ironic way of deprecating everything while, at the same time, deprecating himself."

For Ho the club chiefly served a practical purpose. As a Vietnamese contemporary put it: "He calculated that learning how to speak in public would help him to translate his ideas into words, overcome his timidity and develop his self-confidence." He rarely skipped a session, at which the themes ranged from literature and philosophy to science and technology. Strangely, he dodged political discussions but, perhaps reminded of the Asian penchant for the supernatural, he was intrigued by topics like reincarnation and occultism. He was skeptical toward charlatans. One evening in October 1921, he challenged Dr. Émile Coué, the chic psychologist, whose prescription for self-perfection consisted of chanting the mantra "Every day in every way I am getting better and better." Coúe's ego was ruffled; as usual, though, Ho had been polite, and the club's members applauded his civility.

Suffused with creative energy, he finished a play, *Le Dragon de Bambou,* which mercilessly satirized a fictitious Asian king–in reality Khai Dinh, the puppet emperor of Annam. Ho showed it to Poldès, saying, "This drama ridicules a chief of state, and I doubt that anyone would dare to produce it. You may want to throw it into your wastebasket." But Poldès, who had broad and eclectic interests, generously staged a single performance at the club's ornate premises. Stretching his memory back twenty-five years, he recalled with perhaps a trace of condescension, "Hardly Molière, *n'est-çe pas,* yet carefully crafted, animated by a certain Aristophanic verve and not lacking in scenic qualities."

Sympathizing with Ho's financial woes, several members offered him help, but he proudly spurned anything that even faintly smelled of charity–though he had no qualms about photographing them for his customary rates. One confrere, Vincent Scotto, a popular composer, arranged through his connections in the burgeoning film business for Ho to write for *Cinégraph,* a new movie magazine. In 1922 Ho submitted an article under the byline Guy N'Qua–which the editor, Charles Brouilhet, promptly published. It had nothing to do with the cinema.

The French boxer Georges Carpentier had just trounced the British middleweight champion, Ted Lewis, at the Olympia Hall in London. France went berserk with joy, but Ho scarcely mentioned the bout in his piece. Instead he denounced the Paris sportswriters at the ringside for contaminating their dispatches with such Franglais as *"le manager," "le round"* and *"le knock-out."* He further implored Premier Raymond Poincaré to outlaw foreign phrases from the French press. As he recalled the episode to me, Brouilhet sounded a solemn chord: "No matter what little Ho has done since then, at the time he exemplified the triumph of France's *grande mission civilisatrice.*"

Paris was the world's most tolerant city, which enabled Ho to pursue his double life. If he felt no constraint to mask his radical activities from his companions at Le Club du Fauboug, neither did he conceal his association with the bourgeoisie from his French and Vietnamese comrades. But, over time, he became consumed by his nationalist vocation.

In 1919, President Woodrow Wilson arrived in France to sign the treaty officially concluding World War I. Earlier he had articulated his famous doctrine of self-determination, which promised Europe's ethnic minorities their autonomy. Ho naively assumed that the same formula included Asians. Donning a frock coat, striped trousers and top hat, he went to Versailles, the site of the peace conference, bearing a message for Wilson captioned *"Les Cahiers de Revendications du Peuple Viet-Namien."* A list of France's abuses in its colonies, it affirmed that "all subject peoples are filled with hope by the prospect that justice is opening to them . . . in the struggle of civilization against barbarism." The plea conspicuously omitted any demand for independence, requesting merely that the Vietnamese be guaranteed the same democratic freedoms granted the French residents of Vietnam. Ho's attempt to see Wilson was rebuffed and his faith in the West waned. But his bold gesture caught the attention of Socialists like Paul Vaillant-Couturier, Marcel Cachin and notably

Léon Blum, who was to become premier of the Popular Front government during the 1930s. Jean Longuet, editor of *Le Populaire,* the Socialist newspaper, published his text and urged him to join the party. Ho was not ready to commit himself, however, and would join only a Socialist youth group.

I ferreted out one of his early mentors, Jules Raveau, an old anarchist who claimed to have hobnobbed with Lenin and other revolutionary icons. They would meet at the seedy office of *La Vie Ouvrière* in Belleville, a shabby working-class district at the edge of town. A lively raconteur, Raveau recalled exhilarating Ho with stirring tales of heroic rebels at the Paris barricades in 1848 and martyred Communards summarily executed by firing squads in 1871. Another vintage tutor, Jacques Sternel, gave me a cameo of Ho: "He was as frail as a sparrow, but he burned with the zeal of a crusader. I was then editing a little paper, and an article I had written so touched him that he asked permission to kiss me."

Despite their repressive practices in the colonies, the French authorities permitted expatriate nationalist groups to ventilate their grievances in Paris. The city percolated with them—Algerian, Tunisian, Moroccan, Senegalese, Irish, Polish, Armenian, Korean. They hung out at cheap Latin Quarter cafés, where they confected propaganda, drafted petitions, organized meetings and talked earnestly about their homelands. Ho, persuaded that their resistance to foreign domination would help the Vietnamese, spent much of his precious time in their ramshackle offices, sorting leaflets and stuffing envelopes. He was the only Asian on the executive committee of the Union Intercoloniale, founded in 1921 by African and Caribbean activists in an effort to promote solidarity. Several young Chinese were also then in Paris, among them Chou En-lai and Deng Xiaoping, but apparently Ho never met them.

In December 1920 the Socialist Party convened its annual congress in the Loire Valley town of Tours, and Ho was invited to attend as the "representative from Indochina," an informal designation. A

vivid photograph of him showed him to be a skeletal figure in an oversize dark suit, incongruously surrounded by corpulent Frenchmen with florid faces and walrus mustaches. Speaking extemporaneously, Ho was wrapping up a vitriolic indictment of imperialism when some impatient delegates interrupted him. His eyes aflame, he reproached them, his voice rising to a passionate pitch: "In the name of all mankind, in the name of all Socialists, right-wing or left-wing, we appeal to you, comrades. Save us!"

At that point Ho was confronted by a fateful decision. A multitude of issues divided the Socialists, prime among them the party's attitude toward the new Soviet regime. By temperament Ho was suited to Léon Blum's moderate faction, but he threw in his lot with the pro-Moscow extremists who broke away to form the French Communist Party. His motives were more pragmatic than ideological. The Russians had pledged to unshackle the "oppressed masses" of Asia and Africa, and Ho believed that, sooner or later, they would liberate Vietnam. As he subsequently explained, "It was patriotism, not communism, that initially inspired me."

A prolific polemicist, he often contributed to *L'Humanité* and *La Vie Ouvrière*, a Communist labor journal. He also edited *Le Paria*, a publication aimed at African and Asian nationalists. His pen dripped with acerbic wit; in a treatise called *Le Procès de la Colonisation Française*, for instance, he remarked that "the figure of Justice has had such a rough voyage from France to Indochina that she has lost everything except her sword." Smuggled into Vietnam, where they were covertly circulated, his tracts and essays became required reading for Vietnamese opposed to French rule. Soon he was an agent for the Communist International, or Comintern. He furtively traveled throughout Europe, lecturing, conspiring and proselytizing. Though his Soviet bosses recognized his talents, they did not completely trust him. Contrary to their theoreticians, who had conceived a paradigm for global revolution, Ho maintained that different countries had distinctive characteristics and problems, and each should be allowed to define its own path. Others would be purged for such heresy, but Ho was too valuable.

He derived a perverse pleasure from teasing the French. During the summer of 1922, aware that he was being closely monitored by the Colonial Ministry's security department, he addressed a sardonic letter to Albert Sarraut, the former governor-general of Indochina and now minister of colonies: "I am grateful for your solicitude, which does honor to an Annamite like myself. . . . Your police are excellent chaps and deserve praise, but Sherlock Holmes they are not. . . . Thus, every morning, I shall provide you with a schedule of my daily movements in order to facilitate their surveillance of me."

Meanwhile, Ho had formed a bizarre relationship with the ministry's chief inspector, Louis Arnoux, who kept track of suspicious Vietnamese in France. Arnoux's experience in Vietnam dated back years. Like numbers of his colleagues in the colonial service, he had developed a deep if patronizing fondness for the people they ruled. He spoke Vietnamese, was versed in Vietnamese culture, counted Vietnamese among his friends and had probably had a Vietnamese mistress. Though he considered Ho to be a serious threat to French interests, he admired his persistence. From time to time he and Ho would meet for drinks at a secluded café near the Paris Opéra. Arnoux listened intently as Ho reminisced about his family, childhood and village, and reflected on his aspirations for his homeland. Enraptured by Ho's eloquence, Arnoux suggested to Sarraut that he accord him an audience. Sarraut reluctantly agreed and, summoning

Ho to his office, tried to bribe him into cooperating with France. Offended, Ho bluntly refused, asserting that he could not be distracted from his dream of independence for Vietnam. By one account, Sarraut bared his teeth, thrust out his arm, clenched his fist and warned, "France is magnanimous toward its friends but severe toward its adversaries."

One evening in 1923, as they assembled for their weekly meeting, the members of Le Club du Faubourg observed that Ho was oddly missing—nor did he ever appear again. They speculated on his whereabouts over the ensuing months, then, having always regarded him as mysterious, carried on. But a decade later they somehow heard that he had died in a Hong Kong prison. The secretary pinned a short obituary on the club bulletin board: "Poor Nguyen Ai Quoc! We will never forget his élan, his good humor, his malice. May the gods of Asia watch over his soul."

As it turned out, of course, the reports of Ho's death were greatly exaggerated.

15

La Jeunesse
Française

~~

$\mathcal{A}$ juicy assignment fell into my lap early in March 1955: a blockbuster piece on France's younger generation. As the junior correspondent in the *Time* bureau—I had just turned thirty—I was the logical choice for the task. I had also been living in Paris for nearly eight years, knew numbers of French my own age and spoke the language fluently, including argot. Given a month's deadline, I set forth to assess what youths thought about politics, economics, religion, culture, education, sports and sex, and their hopes for the future. It would prove to be a more complex effort than I initially anticipated. But, I learned, the attitudes of French youth largely matched those of the French in general. So, in many ways, they were a microcosm of France.

Traveling by train or car, I zigzagged through Normandy, Brittany, the Loire Valley and Burgundy across to Alsace, down through the Alps into Provence, up to the industrial belt encircling Lille, and back to factory suburbs outside Paris, chatting with fishermen, dairy farmers, winegrowers, schoolteachers, miners and workers. I interviewed Communist and Gaullist activists, Mendès-France's disciples,

Catholic militants. Revisiting my old Latin Quarter haunts, I talked with professors and students. I canvassed my French friends for their opinions and, in Saint-Germain-des-Prés, listened to highbrows pontificate on the topic—as they did on every imaginable topic. My marriage was then on the rocks and, to console myself, I had taken to pursuing women. One evening I struck up a conversation with a pretty girl on the terrace of a brassy café on the Champs-Élysées. She revealed to me that she was a stenographer in her late twenties, and that her husband had recently deserted her. We had a fling for a couple of weeks, during which she nattered away about her problems and her aspirations. Naturally I incorporated her experience into my dispatch.

Rather than shrink my mammoth file to a few paragraphs, *Time*'s editors flaunted it across three full pages—with my photograph and a blurb about me in the Publisher's Letter at the front of the magazine.

I started my research by looking for similarities between French and American youths. It was a mistake. Though huge compared to France, the United States was far more cohesive, partly a reflection of its sophisticated communications network. So while American youngsters could be stereotyped, their French contemporaries defied easy description. "To try to categorize them is pointless," a Paris acquaintance advised me. "Who are they? Workers, artisans, peasants, students, teachers, doctors, lawyers, scholars, merchants, bureaucrats, office employees, urban, provincial—and they all differ from one another. Each group is confined to its separate fiefdom, discouraged from breaking out by barriers of money, ancestry or both. And each is loyal to its class rather than to its generation."

They also faced a reality curbed by history, custom and the failure of their leaders to govern effectively. Liberty, fraternity and equality decorated the façades of public buildings throughout the country, but the traditions and prejudices of a highly structured society eclipsed its republican slogans. For the younger generation, locked from birth into solid cell blocks, escape was virtually impossible and even parole difficult.

Diverse and often contradictory moods further characterized French youths. Depending on circumstances, they could be tough or flabby, dynamic or languid, articulate or silent, disciplined or tumultuous. In contrast to their American counterparts, who believed themselves to be endowed with limitless opportunities, they were reluctant to take risks that might backfire and obstruct their quest for what they treasured most—security. But they shared a common sentiment: a combination of disorientation, disenchantment and disgust that translated into *méfiance*—a distrust for the powers that be. Beneath this sense of malaise burned an ember of revolt that simmered with a yearning for change.

For youth, as for adults, practically everything had gone wrong. The rosy glow that followed the Liberation had faded. The promising new politicians spawned by the Resistance had abandoned their lofty ideals and joined the entrenched establishment. Skyrocketing inflation had rendered money valueless. The army had forfeited its reputation when France fell to Hitler and sacrificed its best officers in the futile colonial war in Indochina. Already stripped of its meaning by the appeasement policies of the 1930s, patriotism had been stained by the numbers of French who collaborated with the Germans during the Occupation, and was again being tarnished by the Communist Party's slavish obedience to Moscow. The economy, though improving, still remained a Maginot Line behind which cartels defended big industrialists against competition while subsidies and tax breaks cushioned workers and farmers. As they observed the expansion of technology in America and the Soviet Union, youngsters doubted whether the French could ever catch up. As André Labarthe wrote in the quarterly *La Nef:* "Tragically, they are yoked to a chariot that bogged down fifty years ago, and whose drivers can only look backward."

Class boundaries in France during the 1950s were often as rigid as Hindu caste lines. Hardly ever did a dentist's daughter elope with a garage mechanic; a concierge's son was unlikely to become a professor; nor would a businessman's boy have contemplated agriculture as a vocation. Yet some degree of upward mobility existed. A schoolteacher's child could conceivably succeed as a lawyer, and, with connections, capital and luck, a farm youth might own a fertilizer plant or a tractor agency. Mandatory military service had a leveling effect on young Frenchmen, but after returning to civilian life they usually forgot their fellow conscripts.

Class dictated dress, speech and taste as well. Even if he could afford it, a young factory foreman would shun the tweed jacket and flannel trousers of an up-and-coming salesman in a chic perfume company and instead opt for conventional blue serge. A bumpkin's guttural accent was distinct from the drawl of *un titi parisien,* and neither sounded like the clipped diction of upper-crust kids, many of whom affected snobbish English intonations. Just as an apprentice electrician would recoil from taking his *petite amie* to a trendy cellar boîte in Saint-Germain-des-Prés, so *haut bourgeois* students rarely patronized the *bals musettes* of Belleville or Ménilmontant. The *paso doble* and *le jazz hot* were a class apart.

The demographic curve had also punished youth. Medical progress since the eighteenth century had steadily increased longevity, while wars and depressions combined to reduce the birthrate. Thus, by the 1950s, the median age of France's population was nearly thirty-six, the oldest in the world. As a result, young men had to be content with poorly paid jobs until their fathers and uncles retired, and women were relegated to the lowest rungs on the ladder. As evidence of the lopsided age picture, the sociologist René Renod noted that Jeanne d'Arc was barely twelve when God ordained her to rescue France, but that Marshal Pétain, whom most French embraced as their savior after their defeat by the Germans five hundred years later, was approaching eighty-five and virtually senile.

It became faddish for the French to evoke the glorious past, particularly the turn of the century, when France was supposed to have been robust, prosperous and cheerful. Films, festivals and costume balls celebrated the belle époque as a reminder that Paris was once the world's merriest capital. But, to the young, such nostalgia was a gimmick concocted to camouflage the deficiencies of the present. All they had been offered over the recent decade to supplant the nation's antiquated, crumbling institutions was political hypocrisy, economic stagnation and hollow social programs camouflaged in pompous rhetoric. As Jean Sarrail, the rector of the Sorbonne, warned in *Le Monde:* "The youths of today are the leaders of tomorrow. These attempts to deceive them are a blunder that will only aggravate their despondency and cynicism. We must heed their demands or the repercussions will be catastrophic."

But despite their disappointments, few French youngsters were tempted by the notion of emigrating. Intensely nationalistic, they flinched at the thought of settling in a strange land, where they would have to adjust to a strange cuisine, a strange language, strange customs and a strange atmosphere. They were also profoundly devoted to the idea of France's superiority over every other country on earth. So, they concluded, they could only resign themselves to its weaknesses and somehow strive to get by.

Like their elders, they subscribed to the adage "*Chacun pour soi*"—every man for himself. Their egoism was a legacy of the war, when shortages of food, clothing, soap, needles and almost everything else had forced the French to contrive all kinds of schemes to subsist. In the northern town of Roubaix, a sooty landscape of steel mills and coal mines, a young Socialist named Raymond Lahousse confided to me that he had wangled a bargain apartment in a government housing project through a brother-in-law on the municipal council. When I asked him whether he considered his conduct to be ethical, he replied, "Perhaps not, but you can't get by these days without finagling—*il faut se débrouiller.*" Rosalie Durand, a twenty-four-year-old librarian from Joigny, echoed an analogous theme in a letter to *Le Figaro:* "What kept up our spirit during the dark, horrible days of the Occupation was the conviction that the Liberation would be our redemption. Now, with our illusions shattered, we simply struggle for survival." One of the idols of French youth was Georges Brassens, a brawny figure with shaggy hair and a drooping mustache, who strummed his guitar and chanted irreverent songs: "Whatever they say, whatever they say, I will go my own way."

The French proclaimed their system of public education to be the finest in the world, though many Americans might have judged it to be woefully undemocratic. Developed during the Third Republic to wrest control of education away from the Church, it functioned on the egalitarian theory that every citizen was entitled to free, secular schooling up to the age of fourteen. At the same time, however, it was decreed that an elite had to be trained to manage the state and to furnish society with thinkers. At the summit of the hierarchy were the Polytechnique, the École Normale Supérieure, the École Nationale d'Administration and the Institut d'Études Politiques, which produced engineers, intellectuals and civil servants. Lower on the pyramid was a countrywide web of lycées, whose strict, uniform curriculum of philosophy, classics, science, math and foreign languages would put a topflight American high school to shame. During the 1950s, of the nation's three million teenagers, the overwhelming majority of students enrolled in lycées came from well-to-do families. Since admission to a university hinged on a lycée diploma—*le baccalauréat*—the children of peasants and workers were conspicuously underrepresented in the loftier echelons of academe. Accordingly, their chances of entering a profession were slim, and they had to reconcile themselves to lesser jobs. A multitude of other defects blighted the system. Buildings, some of them reaching back centuries, had fallen into disrepair. A scarcity of funds inhibited the recruitment of teachers, particularly for provincial schools and lycées. Consequently, more and more students could not measure up; in 1954 approximately fifty percent of the candidates were denied the *baccalauréat*–"*le bacho*"–for muffing such elementary subjects as grammar and spelling. Yet the universities were bulging to capacity.

Founded in the thirteenth century, the Sorbonne bore no resemblance to an American college. Situated in the city, it lacked a leafy campus or fraternities at which youths gathered for bull sessions or Saturday-night dances. French students, contrary to the popular image of *la vie de bohème,* tended to be serious, even solemn. Without dorms to lodge them, they lived in shabby hotels, and either ate in canteens or cooked on kerosene stoves in their rooms. They shuffled between their classes and neighborhood cafés, where they pored over their textbooks, wrote essays, played the pinball machine or gabbed, chiefly about sports and sex. Unlike American kids, they were too encumbered with courses to pick up extra money by working on the side; in any case, waiting on tables or washing dishes would have been beneath their dignity. Most of them, even if they had affluent families, were on tight allowances and constantly broke. Predicated on need rather than ability, the few available state scholarships amounted to an insufficient twenty or thirty dollars a month, and student groups were chronically lobbying for double that sum. "Our model," as one of their members said to me, "is your GI Bill of Rights."

Culture remains when all else is forgotten," goes a French proverb. This meant that graduates, like potential Chinese mandarins, had to be steeped in the classics to be rated as truly educated. But a knowledge of Greek and Latin, however laudable, was not preparing the younger generation to meet the demands of the twentieth century. An official asserted, "We are afflicted with a dearth of engineers and a surplus of underemployed lawyers."

A case in point was André Millerand, who had completed the Sorbonne's Faculté de Droit in 1948. After finishing his military service, he searched in vain for a position in a law firm. Finally, though his father's contacts, he was hired as a copy editor in a publishing company—a job he detested. By 1955, when we met, he was earning roughly one hundred and thirty dollars a month, not enough to marry his fiancée. One afternoon, over apéritifs at the Deux Magots, he expressed his frustrations to me: "I should have studied chemistry, geology or nuclear physics. In America you can make money doing something you hate. Here you do something you hate, and you don't make any money either."

In the provinces, where close to forty percent of the population lived, some two million youths were involved in farming. The law required the land to be divided among the heirs, so invariably the eldest son reimbursed his siblings for their portion of the property, leaving them to find work in the area as shop clerks or day laborers. For a youngster, village life was sheer monotony. The only entertainment in the evening was the radio or a card game in the local café. On Sunday afternoon it might be improvised soccer, a tryst with a girl in a field or maybe a movie in a nearby town. Every year, out of desperation, one hundred thousand rural youths drifted into the cities, where they were usually shunted into unskilled jobs.

Squabbles between the Communist and Socialist unions emasculated French labor. Most workers, alienated by the constant quarrels, boycotted union meetings or quit altogether—hence the quip "France's biggest union is the disunion of the unaffiliated." The impact on the young was devastating.

In 1936 the Popular Front granted workers such generous benefits as stable wages, family allocations, medical care, annual paid vacations and pensions. But these achievements paradoxically contributed to a generational schism in the labor movement. Their conditions ameliorated, veteran workers became complacent and, in the process, neglected their younger comrades. Novices started at the age of fourteen at half pay, put in ten hours a day and could not rely on the unions to deal with their complaints. As the head of a youth center in Strasbourg portrayed them to me, "They are lepers."

I spent an afternoon with Marcel Le Notre, a muscular twenty-seven-year-old machinist in Tourcoing, one of the grimy towns stretched across the industrial north. His wife, Monique, was employed in a carpet factory. Including an allowance for their only child, their joint income was the equivalent of one hundred and seventy dollars a month. Their dreary redbrick row house, located in a cobblestone courtyard, lacked indoor plumbing and was heated only by a potbellied coal stove in the sparsely furnished downstairs room. When I called on them, Marcel was clad in a stained brown suit and a frayed shirt, Monique in a blue factory smock. To economize, Marcel had ceased smoking, and he mooched my Gauloises as he explained his routine: "It's work, work and more work. We wake up promptly at five-thirty in the morning, grab a quick cup of coffee and a croissant, drop off the baby at my parents' place, walk a half hour to our jobs, retrieve him in the evening, eat dinner and are in bed by eleven. The last time we went to the cinema was two years ago. We never invite over friends, and they never invite us. On Sunday we have lunch with Monique's family or mine. What do we want? A decent life. How do we attain it? I don't exactly know. We just keep going, day by day."

To protect the returning poilus following World War I, the government imposed rigorous rent controls, thereby removing the incentives for new construction. Housing deteriorated, and, in 1954, the Paris authorities reported that seventy percent of the city's dwellings were "substandard." Inadequate housing traumatized Parisians. Conversations revolved around whether to fork over "key money" for an occupied apartment in the expectation that the elderly tenants would soon die, or how to persuade grandparents to give up their flat and move to the country. Matters were critical for young married couples, many of whom shivered in winter or stifled in summer in *chambres de bonne,* minuscule maid's rooms atop luxurious apartment buildings, without heat or baths, and with a single stand-up toilet for the entire floor.

Housing even bugged the well-heeled. Catherine de la Forêt, a designer in a stylish *maison de couture,* earned two hundred and forty dollars a month, a handsome salary for a twenty-seven-year-old. She lived with her parents in a spacious Sixteenth Arrondissement apartment. For her to let an equally comfortable flat would probably have cost half her wage and, to purchase her own place, three or four thousand dollars. "It could be worse," she allowed as we talked in the salon, "but still it's a drag. Here I can't throw a party or ask a friend in for a drink. If I return home early at night, my mother worries that I will become a spinster; if I remain out late, she gets jittery about my virtue. I am head and shoulders above the rest of my generation, yet I'm not really free."

*P*rior to World War II, the Latin Quarter was seething with ideological controversies. Rival leftist and right-wing factions were continually distributing tracts, plastering up posters, delivering speeches and staging demonstrations on the boulevard Saint-Michel, clashing with each other and the cops in street battles. By the 1950s their favorite cafés, La Source and La Capulade, had become a snack bar and an ice cream parlor, and their transformation mirrored the political passivity of youngsters. "Twenty years ago," remarked the editor of a student journal, "everyone was in the fight. Now youth is out of it." When I raised the subject with a young woman, she responded: "What are my political leanings? None. Nobody cares what I think, not even those who agree with me."

This apathy paralleled the pervasive indifference of the French toward politics. They were bewildered by the multiplicity of parties and the complicated electoral laws, bored by the empty oratory and appalled by the scandals and slippery maneuvers of the legislature. As André Malraux, who had shifted from communism to Gaullism, commented in *L'Express,* "Individually we are vigorous, but collectively we suffer from a sickness: the realization that our state is a fraud."

It was symptomatic of their lassitude that, while they revered such fleeting celebrities as film stars, pop singers and champion cyclists, French youths had not had a durable hero since Napoleon. They were cautiously optimistic when Mendès-France, vowing to focus on their grievances during his brief tenure in office, ordered his cabinet to draft an extensive reform plan. But, following his ouster, they slid back into inertia. "If elections were held tomorrow," one expert told me, "a big proportion of the vote would go to the Communists—mainly as a protest."

A sample Communist sympathizer, Pierre Bérard, whom I interviewed in Clermont-Ferrand, was a stocky, bearded man in his late twenties. After attending a technical school, he worked for a while on a farm and now earned forty cents an hour making upholstery for railway carriages. He lived alone in a hotel and commuted to Paris every other weekend on his free railway pass to be with his wife, a department-store assistant. For reasons that baffled him, his repeated applications for a transfer to Paris had been ignored. He had recently switched his membership in Force Ouvrière, the Socialist union, to the Communist-led Confédération Générale du Travail. "I don't want to see the Russians take over France," he argued during our chat, "but the Communists are sincerely concerned with our plight. Besides, when the other politicians see them becoming strong, perhaps they will do something."

From the king's *maîtresse en titre* to *madame la caissière* in the local grocery, French females had always played crucial roles—though only as auxiliaries to men. Not until after the war, indeed, were they awarded the franchise. But by the 1950s young women were beginning to emerge as doctors, lawyers, magistrates, professors, scientists, bankers and managers. They sat on such prestigious public bodies as the Conseil d'État, the supreme arbitration board, and the Cour des

Comptes, the central auditing office. In 1954, for the first time, a woman stockbroker was permitted to trade on the Bourse. Women were prominent in the fashion industry. Several of them, including Françoise Giroud of *L'Express,* had become influential journalists. The brilliant Paris literary salon was a female concept.

In the past, lower-class girls worked and the daughters of the *haute bourgeoisie* did little else than remain at home and, under the care of doting mothers, prepare themselves for a suitable marriage. That situation was reversed in the wake of the war. Thanks to the social security net, less privileged females preferred to rear children and receive family allocations, while numbers of educated, middle-class women longed for careers. Frequently the appeal of a job was more psychological than economic, more a caprice than a necessity. Published in 1949, Simone de Beauvoir's feminist book, *Le Deuxième Sexe,* assured women that they were equal to men and deserved to be emancipated, if only symbolically. I asked a receptionist in an advertising agency what motivated her to work when her husband, an upscale jeweler, could indulge all her whims. "Now I can buy my own clothes without having to nag him for money," she said. An airline hostess emphasized: "Ultimately I want a husband and kids, but I'd rather hand my salary over to a maid than be imprisoned in the kitchen and the nursery."

Young women, however, faced many of the same hurdles that confronted their brothers: low wages, slow promotions, wretched housing, dubious futures. Often, they were also sexually harassed by macho bosses who fancied themselves to be medieval lords eligible to exercise *le droit du seigneur.* But women were less dejected than men, and instead seemed to be grateful for what they had achieved.

France's widespread anticlericalism notwithstanding, the Catholics had made astonishing strides in attracting the younger generation since the end of the war. Though they lagged far behind the Communists, their variety of youth organizations claimed more than one million members. They ran recreational centers for peasant kids and, in industrial regions, provided young workers with shelter and vocational guidance. Headquartered in a dilapidated hotel on a narrow lane in the Latin Quarter, a band of Augustinians was dedicated to helping forlorn students. Attired in black turtlenecks and black berets, they and their volunteer aides referred to themselves as "archangels." Through the night they scoured the cafés, offering a meal, a bath or merely companionship. They never discussed religion, and even less endeavored to convert anyone. "Our goals are modest," said Father Eugene Balm, the tall, rugged Dutch priest in charge of the mission. "If we can do a little good, fifty years from now it will have been worthwhile."

Like their parents, French youths observed Catholic rituals. They commemorated Christmas and Easter, fasted during Lent, abstained from meat on Friday and would summon a priest to their deathbed. Every spring fifteen thousand pious students made the fifty-mile pilgrimage by foot from Paris to Chartres Cathedral. Even atheists and agnostics conformed—at least nominally. Conceded a young Socialist: "We baptized our child. He will have his first communion, get married in church and be buried by a priest. But mind you, I am unalterably opposed to Catholicism."

Except for a small fraction of fervent youths, faith did not interfere with sex. True to Latin custom, the soul and the body were distinct spheres that might touch, if at all, behind the curtain of a confessional box.

By prudish American norms, French youths were immoral. By French norms, they were realistic. "In the United States," recalled a woman of twenty-three who went to college there, "girls were obsessed with sex. My sorority sisters talked about nothing else. Here in France we don't talk—we do." French kids mushed it up in doorways, in streets, in cafés, in bistros during meals and over coffee, while meandering along the banks of the Seine on warm evenings.

The prospects were that they would end up in the sack. An army private gave me his rule of thumb: "No nonsense. If you kiss a girl on the lips, you sleep with her."

There were nuances, however. Workers and avant-garde intellectuals openly lived in sin; among peasants, pregnancy was the common prelude to marriage. For a woman to bear a baby out of wedlock was no stigma; the government, eager to arrest the dwindling birthrate, entitled such women to the same benefits granted to the mother of a legitimate child. But the tony bourgeoisie insisted on decorum, if only as a pretense; regardless of what she did during the afternoon or evening, it was de rigueur for a young girl to come home at night.

Sport was French youth's principal outdoor diversion. A half million kids played soccer in parks and vacant lots, and on balmy Sundays thousands of factory workers and messenger boys donned garishly colored jerseys and riding shoes, twisted a spare tire across their chests, climbed onto bicycles and raced at breakneck speed through the countryside. Snorkeling and scuba diving, inspired by the exploits of Jacques-Yves Cousteau, grew into such a craze that the government had to issue underwater hunting licenses to prevent the extinction of fish. But the vast majority of youngsters were spectators rather than participants. They followed the soccer scores in *L'Équipe*, the sports daily, squeezed into the Parc des Princes on the edge of Paris to watch European title rugby matches and, glued to the radio, frazzled their nerves during the Tour de France.

In addition to their addiction to movies, middle-class youths were fascinated by music. Crowds of them flocked to the Salle Pleyel or the Palais de Chaillot for Bach, Mozart and Beethoven concerts and mobbed the Olympia to hear Édith Piaf and Gilbert Bécaud. Infatuated with jazz, they went bonkers over Sidney Bechet, a permanent resident of Paris, or the French clarinetist Claude Luter, a facsimile Benny Goodman. At Le Discothèque, a Saint-Germain-des-Prés club, they sipped Scotch at a dollar a shot, danced *les slows* and *le lindy,* and sang the lyrics in fractured English. Alarmed by this passion for jazz among their young supporters, the Communists exhorted them to reserve their enthusiasm for such party figures as Yves Montand, whose repertory included proletarian songs, or for politically acceptable exponents of American culture like Paul Robeson.

French students were amazed when I told them that I, along with other young Americans, had worked during the summer. For them vacations were sacred. They would hitchhike to Normandy, Brittany or the Côte d'Azur, and camp on the beach. Or they might trek through the Alps or the Pyrénées, sleeping in youth hostels, or spend a couple of weeks in their ancestral village. In winter, ski resorts like Chamonix and Megève were packed with rich kids.

Irrespective of class or age, the French operated at a leisurely pace, maintaining that it was fruitless to hurry to fulfill their ambitions in a sclerotic economy. Nothing meant more than *le savoir-vivre.* Secure in his family's textile company, a young businessman divulged his strategy to me: "Sow your seeds in your twenties, work hard in your thirties, succeed in your forties, wear your laurels in your fifties—and always remember to enjoy yourself."

My article caused a sensation when *Time* appeared in Paris. Denouncing me for maligning France's honor, a few officials suggested that I be expelled. The big-circulation afternoon daily *Paris-Presse* splashed a translation across its back page under a banner headline, and invited readers to react. The letters, predictably, were mixed. "Monsieur Karnow deserves a slap in the face," remarked Alain Cassin, a twenty-nine-year-old Parisian; said Jacques Auberger, the secretary of a students' federation: "Despite some errors, the report is essentially accurate." Anne Mesnil, a typist, wrote from Nancy: "Humiliating but, alas, mostly true." Analyzing the mail, the newspaper editorialized: "If this were the *baccalauréat*, Stanley Karnow would earn a grade of *assez bien*." Quite good, I thought, was not bad.

16

The Mandarins

*A*mericans ridiculed intellectuals as eggheads, but in France they were venerated as authorities on everything from art, literature and music to politics, economics, religion and complex social issues. Their Olympian status mirrored the respect long shared by the French for the power of ideas and for the elite caste that shaped and spread them. To belong to the intelligentsia approximated deification. Streets bore the names of illustrious and even obscure novelists, poets, dramatists, composers, scientists and philosophers. Their statues stood in parks; their engraved portraits adorned banknotes and postage stamps. The government subsidized their projects or granted them such sinecures as diplomatic appointments to congenial capitals. Fashionable hostesses lionized prominent *hommes de lettres,* while gossip columnists detailed their tastes, idiosyncrasies, quarrels and liaisons in the schmaltzy jargon usually reserved for screen and sports stars. Scores of weeklies and monthlies were exclusively devoted to their latest pronouncements. Their books and essays, which they dashed off at astounding speed, triggered squabbles that, judging from the endless reports in the newspapers, enthralled the public. Multitudes tuned into their radio talks, their plays drew huge audiences, and crowds crammed into halls to hear their recondite, often soporific lectures. As a group they could be, as Simone de Beauvoir suggested in *Les Mandarins,* her Goncourt Prize roman à clef, as parochial, arrogant and chauvinistic as Chinese scholars. They were particularly contemptuous of their American equivalents—deriding them, with a few exceptions, for acquiescing to the temptations of commercialism. Beauvoir sniffed after a trip to the United States: "They allow themselves to be dominated by crass managers and editors, like nude dancers only too willing to display their bodies to impresarios. All that matters is money."

Paris highbrows chiefly congregated on the Left Bank, especially Saint-Germain-des-Prés, where I had lived for years. The district was as intimate as a village, and I had become familiar with its routines.

In the afternoon Jean-Paul Sartre, the existentialist oracle, garbed in a frayed jacket, woolen sweater and beret, a cigarette tucked in his mouth and his pockets stuffed with papers, descended from his apartment on the rue Bonaparte to join Beauvoir and their disciples for apéritifs and chitchat at their habitual haunts—the Flore or the cameo cellar bar at the Pont-Royal hotel. The perceptive political analyst Raymond Aron held forth at the Deux Magots, while Maurice Merleau-Ponty, the eminent professor of philosophy at the Collège de France, presided over his inner circle a block away, at the Rhumerie Martiniquaise. Claude Roy, an astute chronicler of the scene, favored the quiet Méphisto, and Albert Camus preferred the solitude of a rear table in the drab Café de la Mairie du Sixième Arrondissement, in the nearby Place Saint-Sulpice. Now and again, attired in his signature turtleneck, Samuel Beckett would emerge from his secluded studio to nurse a beer at the Montana. Once, before he died in 1948, I discerned the demented poet and actor Antonin Artaud, out on furlough from his asylum. Sometimes I spotted *"l'épiphaniste,"* Henri Pichette, or Isidor Isou and his bizarre sect of *"lettristes."* American expatriate writers, among them Richard Wright,

James Baldwin and Otto Friedrich, assembled at the gaudy Royal Saint-Germain or at the Tournon, a pedestrian *café-tabac* opposite the Jardin du Luxembourg. Montparnasse, the venue for artists between the wars, had largely lost its panache. Even so, such vintage Surrealists as Louis Aragon, André Breton and Paul Éluard periodically appeared on the *terrasses* of Le Sélect, Le Dôme, La Coupole or La Rotonde, or, on gentle summer evenings, in the garden of La Closerie des Lilas. A deferential hush enveloped Chez Lipp when the venerable André Gide shuffled in for dinner; occasionally Jean Cocteau and his Tout Paris cronies flounced into the tony Méditerranée. The lower income bracket ate at banal bistros, like La Brasserie du Balzar, Le Petit Saint-Benoît or Aux Charpentiers.

For entertainment the literati might drop into Le Tabou to catch Boris Vian, a bouncy jazz trumpeter who turned out raffish cabaret skits and tough-guy mysteries à la Dashiell Hammett, advertised for the sake of verisimilitude as *"traduit de l'Américain."* They also flocked to La Rose Rouge or the Club Saint-Germain, smoky basement *boîtes* around the corner from the Flore, to listen to Juliette Greco—a husky-voiced *diseuse* with a parrot nose, ebony eyes and long black mane—croon abstruse lyrics expressly crafted for her by Sartre, Françoise Sagan, François Mauriac and Raymond Queneau. I squeezed as many of their distractions as I could into my schedule—colloquies, concerts, experimental film festivals, avant-garde theater premieres, soirées at voguish salons, jammed vernissages at chic art galleries, receptions at the offices of esoteric magazines, glittering cocktail parties at trendy publishing houses. Much of it may have been artificial, but, it seemed to me, no place else on earth was so exhilarating.

Sadly, though, Saint-Germain-des-Prés had itself deteriorated into a sleazy carnival. Drifters, panhandlers, fast-food stalls and souvenir peddlers clogged the square facing the ivy-clad twelfth-century Romanesque church. Discos bopped with nymphets called *"rats des caves."* Fleets of rubberneck buses paralyzed the traffic along the boulevard. Cafés and restaurants overflowed with *mondaine* couples out on a lark, hayseeds avid for a glimpse of *"les intellos,"* dilettantes and poseurs feigning arcane conversations. To the delight of local merchants, business was booming. The target of all the pandemonium, peculiarly, was Sartre. Scarcely anyone could explain, much less spell, existentialism, but it had vaulted him to overnight fame. Tourists chased after him for his autograph. Reporters for the mass-circulation dailies, *France-Soir* and *Paris-Presse,* ambushed him for interviews—and, when he ducked them, typically concocted exaggerated and often lurid versions of his movements, including his purported escapades with female admirers. He was mobbed by photographers, caricatured by cartoonists, lampooned by *chansonniers.* Jean Galtier-Boissière, the editor of the iconoclastic *Crapouillot,* dubbed Saint-Germain-des-Prés *"la cathédrale de Sartre"* and Beauvoir *"la grande Sartreuse."* Throngs of youths, touting themselves as existentialists, surged through the neighborhood—ponytailed girls in skintight leotards, braless T-shirts and sandals, their long-haired, unshaven boyfriends in tattered denim jeans, duffle coats and espadrilles. Incensed, Sartre repaired to the Flore and scrawled a pompous communiqué: "Be advised that existentialism—the philosophy—has nothing whatsoever to do with these bands of young hooligans. They bear no relation to me nor I to them. The commotion was totally manufactured by the sensationalist press." Enthused by his outburst, the papers inflated the hullabaloo to preposterous proportions—and it provided me with a droll piece for *Time*.

*H*aving studied European literary history in college, I was acquainted with French intellectual tradition, which dated back to the monumental *Chanson de Roland*, sung by itinerant troubadours during the reign of Charlemagne. By the Middle Ages the Latin Quarter had become an ecclesiastical center second only to Rome, its narrow cobblestone lanes packed with seminarians thirsting for knowledge. Frequently, as I roamed around the area, I tried to imagine the fervor that must have permeated it then. Pierre Abélard was skirting heresy by teaching on the Montagne Sainte-Geneviève that Christian canon and rationalism were reconcilable. Thomas Aquinas, the future saint, was there as well, contemplating a similar proposition. In 1257, Robert de Sorbon, the papal legate and confessor to the pious Louis IX, inaugurated the eponymous college that was to expand over the centuries into the sprawling University of Paris. Pope Alexander IV, in a blessing soon after its inception, intoned, "The schools of Paris are the Holy Church's radiant beacon and an eternal tribute to the glory of God."

Persuaded that they possessed the key to education, the French presumed that it was their mission to disseminate the gospel to humankind. Gradually, however, a secular spirit eclipsed the preoccupation with theology. Rabelais's ribald tales of lascivious monks and nuns punctured the orthodox clergy's pretense of sanctity, while Montaigne encouraged the pursuit of pleasure by maintaining that morality and *l'art de vivre* were compatible. A more permissive, cosmopolitan atmosphere began to pervade France during the Renaissance as kings and aristocrats imported painters, sculptors, architects, even tailors and cooks, primarily from Italy. In 1635, concerned that the new mood might threaten the supremacy of the state, Cardinal Richelieu, the canny prime minister to Louis XIII, founded the Académie Française as a device to dampen potential dissent. Its forty members, reputedly the most sagacious men in the realm, were elevated to a position that many a nobleman would have coveted. Known as *"les immortels,"* they ranked a notch below princes and dukes in the court hierarchy, which entitled them to wear brocaded doublets, frilled blouses, lace ruffles, satin knee breeches, silk hose, ostrich-plumed hats, ermine-trimmed cloaks and bejeweled épées at official ceremonies. Apart from showing up at functions, their only responsibility—consonant with the theory that the language and the nation were synonymous—consisted of revising the institution's definitive dictionary. Once a week they would convene in an opulent chamber beneath the dome of the superb baroque palace on the Seine that had been the residence of Cardinal Mazarin and, for a hour or two, sip fine wines and fiddle with the vocabulary. The interminable task had been designed to keep them out of mischief, but they were not always easy to control.

By the seventeenth century, with feudalism crumbling, the prosperous bourgeoisie was challenging the concept of divine rule and an upper crust that derived its privileges from birth. In this changing climate, Descartes envisioned a universal truth predicated on logic and, over the ensuing three hundred years, France was to be consumed by a crucial and sometimes acrimonious dialogue between reason and faith. The giants of the Enlightenment asserted that man was innately good and, once unchained, would propel the world toward perfection. Though often suspected of sedition, they enjoyed the patronage of distinguished figures like Louis XV's mistress, Madame de Pompadour, and, as a consequence, exerted enormous influence. Louis banned Diderot's twenty-eight-volume *Encyclopédie* on the grounds that information could be dangerous, but he covertly procured a set for his private library. Swayed by Rousseau's reveries of an idyllic paradise, Marie-Antoinette masqueraded as a milkmaid at her *petit hameau* at Versailles while her ladies-in-waiting adopted the quaint practice of breast-feeding their babies.

No eighteenth-century *philosophe* made a more profound impression on thought in France and the rest of Europe than did Voltaire. Phenomenally erudite, versatile and prolific, he denounced the injustices and ineptitude of the ossified ancien régime in a steady stream of verses, fables, satires, epistles, madrigals, librettos, impromptus, translations, histories, dissertations and polemical treatises. He was repeatedly imprisoned in the Bastille and later banished to Ferney, a village near the Swiss frontier, but relentlessly carried on his gasconades. Finally pardoned, he was triumphantly welcomed back to Paris and, his wit as keen as ever, sat in the Académie until his death at the age of eighty-four. Inspired by his example, subsequent generations of pundits would be guided by the tenet that, however much the establishment tolerated and even fêted them, their duty was to fasten on its deficiencies.

At the outbreak of the Revolution, determined to build an equitable society, the celebral elite drafted the Declaration of the Rights of Man and the motto "*liberté, égalité et fraternité*," whose lofty precepts became the credo of the French and peoples everywhere. Numbers of journalists, pamphleteers and playwrights rejoiced in their freedom from despotism—only to be guillotined during the Terror by the tyranny of extremism. Recruited by Napoleon as propagandists, many of the survivors idolized him. In March 1815, when he made his famous march back to Paris from exile in Elba, one of them coined a stirring metaphor: "The imperial eagle soars from steeple to steeple unto the towers of Notre-Dame." Nostalgia for the emperor's cause persisted long after his legions had been vanquished at Waterloo. Julien Sorel, the sentimental hero of Stendhal's *Le Rouge et le Noir,* concealed his picture under his mattress. "I will do with the pen," vowed Balzac, "what Bonaparte did with the sword."

The Bourbon restoration introduced the Romantic movement, which sought among its objectives to discredit the Revolution, expunge the Napoleonic legacy, rehabilitate the Church and rewind the clock to a more stable, virtuous era. One of its earliest and most eloquent authors, François-René de Chateaubriand, after exploring the American wilderness, echoed Rousseau's appeals to commune with nature. Dedicated to the monarchy, he served as Louis XVIII's foreign minister but, his conscience awakened by the widening chasm between wealth and poverty, eventually championed a precursor of Christian democracy. The Gothic revival, popularized by Sir Walter Scott, took France by storm, enchanting poets like Alfred de Musset and Alfred de Vigny. Romanticism acquired a social flavor after Louis-Philippe, the bourgeois king, ascended the throne in 1830. A school of economists, among them Fourier, Proudhon and Saint-Simon, hatched schemes for rural utopias that sounded almost medieval. Historians like Thiers, Guizot and Michelet each had his distinct, often controversial, interpretation of the past. It was also the heyday of the historical novelist—Mérimée, Dumas *père et fils* and, above all, Victor Hugo.

France never spawned a national literary icon equal in stature to Shakespeare, Dante or Goethe, though Victor Hugo came close during his eighty-three years, which virtually spanned the nineteenth century. The majestic themes, rich texture, graphic narratives and measured rhythms of his novels, poems and melodramas were models for both his contemporaries and his successors. Driven into politics by his overweening ego, he alienated his colleagues by his rantings and was ignored as a nuisance. In 1851 he rashly attempted to foil Napoleon III's coup d'état, eluded arrest and escaped to the isle of Guernsey, where he languished for eighteen years. But his prestige remained undiminished, and, at the advent of the Third Republic, he returned to Paris and was elected to the Chambre des Députés. After his death, a half-million citizens flanked the route to mourn him as his body was conveyed to the Panthéon—another indication of France's reverence for its writers.

Flaubert's depictions of the ambitious middle classes bridged the gap between romanticism and realism. Fancying himself an aristocrat, Balzac detested the bourgeoisie, and he skillfully dissected its greed and vulgarity. Zola pushed realism further in his naturalistic epics, which vividly captured the ordeals of common folk crushed by the industrial juggernaut—factory workers, coal miners, farm laborers, marginal shopkeepers, prostitutes. Shelving his flourishing career, he embarked on his legendary crusade to vindicate Dreyfus. The intelligentsia, compelled more than ever before to choose sides, divided into hostile factions. At stake for Dreyfusards like Léon Blum and Georges Clemenceau was the fate of the republic, its liberal, anticlerical priorities—and, indeed, the heritage of the Revolution. Hanging in the balance for the royalist, jingoist, reactionary Ligue des Patriotes and Action Française—headed by Maurice Barrès and Charles Maurras, both talented writers—were Christian values and the honor of the army. The Latin Quarter and other sectors of Paris were transformed into battlefields as the competing contingents, wielding crude weapons, clashed again and again. The conflict reminded intellectuals that it was their obligation to abandon their ivory towers and become *"engagés"*—politically committed.

France during the first three decades of the twentieth century soared from unparalleled prosperity into the carnage of World War I and, after recovering briefly, plummeted into the depths of the Depression. But these ups and downs never dampened its phenomenal creativity.

Animated by Henri Bergson's psychological innovations, Proust trained his microscope on the manners and mores of the patrician Faubourg Saint-Germain. Colette's charming vignettes of boulevardiers and coquettes recalled the belle époque. Gide examined his characters with classical rigor, François Mauriac described the oppressive life of a proper Catholic family in his native Bordeaux, while Jean Giono evoked the beauties of Provence. Antoine de Saint-Exupéry exalted the bliss of flying, and André Malraux, back from Asia, pondered man's destiny. The theater offered tragedies by Paul Claudel and Jean Giraudoux, sophisticated comedies by Sacha

Guitry and Henry Bernstein, bedroom farces by Georges Courteline and Georges Feydeau, and a variety of Cocteau's frothy fantasies. Diaghilev's Ballet Russe, with scores by Stravinsky, dazzled the town; Debussy, Satie and Ravel were at their height. Picasso, Braque, Matisse, Dufy, Miró, Klee, Chagall and Brancusi were exhibiting regularly. A brilliant galaxy of movie directors—Jacques Feyder, Jean Renoir, Marcel Carné, René Clair—were pioneering cinematic techniques. Hemingway, Fitzgerald, Dos Passos, Kay Boyle, e. e. cummings, Glenway Wescott and other Americans, lured to Paris by its fecund ambience, were gaining recognition under the tutelage of Gertrude Stein.

Those electrifying years sparked a proliferation of eccentric coteries. One of them, the Dada, signifying "hobbyhorse," preached aesthetic anarchy. It was invented in Zurich in 1915 and brought to Paris by Tristan Tzara and Hans Arp; its shockers included a mustachioed *Mona Lisa.* Following its collapse seven years later, Breton, Aragon, Éluard and Philippe Soupault launched Surrealism, a term borrowed from an Apollinaire poem. They amalgamated Marx, Trotsky, Freud, Goya and Bosch with aspects of Dada and Cubism in a compound defined by Breton as "pure psyche automatism"—meant to prove that, after the slaughter of World War I, life was absurd. Writers produced gibberish; artists like Salvador Dalí, Francis Picabia, Yves Tanguy and Marcel Duchamp fastened on weird combinations of bottles, umbrellas, urinals, sewing machines, birdcages and bicycle wheels. The Surrealists also exhorted their acolytes to defy the law by insulting policemen, screaming obscenities at priests, spitting at passersby, inciting riots, barging into cafés and smashing glasses. Without a positive goal, however, they shortly ran out of steam. But the memory of the nihilistic interlude would resonate through the years, instilling in future highbrows the belief that they had been ordained to rebel. Seeking a more disciplined channel for their revolt, Aragon and Éluard embraced communism.

After France's fall in 1940, a few intellectuals fled to America, where they served as Free French propagandists or taught school. Several of them rallied to de Gaulle's forces in England or Africa. Others stayed behind, entered the Resistance, edited clandestine journals or actually fought as guerrillas. Convinced that Marshal Pétain represented legitimacy, still others worked for the Vichy regime, and some implacable right-wingers cooperated with the Germans. But many of them thrived under the Occupation, even under censorship. Sartre staged *Les Mouches* and *Huis Clos,* his first plays. In addition to publishing *L'Invitée,* her first novel, Beauvoir broadcast commentaries for Radio Nationale, a Vichy station. Cocteau mingled with Nazis and performed his plays, and was hectored only because of his brazen homosexuality. Adapting to the situation, Camus came out with his initial novels, *L'Étranger* and *Le Mythe de Sisyphe,* while running *Combat,* one of the underground papers. Aragon had also solicited German approval as well as precious paper for his novels and poems—though, following the Liberation, he demanded severe punishment for collaborators. Along with the vast majority of French, he conveniently forgot his wartime activities, and implied that he had been in the Resistance. Despite pleas for clemency from Mauriac, Claudel and others, the only intellectual of consequence to face a firing squad was Robert Brasillach, the editor of *Je Suis Partout,* a pro-Nazi weekly. Charles Maurras, then seventy-seven, was sentenced to life imprisonment. Unrepentant, he muttered as the verdict was read, "*C'est la revanche de Dreyfus.*"

Most intellectuals, beneath their façade of individualism, were remarkably conformist. Imbued with *la mystique de la gauche,* they traced their lineage back to the Jacobins, the Dreyfus affair and the leftist struggles against fascism during the 1930s. Only a minority of them were Communists; still, they subscribed to the party's campaigns, orchestrated by Jean Kanapa and Laurent Casanova, its senior ideologues, who received their instructions from the Kremlin's international agitprop bureau, the Cominform. A pivotal figure in the apparatus, Aragon ran *Ce Soir,* its zippy evening paper, and the literary weekly *Les Lettres Françaises,* along with an array of cultural associations. Among its members were such notables as Éluard, Marguerite Duras and Frédéric Joliot-Curie, the Nobel-laureate chemist; as his registration fee, Picasso sketched one of its most effective propaganda gimmicks, the peace dove. The party was proud of blue-blood fellow travelers like Emmanuel d'Astier de la Vigerie, the editor of the daily *Libération* and scion of a family ennobled during the Bourbon restoration. Its supporters included Emmanuel Mounier, the editor of *Esprit,* the progressive Catholic monthly. A spectrum of gullible celebrities— Jean-Louis Barrault, Gérard Philipe, Simone Signoret, Yves Montand, Fernand Léger—enhanced the party's reputation by attending conferences, signing petitions and parading in protest processions.

Not only was it taboo to criticize the Soviet Union, but numbers of otherwise skeptical intellectuals swallowed and even parroted the Moscow line. Refusing to acknowledge Stalin's brutality, they rebuffed evidence that for years he had been deporting millions of real or suspected dissidents to Siberian labor camps. They were conspicuously mute when his satraps in Czechoslovakia, Hungary and Romania executed "deviationist" Communist leaders. Though they were aware of reports of his anti-Semitism, they remained silent, even after a Moscow tribunal convicted a group of Jewish doctors in 1953 on flimsy charges of treason. Their reluctance to speak out mirrored the dogma that anything that tainted the Kremlin's image of benevolence would bolster the enemies of the working classes throughout the world.

Recollections of Gide's experience also troubled them. A passionate Communist sympathizer since the 1920s, he had once pledged to make any sacrifice necessary to advance the Soviet interests. But in 1936, invited to Moscow to deliver the eulogy at Maxim

Gorki's funeral, he was devastated by the spectacle of hunger, lethargy and corruption camouflaged by paeans of praise for Stalin. Returning to Paris, he announced, "The Soviet Union has betrayed my hopes." From then on he was maligned by the Communist press and shunned by nearly all his friends, and his apostasy remained an example for other highbrows. My mother-in-law, Nathalie Sarraute, remembered her own fear following a visit to relatives in Moscow in 1937, at the peak of Stalin's notorious purges. Years later she confided to me: "It was terrible. The secret police were rounding up and shooting people, or shipping them to camps. I was horrified; still I didn't breathe a word back home. They had ostracized the great Gide, and I was just a little fish in the pond. What would have happened to me if I had talked?"

The subject simmered below the surface until, in 1949, an explosive episode catapulted it into the limelight. Five years earlier a minor Russian diplomat, Victor Kravchenko, had defected in Washington and published *I Chose Freedom,* an indictment of Stalin's atrocities. No sooner did the French edition appear than the Communists contended in *Les Lettres Françaises* that the book was a CIA fabrication. Kravchenko promptly filed a criminal libel suit against its editors, and the trial, which promised the first authentic revelations of the Soviet camps, intrigued even ordinary Parisians—as I deduced from the fact that the topic riveted my concierge to her paper. The courtroom was congested, but luckily I had wangled a seat in the press section. Stylish matrons from the *seizième* filled the benches alongside party cadres from the *ceinture rouge.* Photographers, their flashbulbs popping, swarmed around the corridors. In the broad plaza outside, demonstrators for the competing cliques were waving placards and shrieking at each other in contrapuntal cadence, "*À bas les fascistes*" and "*À bas les cocos.*" The Kremlin, worried about the impact of the case on world opinion, shuttled in witnesses from Moscow. After four months of deliberations, the magistrates ruled for Kravchenko and awarded him token damages. Though the decision symbolically condemned the Soviet system, the Communists remained obstinately obedient to the Russians.

A new version of the trial unfolded the next year in the same courtroom. Now the plaintiff was David Rousset, the editor of *Franc-Tireur,* an anti-Communist leftist daily, who had published a devastating exposé of the Soviet camps. A former Nazi concentration camp inmate, he had accumulated mounds of testimony from Stalin's victims, which made him more credible than Kravchenko. Infuriated, the Communists attacked him in *Les Lettres Françaises,* and, like Kravchenko, he sued for defamation and won damages. His effort yielded some results. Sartre, Beauvoir and others conceded the existence of the camps—though, lest they be tarnished as anti-Soviet, added that political prisoners were also being persecuted in Greece, Spain and France's colonies in Africa and Indochina. As they began to fathom the grim reality of Soviet totalitarianism, however, many intellectuals changed. In 1956, after Khrushchev divulged the magnitude of Stalin's abuses, a left-wing friend confessed to me, "*Vous savez,* we were blind. Kravchenko and Rousset, they were correct."

The same myopia prompted intellectuals to disparage the United States. As much as I appreciated their extraordinary urbanity and erudition, I never ceased to be astonished and perplexed by their tendency to harp on such stale clichés as bloated capitalists, gangsters and lynchings. Minimizing America's role in the emancipation of Europe, they ascribed the conquest of Germany to the Soviet stand at Stalingrad. The United States, they insisted, was out to dominate Europe through the Marshall Plan, the Atlantic Alliance, German rearmament—and, of course, Coca-Cola, the *Reader's Digest* and Hollywood. This monotonous litany was not confined to the Communists. Even a moderate like Mauriac warned that, unless America's materialism were checked, the "cohesion of French civilization" would be jeopardized.

These views, however distorted, were symptomatic of the postwar frustrations that bedeviled the French, leftists and conservatives alike. They had been humiliated by the German defeat. Also, with their political structure shaky, their economy in ruins and their social fabric torn by chronic strikes and other turmoil, their pride in *la grandeur de la France* rang hollow. Exacerbating their predicament was their virtually entire dependence on American assistance—which Washington usually dispensed with onerous strings attached. Resentful, they unleashed diatribes against the United States.

Several intellectuals, realizing that reliance on the Kremlin was not a plausible alternative to their tirades against America, groped for a middle path. In 1948, for instance, Sartre, Rousset and Camus formed the Rassemblement Démocratique Révolutionnaire as a vehicle to promote neutralism. A coalition of non-Communist leftists, it quickly faded after Sartre complained that Rousset was too anti-Soviet. Claude Bourdet, the editor of the weekly *L'Observateur,* proposed a united Europe independent of the two titans—a notion that Hubert Beuve-Méry, the director of *Le Monde,* endorsed. It was discussed for a while in the cafés, then evaporated. But Raymond Aron cautioned that only a partnership with the United States would deter Soviet aggression. In June 1950 more than one hundred liberal American and West European intellectuals organized the Congress for Cultural Freedom as a counterweight to the Communists. As imposing a group of brains as ever assembled, they included Salvador de Madariaga, Bertrand Russell, John Dewey, Carlo Schmid, Karl Jaspers, Benedetto Croce, Arthur Koestler, Sidney Hook, Arthur Schlesinger and Jules Romains, the French novelist. It probably never dawned on them that they had been enlisted under CIA auspices. Nor did it occur to me until Cord Meyer, an agency operative whom I had met through a mutual friend, disclosed to me that he had been their supervisor. At the time he frequently fetched up in Paris, and on sunny afternoons we would go sculling on the Marne.

Sartre vacillated during the postwar decade. Late in 1945, alarmed that he might attract young leftists into his fold, the Communists blasted him, calling existentialism a "rancid, nauseating, decadent anti-Marxist pseudo-philosophy." He replied by excoriating them for their complicity in Stalin's evil maneuvers, and they decried his flirtation with neutralism as naive. The rhetorical brawl intensified in 1949, when *Les Lettres Françaises* impugned his play *Les Mains Sales* as an "anti-Soviet screed" written to ingratiate himself with the American "imperialists." As *un homme de gauche*, Sartre was tormented and, three years later, shifted completely in a convoluted article in his magazine, *Les Temps Modernes*. "To oppose communism is to oppose the proletariat," he affirmed—and became an unabashed party apologist. He justified the Red Army's takeover of Eastern Europe as vital for Soviet security and studiously avoided any mention of Stalin's anti-Semitism or the indiscriminate liquidation of his adversaries. Moreover, he constantly fulminated against the United States. He reached a fever pitch during the weeks preceding the execution of Julius and Ethel Rosenberg in 1953. The Left Bank was in an uproar, and he thundered at a turbulent meeting in the Palais de la Mutualité, "*Attention, mes amis!* We must sever our ties to the enraged American dogs, or their rage will infect us."

Though America also appalled him, Camus reproached Sartre for condoning Stalin's egregious violations of human rights. Sartre came under even more withering fire from Merleau-Ponty, his former co-editor at *Les Temps Modernes*. Merleau had leaned toward the Communists until June 1950, when he concluded that Stalin had instigated the Korean War. For Sartre to publicize Moscow's professions of peace was dishonest, he wrote, adding: "If Sartre is so enamored of the Soviet Union, he should live there rather than manifest his allegiance from the comfort of Saint-Germain-des-Prés." The papers, anticipating a kinetic response from Sartre, headlined SARTRE-MERLEAU DUEL IN THE

MAKING. But Sartre said nothing, and instead delegated Beauvoir to answer for him. "Merleau," she said, "is too close to the bourgeoisie to comprehend that a man as sensitive as Sartre can identify with the misery of the exploited working class from afar." Disappointed, *Combat*, a paper favored by the intelligentsia, clamored: "Why doesn't the master speak? We want to feel his anger, his indignation, his wrath!" Still Sartre said nothing—and my dispatch to *Time* on the fuss never got into print.

If André Malraux scorned these debates as abstractions, it was because he had lived them—or claimed to have done so. By his own account, he was the quintessential *homme engagé*, who had conspired with revolutionaries in Shanghai, helped nationalists in Indochina, negotiated with Nazis in Berlin, hobnobbed with Stalinist assassins in Moscow, fought with the Loyalists in Spain and participated in the Resistance. He served as minister of information in de Gaulle's provisional government, and now ranked among his trusted advisers. With all this, he was a connoisseur of art—in particular Ming porcelains, Cambodian bronzes, Japanese scroll calligraphy, Hindu temple sculptures and American Indian totem carvings. I had been fascinated by his novels *La Condition Humaine* and *L'Espoir*, in which he relied on his own adventures to diagnose the plight of man confronted by the upheavals of the twentieth century. Whatever myths he had contrived about himself, at least he differed drastically from France's hothouse intellectuals, and, for that reason, *Time* planned a cover story on him in the spring of 1955.

I had recently moved to Boulogne-sur-Seine, an upscale Paris suburb, and, by chance, Malraux lived nearby. He was jealous of his privacy but, after a well-connected friend intervened on our behalf, begrudgingly agreed to receive me and one of my *Time* colleagues. Arriving in the early evening, we were ushered by a maid into his den. It was strewn with books, papers, magazines, documents, antiques, photos, paintings, drawings and mementos of his travels. On his desk lay the manuscript of what I guessed to be his work in progress, *Les Voix du Silence,* a massive synthesis of the world's art. Malraux entered the room, briskly shook our hands, gestured us to armchairs and offered us whiskey. Short and dark, with a black forelock dropping over his incandescent eyes, he was afflicted with a facial tic that gave him the look of a mad genius. Without indulging in preliminaries, he lighted a Gauloise and started talking, his gush of words interrupted from time to time by bouts of wheezing caused by his chronic asthma.

As though he were absorbed in some clandestine plot, he shrouded his personal background in mystery. I had gleaned from a few newspaper features, however, that his father, the proprietor of a fishing flotilla, had gone bankrupt, leaving André to be raised by his mother, who ran a tiny grocery on the edge of Paris. Unlike Sartre, Merleau and their breed, he had not graduated from one of the *grandes écoles* but had learned instead by plunging himself into events that they observed only from a distance. It was difficult to follow him as he rambled on—twitching, chain-smoking, squirming in his chair. "Our ancestors understood their environment, which was circumscribed by family, church and custom. Ours is the first generation to inherit the whole world, and we can barely grasp it. I have searched for its meaning all my life, through concrete action rather than philosophy. What have I discovered? I am not certain. Perhaps doubt. Maybe the next century will do better."

17

The Glass of Fashion

The bone-damp chill of winter was lifting, and pale sunlight had begun to etch shadows of the leafless chestnut trees on the cobblestone streets. Children were again playing in the parks, café terraces had started to reopen and lovers could be seen smooching on the banks along the Seine. In the district around the Champs-Élysées, the George V, Prince de Galles and Plaza Athénée lounges were shrill with the shouts of Chicago and Dallas department-store buyers as they cruised from divan to divan, hailing California and Florida dress-chain representatives. At plush restaurants like Lasserre, Ledoyen and Maxim's, stocky, cigar-chomping Seventh Avenue manufacturers in silver ties and white-on-white shirts shared tables with New York designers in jangly bracelets and rhinestone-rimmed glasses. Powder-puff bars were packed with the female editors of women's magazines, photographers, wire service reporters, gossip columnists, press agents, public relations hustlers, titled ladies, rich bourgeois hostesses, stage and screen stars, and the usual celebrities and playboys. This effervescent reunion was a rite of spring—the mystic and sacred moment when the city's top couturiers unveiled to the world the latest variations and dissonances on the theme of the Eternal Feminine.

Though I might drop in on a show once in a while to ogle the mannequins, fashion was not my terrain. In March 1957, however, I was assigned to a mammoth story on the subject. Compared to such industries as food and cars, haute couture contributed little to France's economy. Its income stemmed primarily from serving elite Parisiennes and foreigners, and from exporting designs—especially to America. The thirty or forty *grandes maisons* employed only about seven thousand workers and grossed less than a million dollars a year—in contrast to the four billion dollars' worth of dresses sold annually in the United States. But whatever the balance sheet, Paris fashions swayed the tastes of women everywhere, thereby confirming in the French the conviction that, when it came to producing prestige goods, they were peerless—a belief that, in turn, reinforced their overweening sense of cultural superiority.

Day after day for nearly a month, I crisscrossed the small Right Bank *quartier* where the major fashion houses were clustered. I dutifully viewed the Fath, Balenciaga, Balmain, Castillo, Dessès, Givenchy, Lanvin, Laroche and Patou collections—some of which, for promotional purposes, featured gimmicks like a giraffe-hide coat and a suede bolero lined with alley cat skin. But mainly I focused on Christian Dior, then the preeminent Paris couturier, who was slated to appear on *Time*'s cover.

One morning I took a taxi over to Dior, a baroque granite mansion situated on the Avenue Montaigne, a broad, shaded street between the Rond-Point des Champs-Élysées and the Place de l'Alma. The security reminded me of Fort Knox. Roughly three hundred embossed invitations had been issued to a select list; and, to bar gate-crashers, handsome girls in nondescript black and lockjaw accents guarded the entrance, carefully checking credentials and allocating seats according to a rigid protocol: professional buyers according to their previous purchases, journalists according to the influence of their publications, luminaries according to their current reputations. Punctuality was de rigueur, and absolutely no exceptions. Some months before, the Duchess of Windsor had arrived late, expecting VIP treatment, and she was relegated to a staircase.

The large gold-and-olive salon was a hall of mirrors, the subtle glow of its giant crystal chandeliers overwhelmed by the glare of floodlights. Tucked into alcoves were urns filled with roses, gardenias and carnations whose mélange of fragrances pervaded the chamber. Squeezing into a flimsy gilded chair in the press section, I glanced around. The front rows were crammed with American and European merchandisers cradling pens, notepads and programs. Svelte women in toque hats and pearl chokers leaned forward anxiously; prosperous provincial matrons sat ramrod-upright, clutching stout handbags; a few privileged tourists gazed in awe at the opulence. The mood was as tense and as promising as a Broadway premiere; then the babble subsided as a stereo emitted a medley of waltzes, polkas, ballads and pop tunes—and, in threes and fours, the first of thirteen mannequins glided out from behind a gauze curtain.

Lanky and remote, they seemed to be rapt in an asexual trance as they sashayed up and down the runway in movements and gestures as studiously choreographed as a ballet—hips swiveling, arms akimbo, heads tossing. A woman assistant in basic black, speaking through a microphone, identified their lavish ensembles, tailored sheaths and cocktail casuals in a noncommittal monotone: *"Ariane, trente-trois, zirty-zree," "Chloë, quarante-et-un, fawrty-wan," "Papillon de Printemps, cinquante-cinq, feevty-feeve."* The mannequins would twirl, hover, twirl again, pause, slip off a jacket or a mantle and hand it to an invisible aide, who accepted it silently, like some ancient hetaera. Then yet another pirouette, and they evaporated into the wings. The session lasted three hours, culminating in an array of classic bridal gowns. Most of the audience burst into enthusiastic applause punctuated by cries of *"Magnifique!"* and *"Bravo!"* But, lest the faintest flicker betray their interest in an article to a rival, the pros feigned indifference.

Amid it all, a woman reporter for a Fleet Street tabloid nagged me with a torrent of gush: "Isn't that a witty pebble weave?" or "Don't you think that there's a certain je-ne-sais-quoi texture to that velour?"

The frothy pageant was the indispensable prelude to the serious business that began only after the lights had faded. At that juncture, buyers for Henri Bendel, Saks, I. Magnin, Bonwit Teller, Neiman-Marcus and other establishments that catered to the carriage trade huddled with the solemn, black-clad *vendeuses* strategically stationed in the corridors. Every buyer had her personal *vendeuse*, every *vendeuse* her jealously coveted clientele—and, after years of making deals, they trusted each other. Some buyers, enraptured by the models they had just seen, instantly signed contracts, but most of them would shop around and deliberate before deciding. With big bucks at stake, the risks were enormous. An item that glittered in scintillating Paris could bomb in sober Scarsdale.

A spectrum of options was available to wholesalers. I discussed one of them with Sydney Blauner, a chunky man in his fifties whose Manhattan firm turned out a line under the label Suzy Perette. For an ante of two thousand dollars and royalties, he acquired the right to incorporate Dior's notions into dresses that retailed in the United States for fifty or sixty dollars. Thus, on a slim budget, an Atlanta stenographer or a Cleveland nurse could emulate a glamorous Parisienne. As Blauner told me, "If you don't come to Paris, you're missing the boat. There are more ideas in a thimble here than in all of America."

Pirates chronically menaced the couturiers. A case that hit the headlines unfolded in 1948, when a customer complained to Dior that she had paid a whopping sum for an exclusive gown and, at a ritzy nightclub, spotted another woman in exactly the same number. "This is not a joke," she wept, "but a tragedy." Promptly summoned by Dior, the gendarmes launched an investigation that ended six years later in the arrest of a gang of fashion thieves. They had been stealing designs, which they shipped to London, Brussels, Beirut and elsewhere for conversion into cheap facsimiles. Documents compiled by the police divulged their methods. They would bribe a seamstress or a *midinette* to purloin patterns, or coax a mannequin into borrowing a dress for an evening and copy it. Indicted for violating French copyright law, they were convicted and fined. But one couturier, voicing doubts that forgers could ever be stopped, said, "Maybe we ought to take it as a compliment when they rob us."

As I sought to understand fashion, I discovered that it was misty and nebulous—easier described than defined. I reread Proust's passage on Odette Swann: "Attire to her symbolized the delicate and spiritual mechanism of a whole form of civilization." For Jean Cocteau, fertile artist, playwright, filmmaker and aesthetic arbiter, fashion "thrills us briefly with its insolent, enigmatic bouquet—then, like a frail blossom, dies." Cecil Beaton, the chichi English photographer, differed: "Fashions are ephemeral, but fashion is enduring." Over an apéritif at a Saint-Germain-des-Prés café, the sassy Comtesse Louise de Vilmorin discarded all this rhetoric as poppycock: "Fashion is a veneer foisted on naive women by despots. Give me sincere blue jeans."

Late one afternoon I spent an hour or so with Dior in his green-paneled sanctum above his salon. A plump, balding bachelor of fifty-two whose pink cheeks might have been sculpted from marzipan, he resembled an ambassador or a banker in his charcoal double-breasted suit, the rosette in its lapel denoting his grade as an officer of the Légion d'Honneur. Relaxed after the day's grind, he appreciated the chance to talk. His bland, courteous exterior concealed an inner tension, presumably the result of his dedication to a strenuous, competitive field. When I suggested to him that fashion would wither unless women felt compelled to comply with the latest modes, he peered up his aquiline nose at the ceiling, chuckled and replied, "I'm no philosopher, but it seems to me that women—and men too—instinctively yearn to exhibit themselves. In this machine age, which esteems convention and uniformity, fashion is the ultimate refuge of the human, the personal and the inimitable. Even the most outrageous innovations should be welcomed, if only because they shield us against the shabby and the humdrum. Of course fashion is a transient, egotistical indulgence, yet in an era as somber as ours, luxury must be defended centimeter by centimeter." He resented the charge that dressmakers imposed their will on their clients: "It's a calumny to call us dictators. *Le couturier propose, la femme dispose.*"

The following evening Dior invited me for drinks at his *hôtel particulier* in upscale Passy, near the Château de la Muette. His butler uncorked a vintage Dom Pérignon and, enveloped in magenta upholstered armchairs under a stilted Bernard Buffet portrait of him above the fireplace, we sipped a glass or two. Then, realizing that I was there to gather information for my story, he gave me free rein to poke around. The decor was a ragout of the sublime and the grotesque. Tiers of shelves held sets of leather-bound volumes, odd pieces of bric-a-brac and autographed photos of French and foreign dignitaries, famous writers, composers, opera singers, movie directors, actors and actresses. The vermilion damask walls were a quilt of engravings and aquarelles, Impressionists, Neo-Impressionists, Cubists, Surrealists, Dadaists and kitschy fin de siècle paintings of verdant landscapes and beefy nudes. Ancient Greek amphorae and Roman busts, antique Gallic ceramics and Ming porcelains sat on inlaid medieval Spanish and Italian chests alongside such carnival souvenirs as stuffed animals, plastic *poupées* and plaster statuettes. The boudoir was furnished with a crimson-canopied Second Empire bed, a purple Louis XIV *prie-dieu*, mauve draperies and a white bearskin rug. Dior frequently switched clothes three or four times a day; and his closets and drawers, I guessed, contained hundreds of suits, pajamas, ties and pairs of socks and shoes. Peeking into the Florentine-tiled bathroom, I noticed a colossal green marble tub lined in zinc and equipped with swan's-head faucets. "My friends tease me for accumulating this stuff," he said, "but valuable or trashy, it inspires me in some way or other. I regard it as my own flea market."

Unlike many of his fellow couturiers, who publicized themselves by mixing with *le tout Paris* at glittering galas, Dior was a hermit and, prizing his privacy, seldom went to the opera, the cinema or the theater. He preferred to dine quietly at home and perhaps play a rubber of bridge with a few intimates. His domestic staff of six included a cook, and, defying his doctor's orders to curb his weight, he was partial to earthy peasant casseroles accompanied by choice wines and liqueurs, among them a fine framboise bottled at his château in the forest of Fontainebleau, near Paris. A devout Catholic, he rarely skipped Sunday mass, but he was deeply superstitious, regularly consulted an astrologer and swore by her communion with the zodiac.

Pursuing our chat, I asked Dior to explain why fashion thrived in France. "First," he responded, "we inherited a tradition of craftsmanship rooted in the anonymous artisans who constructed the cathedrals and expressed their genius in chiseled stone gargoyles and cherubs. Their descendants—skilled automobile mechanics, cabinetmakers, masons, plumbers, handymen—are proud of their métiers. They feel humiliated if they've done a shoddy job. Similarly, my tailors, seamstresses, even novice *midinettes,* constantly strive for perfection. We also benefit, paradoxically, from having a singularly difficult consumer: the Parisienne. At a fitting she behaves like a contortionist. She stands up, sits down, bends and wriggles around; actually she is testing a dress because, she knows, an unhinged strap or a clasp could mean disaster at a fancy soirée. Often she brings along her husband or her lover, and they fidget as well over stitches, seams and buttonholes. They exasperate us, but we cannot afford to ignore their fussing, however petty it may seem. Unless they leave Chez Dior in complete self-confidence, we have blundered and our image will be tarnished as a consequence."

To create his collections, Dior would seclude himself in his château or soak in his bathtub, drafting thousands of spidery sketches on scraps of paper—a kind of hieroglyphic of silhouettes and contours. "Suddenly," he said, "one of them astounds me, as though I have accidentally encountered an acquaintance on a country lane. I embrace it as my motif for the season and give it a name—the A-line, the H-line, the *haricot-vert* line, whatever. Then I refine and color about seven hundred of these *petites gravures*, and they will make up the core of the collection."

Next he conferred with his principal deputies—three female fashion veterans whose opinions he respected. After much debate, they approved about sixty designs, which were then cut into tulle patterns and modeled by mannequins in Dior's spacious atelier. Wearing a white butcher's smock, perched on a high stool and wielding an ivory-tipped bamboo swagger stick, Dior repeatedly reviewed them for weeks. A stickler for detail, he would point his stick at a mannequin and insist on adjusting a pocket, altering a pleat, revising a collar, moving a belt, shifting a bow. Nothing eluded his sharp eye—purses, necklaces, earrings, stockings, parasols and the myriad other accessories vital to every smart lady's wardrobe. Particularly troublesome for him were so-called Trafalgars, fragile, elaborate ball dresses that easily came unstuck and had to be stiffened without losing their flossiness. He rehearsed the mannequins tirelessly, displaying surprising grace as he stepped onto the floor to demonstrate their routines himself. As the show approached, he toiled around the clock, pushing his team to the brink of exhaustion. Spinster *midinettes*, clinging to custom, would sew a lock of their hair into the hems of the wedding gowns in hopes of snaring a husband during the year ahead.

"After all the horrors of preparing a collection," Dior confided to me, "I wouldn't think of attending a show." One day, however, he authorized me to hang out backstage during a presentation, and it was a zoo. Helpers and apprentices raced around, pushing racks of dresses and bolts of cloth and other paraphernalia. The mannequins, so cool and distant on the runway, were now half nude, disheveled and frenetic as fitters brushed their garments, hairdressers rearranged their coiffures, and cosmeticians freshened their lipstick, rouge and mascara. Sounding like a railroad conductor, a dispatcher brandishing a watch and a schedule gently patted their derrieres as he thrust them into the salon under their pseudonyms: "*Diane, Columbine, Fleur de Lis, Mirabelle . . .*" A supervisor remarked to me as we stood in a corner, "*C'est de l'anarchie, n'est-ce pas, mais ça marche quand même.*"

One of four children of a wealthy fertilizer manufacturer, Dior grew up in an immense, chalky stucco house located on a windswept cliff above the rugged Normandy coast. Exploring its vast grounds on summer days was a pleasure that he never forgot. He was pampered by German nannies and coddled by his mother, from whom he learned to treasure flowers and to decorate the dinner table when company was coming. Chubby and awkward, he would linger belowstairs, where the maids regaled him with fairy tales and folk songs, and taught him the rudiments of sewing. He delighted in designing costumes and organizing fancy-dress parties for his playmates. After he began school, his teacher scolded him for doodling leggy women in gowns on his exam papers and work sheets. "Despite the reprimands," he told me, "I felt this compulsion to make sketches."

In 1914, when Dior was ten, his parents moved to Paris and bought a house in Passy, where he himself subsequently resided. Many years later, a fortune-teller predicted after reading his palm, "Women will assure your success." He was then contemplating the notion of becoming a couturier, and floated the idea past his father, who laughed and said, "At your age I dreamt of undressing women, not dressing them." Deflated, Dior entered the École des Sciences Politiques, which trained diplomats. He graduated but, instead of enrolling in the civil service, plunged into artsy Paris. Granted a fat allowance by his family, he sported a bowler hat and a fur coat, and mingled with experimental musicians like Satie and Poulenc, and such avant-garde painters as Dalí, Max Jacob, Kandinsky, Klee and Miró. He also rounded up several Braques, Dufys, Chagalls, Matisses and Picassos and, with a partner, opened a gallery. His father agreed to finance him—on condition that the family name never appear on the door.

One day in 1930, Dior was panicked to find a shattered mirror in his room—and justifiably so. Within two months his mother and a brother had died, and shortly afterward the Depression ruined his father. He himself was afflicted with a lung ailment and spent a year recuperating in the Alps. On his return to Paris he was flat broke and had to liquidate the Passy house, his gallery and its canvases. But, during his convalescence, he studied embroidery, which led him to try his hand at designing dresses. To his amazement he sold six sketches to Robert Piguet, a Swiss couturier based in Paris, for twenty francs each. Soon he started to work full-time for Piguet, and was later engaged by Lucien Lelong. "At the age of thirty," he recollected, "I had found my career."

He was inducted into the army on the eve of World War II and put into a labor battalion. Demobilized when France surrendered to Germany, he joined his father and a sister in Provence, where they survived by growing and peddling fruit and vegetables. Dior enjoyed the countryside, but in 1942 he went back to Paris and to a job with Lelong. During the Occupation, women were desperate to preen themselves as a way of boosting their morale; and couturiers, wrestling with shortages of materials, contrived to infuse straw hats, burlap skirts and ersatz leather shoes with a dash of verve. "The styles were incredibly hideous," Dior recalled, "and I couldn't wait to do something better."

His opportunity arose after the Liberation. New York was then threatening to eclipse Paris as the world's fashion center, and France's leading textile tycoon, Marcel Boussac, feared that the decline of French couture would affect his plants. He searched for a designer to

rejuvenate the sluggish Paris salons, and considered Dior. Exhilarated by the prospect of managing his own house, Dior envisioned "a venture aimed at serving a few discriminating women." But before long he had qualms about burdening himself with the responsibility, and again turned to a fortune-teller. "*Imaginez! Chez Dior! Acceptez!*" she exhorted him—and he did. Boussac put up a million dollars, and, among his initiatives, Dior began to recruit mannequins. He inserted an ad in the newspapers, and a legion of beauties appeared. By coincidence the city authorities had recently closed the brothels, and the girls were shelterless prostitutes who thought that a clandestine bordello had just been inaugurated.

In December 1946 Dior retreated to his house near Paris and, working steadily for three weeks, completed his first collection. "The hardships of the war were finished," he later said. "I revived the ripe bosom, the wasp waist and soft shoulders, and molded them to the natural curves of the feminine body. It was a nostalgic voyage back to elegance." He labeled it the New Look and, the critics ecstatically wrote, made fashion history.

ashion haunts this land," observed a visitor to Paris in 1723. "A fishwife can pass for a marquise with impunity." The phenomenon reached back hundreds of years. During the Middle Ages ladies favored sleeves so narrow they had to be sewn together after a women put on her dress. Feudal lords wore fine linens and cottons loomed in France, and even normally ragged vassals gussied up for festivals. As early as the thirteenth century, guilds of tailors, tanners and drapers monopolized the commerce in Scottish tweeds, Flemish woolens and Russian sables, along with Chinese silks imported through Venice. The pious Louis IX, later canonized for his role in the Crusades, swaggered around in a turquoise corsage and a lemon soutane. Charles VII warned that "excessive expenditures on clothes will provoke God's wrath." Nobody heeded him; a profligate fop, he employed seven Neapolitan haberdashers solely to spangle his shirts. Royalty set the tone: in 1559, when Catherine de Médicis donned black for the funeral of her husband, Henri II, widows abruptly abandoned white. Her effeminate son, Henri III, sparked a passion for ruffs, which he would iron himself until they "crackled like parchment." He presided over one function in five thousand yards of lace.

Sartorial flamboyance attained its apotheosis at Versailles. A determined clotheshorse, Louis XIV accoutred himself in satin doublets, velvet sashes, frilly blouses, high-heeled boots, plumed hats and cascading perukes of ringlets. To keep his courtiers out of mischief, he encouraged them to concentrate on dress. He prescribed what they should wear, when and how; and, dreading banishment to their estates, they obeyed without a murmur. One of his edicts regulated the height of necklines, another the length of trains; seeking to attract his attention, many ladies wore mountainous wigs that required ladders to assemble. A convenient manual, *Les Lois de la Galanterie,* cataloged the rules for everything from carrying swords, canes and fans to the use of gloves, buckles, rings, hose, capes, girdles, gorgets, wimples and cummerbunds. As rigorous as they were, these modes excited the rest of Europe, and the king's minister, Jean-Baptiste Colbert, a dynamic mercantilist, reckoned that selling them could be lucrative. As he put it, "French fashions must be France's answer to Spain's gold mines in Peru."

By the latter half of the eighteenth century, partly bewitched by Rousseau's pleas for simplicity, styles were becoming less rococo. Men adopted knee breeches, three-cornered hats and *la redingote à l'anglaise,* the Gallic version of the English riding coat. Women were enchanted by the *circassienne,* the *caraco* and the *polonaise,* full-skirted, loose-bodiced frocks made of Indian muslin or calico. Fleeing the confinement of the palace, Marie-Antoinette and her retinue played peasant in dirndls and sabots at her bogus hamlet in the gardens of Versailles. A satirist ridiculed them as "sophisticated rustics."

It was dangerous during the Revolution to be caught in ancien régime garb. Proper patriotic apparel consisted of knickers, bonnets and the *carmagnole,* a vest introduced to France by Italian workers, which lent its name to a rollicking dance. Craving a bit of color, citizens added red, white and blue cockades to their caps. A period of frivolity followed the Terror. Audacious women called *les merveilleuses* strolled around naked under tunics, even baring a breast. Some of them pretended to be guillotined—a macabre style known as "*à la victime.*" They cropped their hair, bound their necks in thin red ribbons and tilted their heads to simulate their decapitation. Madame Récamier, the darling of the literati, posed for David in a diaphanous Grecian robe, the craze for *déshabillé* spread, and soon ladies were wearing transparent togas.

In 1798, Napoleon returned from a campaign in Egypt, and his expedition spurred a demand for turbans, harem pants and cashmere shawls. Like Louis XIV, he emphasized dress as a device to distract his courtiers, and chided them if they failed to measure up to his standards. He was aware that revenues could be reaped from exporting French fashions to the rest of Europe and, to advertise the latest styles, sponsored tours to London, Berlin, Vienna, Rome and Saint Petersburg by *La Grande Pandore* and *La Petite Pandore,* a pair of life-size dolls. The Bourbon restoration in 1815 resurrected the romantic past. Rejecting the licentiousness of *les merveilleuses,* ladies covered their arms with long gloves and their throats with high collars. Balzac wrapped himself in a Benedictine cassock and cowl, while Alfred de Musset, attired in orange trousers, wrote melancholy poems lamenting the *mal du siècle.* In an effort to appear ashen, cadaverous and languid, the *jeunesse dorée* drank vinegar and dilated their pupils by dosing themselves with belladonna. The wealthy erected neo-Gothic castles replete with turrets, portcullises, crenellations, dungeons, cressets and moats, and freighted their rooms with suits of armor, ancient weapons and counterfeit heraldic escutcheons. All this lunacy, a symptom of France's evolving society, left an imprint on fashion.

Nobles were recognizable by their titles and their genealogy, but the affluent bourgeoisie then emerging had little to show for its achievements except money. One way for *nouveau riche* merchants to gain status, however, was to adorn their wives, daughters and mistresses in expensive clothes. They fell prey to the couturier, a breed pictured by the historian Hippolyte Taine: "Women will stoop to any depths to be dressed by him. This arid, nervous, dwarfish creature receives them nonchalantly, stretched out on a couch, a cigar between his lips. He growls, 'Walk! Turn! Good! Come back in a week, and I will have an appropriate toilette for you!' It is he, not they, who chooses. They are only too content to be dominated by him—and even so they need references."

Taine's couturier was in fact Charles Frederick Worth, the czar of French fashion through the Second Empire into the early twentieth century. Formerly a draper's apprentice from Lincolnshire, he moved to Paris and began to serve Eugénie, the wife of Napoleon III. When she protested that one of his designs made her look obese, Worth argued that, if she accepted the gown, it would resuscitate Lyon's flagging silk mills and avert a strike by disgruntled workers. The emperor ordered her to wear it, other ladies rushed to Worth for imitations and, within less than a year, Lyon's economy was booming. Ashamed of her ballooning pregnancy, Eugénie begged Worth for help, and he invented the crinoline. Now, instead of grappling with cumbersome layers, women had a dress that fit easily over a circular frame of steel hoops. It was, in short, an engineering feat.

Eugénie's patronage vaulted Worth to fame. The hitherto obscure rue de la Paix, the site of his studio, became the fashion hub of Europe. His prices were astronomical: the equivalent of twenty thousand dollars or more for a dress. Insufferably vain, he rated himself alongside Delacroix as a "great artist," and rudely dismissed customers who dared to question his virtuosity. He was also a monumental snob. If a countess was in a hurry for a gown, he would deliver it in an afternoon. He created taste with equal speed. Brown was absent from his palette until the wife of a Brazilian coffee millionaire disclosed to him that she secretly hankered for brown. Overnight, ladies were in acorn, beige, cinnamon and hazel; a few of them even dyed their hair russet.

Worth's spell was broken by Paul Poiret, who reigned supreme during the belle époque, the most sumptuous interlude since Versailles. A swarthy man with a pointed beard and a handlebar mustache, he was extraordinarily versatile. He painted, wrote, acted in a repertory troupe, ran a theater and a restaurant—and, when he was not designing dresses, decorated interiors. After a stint as a clerk in an umbrella store, he worked for Worth before founding his own *boîte*. In 1909, Serge Diaghilev's Ballet Russe made its debut in Paris, and the sensational spectacle, with its evocation of the mysterious Orient, dazzled the cognoscenti. "*C'est d'un mauvais goût épatant!*" they rhapsodized—and Poiret concurred. Electrified by the gossamer costumes, he pledged to unchain women. "I declared war on the corset," he said. "My slogan would be freedom for the tummy."

Convinced that he was the reincarnation of a Persian sultan, Poiret opened his magnificent mansion in the Faubourg Saint-Honoré to ostentatious parties. He called one of them "*la mille et deuxième nuit*" and surveyed the scene from a throne while live cockatoos and monkeys scrambled among the four hundred guests. Posturing as odalisques, women lolled around in negligées. Nubian slaves, their trays laden with caviar, shrimp, lobster and gallons of champagne, threaded through the horde. A poet disguised as Omar Khayyám recited sensual verses, and a dancer recently jailed for indecent exposure performed, wearing only an emerald in her navel. Rich aristocratic and bourgeois hostesses outdid themselves to throw even more exotic evenings, and Poiret cashed in on the vogue by providing them with extravagant dresses. His clients also included demimondaines and *grandes cocottes,* for whom he fabricated chinchilla stoles and towering hats embellished with peacock feathers. He died penniless and bitter in 1944, contending that he had been swindled.

Ornate styles were obsolete by the 1920s. Emancipated during World War I, females were now working in factories, offices and shops; riding subways, buses and bicycles; and, in some instances, driving cars. They had neither the time nor the patience for fastidious trimmings, and the designer who intuitively sensed this transition was Gabrielle Chanel—"Coco." Conceiving *le genre pauvre,* she put women into men's shaggy sweaters, sailors' *tricots,* carpenters' coarse corduroys, ditchdiggers' grainy denims, waitresses' bleached aprons, soccer players' striped jerseys, students' sturdy gabardines. Nothing was too banal for her—sandals, bandannas, berets. Slender and athletic, with the lissome gait of a racehorse, Chanel made the kinds of clothes that she herself liked to wear. Her gamine creations presaged unisex, yet essential chic in her mind was a prosaic dress drenched in diamonds, rubies and sapphires. Fashion, she asserted, ought to appeal to the masses rather than be restricted to a precious few. When a coalition of couturiers petitioned the government to enact tough legislation to prevent piracy, she dissented, maintaining that fraudulent copies earned them popularity. The conceits of her confreres, she said, were preposterous. "We are furnishers, not artists. At first art seems ugly and then becomes beautiful; at first fashion seems beautiful and then becomes ugly."

The daughter of an Auvergne wine dealer, she was reared on a farm by two maiden aunts and, at the age of seventeen, fled to Paris to escape the boredom of the provinces. After a stint as a milliner, she opened a dress shop adjacent to the Ritz, and it remained her headquarters. She would turn on her charm to induce boulevardiers to escort her to trendy spots like Maxim's, Fouquet's and the Pré Catalan, where she could parade her own raiment before the crème de la crème. Her styles clicked, and, by the 1930s, she was raking in an estimated four million dollars a year—and reportedly had assets of ten million. "Under her glossy façade," commented a Paris banker, "she is a shrewd, calculating peasant." Her penchant for the common touch notwithstanding, Chanel rattled around in a mansion on the rue du Faubourg Saint-Honoré and consorted with snooty cronies at their châteaux and ski chalets, or aboard their yachts in the Mediterranean. Yet she fiercely protected her individuality. When the Duke of Westminster asked her to marry him, she demurred, saying, "There have been several duchesses of Westminster; there is only one Chanel."

Coco's main challenger, Elsa Schiaparelli, emigrated from her native Italy to Paris in 1925 and, with more panache than experience, began designing. She befriended painters and writers, and they showered her with ideas, some of them surrealistic—Cocteau, a cloak covered with skulls; Dalí, a hat in the shape of a shoe; Aragon, a tiara studded with seashells. An indefatigable traveler, she accumulated serapes in Mexico, saris in India, djellabahs in Morocco and caftans in Siberia. She pioneered the use of synthetics like rayon and nylon, which she blended with taffeta and crepe. Her signature was an aggressive if bilious puce dubbed "shocking pink," which won her acclaim. Madly gregarious, she cultivated everyone who was anyone, from the Prince of Wales and the Maharajah of Bangalore to Lady Mendl and Mae West—and extracted blurbs from all of them. Probably close to eighty, she was still active when I saw her amid the safari trophies in her salon. "Making clothes is architecture," she told me. "The body is the fundamental structure, and you build on it."

During the years following World War II, the French fashion industry recovered and began to flourish. Women were eager for a breath of fresh air after a dismal decade, and a new generation of couturiers had appeared to satisfy them. They put Paris back on the map—though not everyone was pleased. Françoise Giroud, the ardently feminist editor of L'Express, said: "Dressmakers were once virtually all women and real men. Now they are homosexuals who detest us. What happens when your lover attempts to disrobe you? He wrestles with the intricate catches, loops and geegaws for an hour, and ends up by ripping the gown. That is a masculine form of revenge."

Cristóbal Balenciaga, the dark, gaunt son of a Basque boat captain, was nicknamed "the monk of mode" for his aloof manner. His clients revered him as though he were the chief of a weird sect. He was steady and reliable; then, out of the blue, he would flabbergast Paris with a skirt cut at the knee. His antithesis, curiously, was his companion—Hubert Taffin de Givenchy, a marquis whose ancestry dated back four centuries. Givenchy was adept at splashing around brilliant colors, like an organdy dress speckled with tropical fruit. Acclaimed for a garish line he labeled "la super-fantaisie," Pierre Balmain roamed the globe plugging French fashion with the aphorism "I want to hear people say, 'There goes a beautiful woman,' not 'There goes a beautiful gown.' "

Dior's New Look triggered a storm of controversy. He amplified skirts, tightened waists, brought back petticoats and lowered hems to below the calf—intending through his generous use of material to dramatize the end of austerity. But some mavens cautioned that most women were conservative, and would shun the drastic change.

"Again the capitalists are squandering resources while poor children go hungry," thundered *L'Humanité,* while *Combat* blared: "*Aux ciseaux, les citoyennes!*" At the other extreme, Fernand Gregh, a member of the Académie Française, noted: "The more we clothe a woman, the more desirable she becomes." The publicity sent Dior's stock skyrocketing. He was given a six-page layout in *Life,* and American stores anticipated brisk sales.

But, perceiving that haute couture was at best only marginally profitable, Dior quickly expanded his operations. He was the first couturier to develop the boutique, which enabled women to procure *prêt-à-porter* renditions of his premium dresses at relatively modest prices. The outlets also carried a gamut of spin-offs bearing his logo—scarves, handkerchiefs, lingerie, jewelry, sunglasses. In our final talk I returned to the question of what sustained fashion. He countered with a question: "Have you ever seen a woman enter a shop and ask for 'something just like the one I'm wearing'?"

18

Le Poujadisme

~~~~~

One of my assignments was to track the strikes, boycotts and other disorders that periodically roiled France. Often they consisted more of sound than substance, but late in 1953 my interest was kindled by a potentially serious wave of unrest gathering momentum in the southwestern provinces. Hoping to get some sense of its dimensions, I drove there from Paris, a distance of three hundred miles, and arrived on a frosty evening in Rodez, the capital of the Aveyron *département,* a hardscrabble landscape of scrub vegetation interspersed with vineyards and potato, rye and barley fields. I located a hotel room, grabbed a *casse-croûte* and went out for a walk. Apart from a nearby café, everything was shut—invariably a symptom of tension. Knowing from experience that it would be the best place to learn what was happening, I stepped in. It was crammed with clients—by their look mostly peasants, shopkeepers and craftsmen—smoking, drinking and chattering away at top speed. Over a glass of white wine, a couple of them informed me that a pair of tax investigators had just come to town to inspect the ledgers at Ferdinand Salvan's *boulangerie.* Their voices trembling with indignation, they said that they intended to resist this intolerable intrusion into their neighbor's privacy and were braced for trouble. Perhaps, by luck, I had strayed into a story—or part of a bigger story.

Early the next day, peering from my window, I spotted a truckload of the Corps Républicain de Sécurité, paramilitary police especially trained to quell disturbances. They wore blue uniforms and helmets, and toted rifles, gas masks and truncheons, as though they expected a full-scale clash. I had already seen such units in action against strikers and rowdy students, and they could be brutal. They had pulled in at dawn to guard the examiner and were deployed in front of Salvan's bakery. Dressing hastily, I rushed out in time to observe hundreds of townsfolk pour into the narrow streets, brandishing placards proclaiming JUSTICE AUX CONTRIBUABLES and screeching, "À bas les flics." The police stood their ground until, their patience exhausted, they surged into the throng, swinging their cudgels; after an hour of shoving and shrieking, an ambulance trundled a dozen citizens off to a clinic with minor injuries. Meanwhile, scared by the violence, the tax official had jumped into his Citroën and fled without fulfilling his mission, and the cops, no longer needed, climbed back into their truck and quietly withdrew. Jubilant, the crowd paraded to the cathedral to chant the "Marseillaise"; the detested fisc had been routed.

Week after week, similar incidents were convulsing the region. In Périgueux, a mob of irate tradesmen linked arms to defend a butcher against a tax man, and not far away, in Castelsarassin, militants unceremoniously hustled a revenuer and his police escort out of town. Elsewhere merchants had erected roadblocks and improvised a telephone network to alert each other to approaching collectors; women ran mimeograph machines, and children distributed tracts. Mayors and their staffs were aiding the endeavor by shelving audit notices, and priests offered to ring their church bells as a warning. In Limoges several businessmen concocted an ingenious scheme to rescue a delinquent colleague whose property, seized by the authorities, was being auctioned off to repay his debt. They packed the salle des ventes and, amid much hilarity, bid fifty centimes or a franc for articles like his radio, couch, pots, pans and dishes, purchased the entire stock for one hundred and twenty-five francs—about thirty cents—and handed it back to him.

By early 1954 the turbulence had engulfed virtually all of France south of the Loire Valley and threatened to spread north. The government was worried but helpless. "We can only wait," a finance ministry bureaucrat confessed to me. "When it grows colder they'll have to stay indoors, and maybe that will discourage them."

But the prospects were dim that the insurrection would shortly cool off. On the contrary, before it faded four or five years later, it had burgeoned from a tax revolt into a full-fledged political party whose deputies played a pivotal role as allies of the ultraconservatives in the perennially splintered National Assembly. Grandiloquently labeled the Union de Défense du Commerce et de l'Artisanat—the UDCA—the movement owed its spectacular if transient success to its chubby, handsome, truculent leader, Pierre Poujade, who at thirty-four was one of the most charismatic figures to surface in France since the war. Extolled by his disciples as a savior and denounced by his enemies as a demagogue, he endowed the French vocabulary with a new idiom for dissent: *le poujadisme.* I covered him on and off during his meteoric rise, and was fascinated as much by his dynamism as by the phenomenon he represented.

*I*nitially, seeking clues to Poujade's magnetism, I explored Saint-Céré, his native town in the barren Lot *département,* which before the Revolution had been a part of the province of Quercy. This was the heart of the *désert français,* the country's stagnant lower half as opposed to the throbbing if blighted industrial belts encircling Paris and the northern cities. Formerly a flourishing medieval town of spires and turrets, Saint-Céré had slid into decay. Its population had dwindled in a century from more than five thousand to three thousand, and its distilleries, tanneries, woolen mills and brick kilns were relics. Now it depended for its livelihood primarily on tourists, most of them French, who came during the summer to gaze at the prehistoric drawings in the nearby caverns, to dance and gamble at the casino, and to linger in the candlelit gardens of its few restaurants, savoring such *spécialités* as truffles, pheasant, snails, freshwater crayfish and robust Cahors wines. But after the tourists departed and the gloomy winter set in, the inhabitants would languish in a monotony relieved only by the weekly cinema. Strolling around reminded me of many other desolate French towns—the crumbling houses, the sagging church and weathered tombstones, the mildewed *monument aux morts* in the square testifying to generations of sacrifice for *la patrie*.

Still, Saint-Céré tenaciously clung to its precarious enterprises. I was told by the president of the Syndicat d'Initiative, an insurance agent, that the town boasted more than two hundred stores—approximately one for every three families. They included thirty-two cafés, thirty groceries, eight butcher shops and seven bakeries, many of them run by wives whose spouses farmed or labored as plumbers, carpenters or handymen. Madame Léon Jeffret, who operated a *salon de thé* while her husband worked as an electrician, explained to me, "Without his salary I would have to close the shop, and without the shop we simply could not get by." The local capitalist, a Communist, owned the cinema, the casino and acres of prime real estate. Bored and stymied by limited horizons, youths migrated to the cities in quest of jobs. The elderly sat in their cafés and mused on happier times.

To promote his populism, Poujade advertised himself as a "common man," and the portrait was not inaccurate. He was the youngest of eight children of a penniless architect who, in a burst of patriotism at the start of World War I, had sold his tiny parcel of inherited land, bought government bonds and marched off to the trenches. Like many other veterans, embittered at being neglected after their ordeal, Poujade *père* enlisted in Jacques Doriot's fascist Parti Populaire Français. He died in 1927, leaving his widow impoverished. To make ends meet, she took in laundry and raised chickens. Pierre attended Catholic school, where he devoured French history and revered Napoleon; he quit at the age of fourteen. Emulating his father, he briefly flirted with the fascists, then knocked around France at various jobs—professional bicycle racer, apprentice typographer, grape picker, ditchdigger, soccer player, stevedore. Later, recalling those years, he said, "They were a better education than being cooped up in a classroom."

When World War II erupted, Poujade went into the air force and, following France's surrender, joined the Compagnons de France, a Pétainist organization. He adored its camaraderie and rigorous discipline, and enthusiastically remembered it as "a true French fraternity." After the Wehrmacht occupied the country's southern sector, he escaped to Spain and was interned for five miserable months before making his way to Algiers. There, ill with a skin disease, he was restored to health by Yvette Seva, a dark-eyed French army nurse whose family of *pieds-noirs* had resided in Algeria for a century. Their love affair blossomed into marriage, and they were both transferred to England, where Poujade served as a deskbound sergeant in the Royal Air Force. On their return to France, they settled into his mother's ramshackle house in Saint-Céré, which had neither central heating nor a toilet. Yvette proceeded to bear four children, but, an iron-willed woman with antediluvian opinions, she was to be a decisive influence on Poujade.

At first he scratched out a living as a traveling book salesman, an odd métier considering his sporadic education. After a while he rented a bit of space in Saint-Céré, and opened a stationery store that chiefly carried picture postcards and tacky souvenirs. His mother would mind their kids and Yvette tended the business as Poujade plied his rural route peddling books, magazines, pens and paper from the back of his dilapidated Renault *camionnette*. To supplement his meager income, he obtained a taxi license and conducted tourists on excursions. He was respected as a star of the town's rugby team, an energetic entrepreneur and a pillar of the community, but he could barely keep afloat. "If I paid my taxes, I would've gone bankrupt," he confided to me during one of our conversations. "Cheating is our only alternative. It's the same for everyone in Saint-Céré, and for everyone in France."

In 1952, reckoning that politics might be a channel for his frustrations, Poujade ran for the municipal council as a Gaullist—the only ticket that would have him. A bombastic orator, he emphasized the theme that subsequently resonated through all his rhetoric: the unscrupulous politicians were ruining the nation and deserved to be ousted. He won easily, but beyond his gift for invective, he was bereft of a vision on which to build a career. His political notions, such as they were, had intuitively filtered down to him from the dogmas of Charles Maurras, the reactionary, monarchist, anti-Semitic swami of the prewar era, who had been convicted of treason for collaborating with the Germans. Maurras, a brilliant if venomous polemicist, had propagated the idea that France was divided into *le pays légal* and *le pays réel,* the rulers and the ruled—on one side the affluent, venal, secular, sophisticated Paris elite, on the other the pious, honest, frugal, hardworking people of the provinces. By his own definition, Poujade belonged to the latter category.

He fumbled around for a program until one day in July 1953, when twenty-seven shopkeepers and craftsmen received notices that inspectors were coming to Saint-Céré to check their ledgers. The same notice reached Georges Frégeac, a blacksmith and Communist member of the municipal council. Behind in his taxes and flat broke, he was distraught. He summoned his fellow councillors to an emergency meeting in a café and outlined a tactic. The following morning, at his instigation, three hundred tradesmen in their aprons were in the streets, shouting "*Vous nous emmerdez*" and "*Foutez-nous la paix!*" Flabbergasted and frightened, the officials and the gendarmes flanking them scurried away. Poujade had not been involved in the demonstration but, as he watched from the sidelines, he sensed that the hostility toward taxes was an issue waiting to be exploited. Later he wrote with his typical hyperbole: "I would symbolize David against Goliath, justice against the inquisition, freedom against slavery—and all in the great French tradition of our forefathers."

He forgot his book business and launched his antitax crusade. Assisted by Yvette and a few volunteers, he held forth from a corner of his store or from a table in an adjacent café. He also scoured the countryside behind the wheel of his junk heap, speaking in dinky bistros and on village greens, wherever he could induce the alienated and disgruntled to listen to his doctrine of discontent—and, in the process, marshal their support. The perfect bumpkin, an image he cultivated, he fit comfortably into provincial France. He spoke a barnyard patois laced with crude, even scatological idioms. His clothes were unpressed, his shoes unshined, his light beard unshaven, his fingernails filthy. He preferred the kitchen to the dining room, favored coarse *pinard* over champagne, dunked his bread into his coffee and slurped his soup from his bowl.

One rainy night I caught up with him in Figeac, about thirty miles southeast of Saint-Céré. He had just driven in, and three or four hundred citizens awaited him in the flag-draped *salle des fêtes* of a hotel. I guessed them to be mostly peasants and petit bourgeois, the men in berets, the women in flowery hats. Poujade shed his tweed sports jacket, loosened his tie, unbuttoned his sweater and unleashed an extemporaneous harangue. "*Écoutez, mes chers amis*, we must not buckle under to a corrupt administration that spares the giant profiteers who are pillaging France. Only through solidarity can we compel them to renovate the rotten regime that imperils us, we the country's backbone, we little guys, we the mules. We are being beaten, choked, humiliated by unconstitutional laws when our rightful place is at the helm of the nation." Two hours later, drenched in perspiration, he was grinning, guzzling beer and vigorously pumping the hands of his new fans.

In the morning he headed for Vitrac, in the Dordogne, where the scene was much the same. Perched on a chair in a café, he said, "Poujade and all you little Poujades, we are not against taxes. We just don't want to pay anyone else's taxes. This unmitigated tyranny must stop—and stop now." It occurred to me that, despite his pretensions to humility, he had begun to refer to himself in the third person, like General de Gaulle.

Appealing to the chauvinistic streak that pervaded the views of many French, he decried multinational corporations and asserted that foreign imports were contaminating France. He digressed into wild theories, like the allegation that the United States and the Soviet Union were secretly plotting to dominate Europe. Nor did he have any qualms about preaching the most egregious brand of anti-Semitism. "They can malign me as a racist," he would repeat, "but the fact is that I am called Poujade, a good old French peasant name, a name from the banks of the Seine and the Garonne, not from the Volga or the Danube, not Hirsch or Salomon or Ollendorf, as some of the men who govern us were called before they disguised their real identities." He never ceased to evoke Premier Mendès-France's Jewish lineage. When Mendès embarked on his crusade against alcoholism by sipping milk for the cameras at a diplomatic reception, Poujade sneered, "France is the world's largest wine producer, so obviously there's not a trace of Gallic blood in his veins."

Poujade's platform was more a catalog of gripes than an agenda for reform. They included his insistence on disbanding the *polyvalents*, inspectors authorized to descend unannounced on a taxpayer to examine his books. He further demanded the repeal of a statute that slapped stiff fines as well as jail sentences on anyone judged guilty of abetting dodgers or thwarting collectors. But mostly he excoriated politicians. "Our ancestors," he would bellow to hysterical audiences, "beheaded a king for doing far less than those masturbators, fags, phonies and piles of *merde* are doing today. After the Liberation they closed all the brothels in France except the biggest one—the National Assembly."

In November 1954, overflowing with confidence, Poujade convened the UDCA's first national congress. As its venue he chose Algiers, where the overwhelmingly right-wing *pieds-noirs* ardently greeted the delegates. He claimed that his movement, now informally known as the Poujadistes, counted more than four hundred thousand registered followers and an equal number of sympathizers. In exchange for annual dues of one thousand francs a year, its members would be insured against confiscation of their assets, get a subscription to his weekly journal, *Fraternité Française,* and receive a handy guide to contending with fiscal snoopers. Among its other advice, the manual cautioned them to "close your enterprise in case auditors pursue you," "pay nothing until you have conferred with one of our counselors"—and, when in doubt, "stall as long as you can." Now, persuaded that he had cemented his ranks, Poujade was ready to storm Paris.

Their legacy of onerous and often arbitrary levies had instilled in the French the belief that eluding taxes not only guaranteed their survival but was ethically acceptable. So, as an old adage went, France was a country of excessive taxation tempered by excessive fraud.

Until the fourteenth century, land was the chief source of wealth, and the king, the nobility and the clergy enjoyed the privilege of saddling their tenants with levies like the *taille*, a percentage of their crop. But, with the expansion of commerce and the centralization of government, feudalism declined and the hierarchical fiscal system gradually began to collapse. Though a panel of scholarly Sorbonne jurists had established the Crown's right to impose taxes under the principle of *defensio regni*—"for the protection of the realm"—their thesis was widely challenged. The Comte de Foix, for example, was exiled to his château in the Pyrénées for refusing to pay the *centième* and the *cinquantième*, tolls on capital and income devised by Philippe le Bel to finance his interminable wars against the English and the Flemish. The emerging bourgeoisie also balked at footing the bill for his expenditures. Bedeviled by defeats and costly quarrels with the Vatican and the Knights Templar, Philippe ordered the population to melt down its silver to replenish his depleted exchequer and invented still another tax, the *cinquième*. In 1302, to allay a mounting tide of objections, the king formed the États Généraux, an institution composed of the aristocracy, the clergy and commoners, which he pledged to consult before introducing fresh fiscal measures. An embryonic parliament, it was a degree toward democracy; soon, however, its members started to sanction abusive taxes of the kind that they had themselves earlier resented, and uprisings multiplied.

In 1358 peasant gangs known as *jacqueries* terrorized the region around Paris, burning, looting, raping women and torturing babies. A contemporary chronicler described them as "insane savages," but the provost of the Paris merchants, Étienne Marcel, perceived the rampage to be a chance to coerce the throne into reducing taxes. His maneuver aborted, he was murdered by his rivals, and royal soldiers retaliated by massacring twenty thousand dissidents in a day. Fifty years later Simon Caboche, a skinner at the town abattoir, sparked a rebellion against the prodigal Charles VI. Shopkeepers and craftsmen flocked to his colors and, in a portent of the future, besieged the Bastille for eight months. Eventually subdued, Caboche was confined to a dungeon until 1418, when the Burgundians occupied the city.

Over the decades ahead, protests recurrently disrupted France. One of the bloodiest exploded during the reign of Louis XIII, when Cardinal Richelieu, his shrewd and powerful minister, in an attempt to solve a crippling budget deficit, borrowed against uncollected taxes and, to service the loan, exacted harsh new levies on items like tobacco and playing cards. In 1637 peasants proudly calling themselves *croquants*—clodhoppers—ran amok through the southwestern provinces, wantonly slaughtering officials. The upheavals mushroomed north into Brittany and Normandy, where peasants, merchants and artisans nicknamed *va-nu-pieds*, the barefoot, combined with a group dubbed *bras-nus*, the naked arms. They torched government warehouses and, wielding hachets, scythes and barrel staves, cut down anyone who stood in their path. The reprisals were ruthless, but they did not deter revolts. In many instances they were triggered by the local gentry in defiance of the king.

"Taxation," advised Louis XIV's treasurer, Colbert, "requires plucking the goose to obtain the largest amount of feathers." So, an assortment of oppressive levies increasingly afflicted France. By the eighteenth century, in addition to the *taille*, they included the *dîme*, the *vingtième* and the *octroi*, a duty on goods. Another was the *corvée*, which forced peasants to labor for the state. But worst of all was the *gabelle*, the salt tax. As a device to generate funds, the ancien régime obliged households to consume a specified quantity of salt annually, whether or not it was needed. Before the days of refrigeration, salt was also indispensable for preserving perishable food, and the tax made its price exorbitant. A black market naturally sprang up, inspiring the mobilization of a brigade of inspectors called *gabelous*. In 1768 alone they arrested eleven thousand culprits, whose punishment ranged from prison terms to long years in the galleys. The inequitable fiscal structure was abolished during the initial flush of the

Revolution, only to be resurrected by Napoleon to sustain his army. His coffers drained, he even revived the hated *gabelle*. Constantly insolvent, the Third Republic continued to burden the French with taxes.

Inevitably they became skilled evaders. Apart from workers, whose salaries were docked for taxes, everyone had a scam. Barbers concealed their tips, dentists requested their fees in cash, businessmen kept two sets of records, millionaires with lavish weekend châteaux claimed deductions as cattle breeders. Digging into the books of a two-bit circus, an auditor ran across write-offs for peanuts for fictitious elephants. In 1952, a government study revealed, the average profit disclosed by the vast majority of France's nearly two million tradesmen and artisans was less than an average office employee's wage.

To approximate incomes, inspectors relied on *les signes extérieurs de richesse,* the visible indications of wealth. They would scrutinize a citizen's apartment, appraising his furniture, paintings, antiques, vintage wines, wardrobe and wife's jewelry. A taxpayer could also be interrogated in detail: did he have a dog, a horse, servants, a nanny for his children, a mistress, a vacation house, a yacht, and what was the size of his car? In contrast to America, where massive finagling was a felony, France treated violations leniently. The law precluded jail for offenders; instead the examiner and miscreant would amicably negotiate a reasonable compromise. Overeager officials were a menace to this eminently humane procedure. One zealot, who scrupulously jotted down the license numbers of the automobiles parked outside a three-star restaurant, discovered that many of their owners could not possibly have afforded to dine in such style on their declared earnings, and duly reported them. Unfortunately for him, his list contained several dignitaries with friends in high places. He was shunted off to a position in a remote province.

Because incomes were difficult to gauge, the government derived seventy-five percent of its revenues from indirect levies. Rich and poor thus paid the same tax for beer, wine and cigarettes. But, despite their egalitarian convictions, the French seemed to be impervious to the manifestly unfair assessment, since it was invisible. The fiscal bible was the *Code Général des Impôts,* a labyrinth of some three thousand rules, regulations and codicils, many of them archaic, such as a levy on windows facing the street. Scanning its pages, I encountered incomprehensible clauses, like one exonerating from certain taxes "chauffeurs or coachmen who possess one or two vehicles that they operate themselves, on condition that the two vehicles are not simultaneously in service." These ordinances compelled an entrepreneur to file separate returns on his volume, sales, gross and net profits, wages of his staff, their pensions, health insurance and family allocations. His only recourse was to doctor his books.

At the same time, to shield them from competition, the government accorded mom-and-pop shops and artisans an array of subsidies and exemptions. Peasants were equally coddled; they paid taxes based on land values fixed in 1908—or no taxes. As a result, nearly half of France's working population was self-employed, and the loss to the nation through this fiscal generosity totaled four hundred billion francs a year—about one billion dollars. So, logically, Poujade and his faithful should have had little cause to complain. But their fulminations reflected a deeper malaise. At the time, the country was modernizing, and, they feared, the advent of chain stores, discount outlets and assembly lines would spell their doom.

Some officials suggested that one way to muzzle Poujade was to charge him with "disturbing the peace," then discarded the idea. Suspecting that he was dipping into the UDCA's war chest of more than five million francs, the government also hired a squad of detectives to probe his finances, but they turned up nothing. Poujade gloated, "It just proves that they're desperate."

In January 1955, after nineteen months of focusing on the provinces, he scheduled his first show of strength in Paris, and the government did all it could to hinder him. The state railways denied his followers the cut-rate fares customarily granted conventioneers, while the transportation department, pointing to the floods then devastating France, tried to ban their chartered buses from the roads. He was also barred from the city's three largest auditoriums, and instead staged the rally in two hangars in the Parc des Expositions at the Porte de Versailles, on the western fringe of town. The armed security police lurking in the backstreets, he knew, were poised to provoke a battle as a pretext to annul the event, and, in case of a skirmish, he had his own vigilantes, supervised by Jean-Marie Le Pen, a brawny paratroop veteran of the Indochina war. Dropping in, I witnessed Poujade putting on a virtuoso performance for the more than one hundred thousand delegates. His shirtsleeves rolled up and his face dripping with sweat, he was shuttling between the hangars, speaking for a half hour in each.

"We want our piece of the cake, too!" he yelled. "From tomorrow on, we don't pay taxes until they give us genuine fiscal reforms. *D'accord?*"

"*D'accord,*" echoed the crowd.

"We fight together?"

"*D'accord.*"

"To the limit?"

"To the limit."

But the atmosphere seemed to me to be more cheerful than angry. When Poujade uncorked one of his usual tirades against Mendès, some of the delegates hissed and hooted, "*Les Juifs au Jérusalem.*" As they dispersed, though, most of them were laughing and joking, as though they had been to a carnival.

Realizing that its effort to obstruct Poujade was only boosting his reputation as an underdog, the government reluctantly allowed him to hold his next meeting in Paris. Three weeks later, filling the huge Vélodrome d'Hiver, the site of the celebrated six-day bike race, he reiterated his diatribes, again to a thunderous ovation. At this juncture his strategy was explicit: having conquered the provincial butchers, bakers and grocers, he now sought to lure their urban equivalents into his camp. To the popular dailies, always lusting for sensational copy, he was "Robin Hood," while the liberal papers, comparing him to Hitler, labeled him "Poujadolf." Jacques Fauvet, the prestigious political commentator for *Le Monde,* wrote, "He endangers the republic." The Communists, who had hoped to manipulate him for their own purposes, dismissed him as unmanageable. As *L'Humanité* remarked: "He is merely an enraged petit bourgeois with no appreciation for the class struggle."

Shortly afterward Mendès fell, and Edgar Faure stitched together a rickety coalition cabinet. Flexing his muscles, Poujade sent the new premier an ultimatum: "We presume that you are familiar with our grievances. Unless you satisfy us, you will suffer the consequences." It was not a message that Faure could ignore. He had a slender majority in the National Assembly, and, with a ticklish tax bill up for debate, he could be toppled. Either under pressure from constituents or out of opportunism, roughly half of the deputies leaned toward Poujade. To mollify them, Faure proposed to curb the *polyvalents* if they agreed to delay a motion to ease the penalties for evaders. The session dragged on into the wee hours of the morning; and so brittle was the mood that when Poujade, sitting in the visitors' gallery, casually rose to remove his sweater, the jittery speaker interpreted the gesture as a signal for a riot and pushed the alarm button on his desk. Sirens screamed, guards urgently closed the exits and ushers scrambled to evacuate the chamber. Faure's bargain squeaked through by a slim margin and Poujade, seething, sputtered to a group of reporters clustered outside, "They are all a bunch of *salauds,* but, mark my word, we'll get them in the end."

Over the ensuing months, the Poujadistes intensified their agitation. Their strikes, boycotts, road barriers and brawls with the gendarmes brought small towns and big cities like Lyon and Bordeaux to a standstill. But it was becoming clear to Poujade that, to be really effective, he had to transform his movement into a political party. As a test, one of his acolytes ran for municipal council in La Bourboule, in the Auvergne–and was trounced. Henceforth, Poujade concluded, he would concentrate on broadening his ranks to include industrialists, doctors, lawyers, students, schoolteachers, workers, women–anyone with a pet peeve. "We are all being persecuted!" his pamphlets and posters read. "Let us stand together!" The responses were mixed, yet he remained buoyant.

Before long he began to contemplate the possibility of fielding a ticket in the National Assembly elections slated for January 1956. The gamble seemed to be feasible, and, to prepare for the contest, he leased a hotel near Saint-Céré, where he trained a regiment of amateur commandos to heckle rivals, pelt them with ripe vegetables and break up their meetings. Maintaining that he had no political ambitions, he recused himself from the race and recruited some eight hundred candidates, whom he made swear loyalty oaths to him. He scripted their speeches, exhorting them to pound away at the same leitmotif: "Throw the rascals out!"

A legislative election had not been held in the middle of winter since 1876, partly on the theory that the French were too hung over after their bibulous Christmas holidays, and also because they would brave the cold only when absolutely necessary. Nevertheless, this time they went to the *urnes* in enormous numbers and booted out nearly one hundred and fifty of the National Assembly's six hundred or so members. At best, Poujade had speculated, he would capture forty seats; he accumulated two and a half million votes, which translated into fifty-two seats. A butcher, who told me that he had cast his ballot for the UDCA, shrugged: "I'm a lifelong Socialist, but what else could I do? The stables must be cleaned. Perhaps Poujade is the broom."

The pundits, who had unanimously predicted that Poujade would fizzle, were astonished by the outcome and mortified by their miscalculation. Later, in a district-by-district analysis of the returns, they attributed his victory to the electorate's revulsion against the incumbents—especially the moderates. One of them observed that the Poujadistes and the Communists, two parties committed to the destruction of democracy, would now command one third of the parliament. Exulting in his triumph, Poujade crowed, "We have been vindicated." And, he added with remarkable prescience, "The Fourth Republic is hovering on the brink of death."

Journalists from around the world dunned him for interviews, photographers shot him from every angle and *Time* immortalized him by featuring him on its cover under the caption "An Ordinary Frenchman." To be close to Paris, he had borrowed a spacious house in a village outside town. Owned by a nouveau riche grocer, it was decorated with hideous statues and ersatz objets d'art. I went there early one morning to find Poujade sprawled across a quaint feather bed, perusing piles of newspapers over café au lait and a slab of buttered baguette. His wife sat next to him, her typewriter propped up on a suitcase, taking down his directives and memos. The telephone rang incessantly and, cradling the receiver on his shoulder, he barked orders to confederates in the provinces.

After a while he donned a turtleneck sweater, and we drove to his temporary headquarters in a suite in a modest hotel near the Tuileries. It was pandemonium. The three or four rooms were thick with cigarette smoke and littered with empty wine and beer bottles. Aides, men and women alike, bustled back and forth, making telephone calls, drafting statements, confiding tidbits to reporters, promising the moon and the stars to constituents. I stuck around for the rest of the day, watching Poujade function.

None of his novice deputies had ever been inside the National Assembly, and he set up a series of lectures on parliamentary practice—a subject about which he knew next to nothing. Every day he would also go to the legislature to control their activities, either from a back room or from a corner in its marble corridors. But, after years on the barricades, they were still surly and rambunctious: Le Pen had first swaggered into the chamber saying audibly, "I'm different from everybody else here—I like women." Above all, they were naive yokels, no match for their seasoned, cunning adversaries. Hardly had they warmed their benches on the extreme right side of the hemicycle than the rules committee expelled eleven of them for faulty credentials. Reacting in their usual fashion, they raised a rumpus that spiraled into anarchy when a prankster in the gallery fired four shots from a cap pistol. "This place," one political reporter muttered to me, "is a complete farce."

As the months passed, Poujade floundered. The public, feeling that elected officials ought to display at least a modicum of decorum, had become disgusted with the cockeyed antics of his legislative bloc. More important still, it was apparent that he had nothing much to offer except a lot of fury signifying very little. Aware that his impact was waning, he rehashed his notion of resuscitating the États Généraux. But the idea was too ambiguous to understand; and besides, as some historians noted, that body in its day had only paralyzed the government and spurred the creation of the National Assembly, which had been plaguing itself—and France—ever since.

In the 1958 elections the Poujadistes, who had never really grasped the complexities of parliamentary politics, got less than one half of one percent of the vote. Poujade vanished into memory. The tax structure remained a bewildering maze, and the French continued to cheat—thereby confirming the old cliché, "*Plus ça change . . .*"

19

Turnstile Politics

Covering politics, one of my beats, was a riveting though daunting experience. I spent hours in the National Assembly, which
was housed in the Palais Bourbon, a majestic eighteenth-
century, Corinthian-colonnaded replica of a Roman temple situated
across the Seine from my office on the Place de la Concorde. Perched
in the press gallery, I peered down on the baroque chamber, trying to
fathom how the six hundred or so *députés* functioned. Most of them
were usually absent, and those present seemed to be oblivious to the
proceedings. Ensconced in their plush, crimson-upholstered banquettes, they scanned the newspapers, snoozed or, if they were alert
enough to disagree with a speaker, harangued him with earthy epithets or pounded their desks like rowdy schoolboys. When I needed
a tidbit for a story, they could be cornered for a talk in the corridors,
where they consummated deals in conspiratorial whispers while pac-
ing back and forth, arms interlocked, through a musty decor of allegorical paintings and statues of forgotten statesmen. Now and again
we would chat over a winy lunch at a nearby restaurant, preferably
Chez Lipp; occasionally they might invite me along on one of their

fence-mending trips back to their constituencies. As always I relied on my French confreres, whose encyclopedic memories supplied me with obscure statistics and droll anecdotes. But eventually, thanks to my fortitude, patience and taste for opéra bouffe, I acquired a grasp of the interminable maneuvering and squabbling that characterized the Fourth Republic.

The legislature was manipulated by special interests capable of toppling cabinets that repulsed their demands. Vintners, distillers and sugar beet farmers produced twice the quantity of alcohol that the French could consume and, represented by a potent lobby, compelled the government to buy their surpluses at three or four times the world price. Through their formidable pressure group, the North African *colons* consistently thwarted efforts to settle the Algerian war. Ministers were often on the payroll of companies under their jurisdiction; as finance minister, for example, Edgar Faure had no qualms about carrying on his law practice and even accepted fees from private firms for counseling them on their tax problems. Pervaded by cronyism, the structure was nicknamed "*la république des copains.*"

But many of the deputies, if not exactly paragons of rectitude, were sophisticated, cultivated and witty. They included esteemed jurists, doctors, authors and scholars, some of them Resistance heroes.

Eloquent orators, they converted monotonous debates into dazzling exhibitions of rhetoric embellished with classical allusions and erudite digressions. Their forensic talents, however, were usually irrelevant; as an old and cynical maxim of French politics went, "A great speech may change an opinion, never a vote." Consequently, they focused less on enacting legislation than on stitching together flimsy coalitions designed to preserve their seats. Between 1944 and 1958, there were twenty-five cabinets—an average survival rate of seven months. The rondo of musical chairs resumed after each collapse, and the same faces reemerged in other ministerial posts. Such was the rotation that nearly one out of every four deputies could expect a portfolio. The bargaining for coveted jobs, a complicated process known as *dosage,* could stretch out for weeks. Appalled, the French contemptuously dubbed the assembly *la maison sans fenêtres*—a cloister sealed off from the country. Amid all this, the permanent bureaucracy kept the vital services going while technocrats like Jean Monnet shaped plans for the future. Frequently, though, the sclerosis delayed crucial decisions, making France an object of ridicule for both its allies and its adversaries—or, as the old phrase had it, "the sick man of Europe."

History largely accounted for the chronic instability. Since 1789, the French remembered, they had repeatedly manned the barricades against oppression—a series of upheavals that had endowed them with fifteen separate regimes and a visceral distrust for authority. As he prepared to retire as president of the postwar provisional government late in 1945, de Gaulle cautioned the framers of a new constitution that only a strong executive would prevent a return to the flaccid Third Republic. But, suspecting him of harboring ulterior motives, they rejected his admonition and vested absolute power in the parliament. They further confected an intricate electoral procedure that, in addition to making it virtually impossible to dislodge the deputies, effectively ensured that no party could marshal a majority. With women exercising the franchise for the first time, the document was endorsed in a referendum. It perpetuated the fissures that had traditionally fragmented France: urban versus rural, management versus labor, big corporations versus small enterprises—and the most stubborn of all, secular versus religious.

The chamber reflected these divisions. Arranged around the semicircle from left to right like a multicolored fan—an ideological protocol dating back to the Revolution—were six main blocs interwoven with splinters that could, at key moments, tilt the precarious balance. It was a formula for incoherence.

Clustered on the extreme left were approximately one hundred Communists and four or five Progressistes, a couple of them aristocrats presumably atoning for the sins of their feudal forebears. Their whip, Jacques Duclos, was a rotond former pastry cook from Toulouse whose singsong accent and folksy manner masked a rabid sectarian. They vaunted the party as the paladin of the "exploited masses" but pursued a devious *politique du pire*—a strategy predicated on the theory that a deteriorating situation would enhance their appeal—and, among their tactics, impeded enactment of such measures as a boost in health benefits and the minimum wage. Also devoted to advancing the Soviet cause, they uncorked demonstrations against "Yankee imperialism." One of their noisier rallies, staged in January 1950, singled out as its target Coca-Cola, then making its debut in France. Orchestrated mobs surged through the streets shrieking "*À bas la Coca-colonisation,*" while *L'Humanité* alleged that the local Coke bottlers were actually CIA surrogates. The preposterous gambit swiftly fizzled, though for a time many French fretted that this foreign concoction would pollute their civilization. "It is not the drink," brooded *Le Monde,* "as much as the style of life it connotes—gigantic red trucks, garish neon signs, vulgar advertisements. At stake is the very soul of our culture." Even the finance minister, Maurice Petsche, had misgivings until David Bruce, the astute United States ambassador, reminded him that, under its contract,

Coke was obligated to share its profits with its French partners, Pernod and Les Glacières de Paris.

The Communists depended for their routine operations on a legion of militants, many of them youths rebelling against their bourgeois families. As dedicated and disciplined as monks, they pasted up posters, distributed tracts, peddled brochures, hawked souvenirs at jamborees and submitted to weekly cell meetings at which they recited tedious Marxist mantras. They selected their spouses—and their lovers—from among their comrades. Their wives used the approved cookbook; their children read an approved comic strip titled *Pif le Chien,* an anticapitalist underdog. Within this snug orbit they were furnished with their necessities and their diversions—housing, loans, canteens, kindergartens, summer camps, soccer teams, women's circles, cinema clubs, theater troupes, performances by Bulgarian folk dancers and package tours to Poland. Loyal writers, artists, journalists and musicians were treated to junkets to conferences in East European resorts. These activities were subsidized either by party dues or by Soviet funds funneled into France through a web of occult banks. Remarked Jacques Fauvet of *Le Monde* with grudging respect, "The Communists possess the most competent machine in the country."

A "typical" sympathizer, I gathered from one survey, was a worker or farmhand in his late twenties, with a wife and two children. He tended to be neutralist rather than either pro-Russian or anti-American, though party propaganda had convinced him that the Soviet Union was a paradise and the United States a wasteland blighted by bloated capitalists, vicious gangsters, endemic lynchings and chewing gum. What little he knew about Marxism bored or bewildered him. Frustrated and embittered, he was primarily preoccupied with improving his living conditions and believed that only the party, whatever its flaws, had the answer. With five or six million others like him, the Communists habitually racked up one quarter of the ballots in elections.

But, by the early 1950s, they had become increasingly isolated. Their membership, roughly one million following the war, had plummeted to fewer than four hundred thousand—largely because the party's slavish obedience to Moscow offended the chauvinistic French and also because politics fatigued people. The decline was particularly drastic in the industrial zones around Paris and Lille, and in the hardscrabble areas of Provence. Similarly, *L'Humanité* and its companion papers had dropped circulation and, desperate to recapture readers, were running astrology and advice-to-the-lovelorn features, crossword puzzles and even cheesecake. The defections, which had been debilitating the party for years, suddenly accelerated after October 1956, when Soviet tanks quashed the prodemocratic uprising in Hungary. The French Communists applauded the action, enraging fellow-traveling politicians and intellectuals. Jean-Paul Sartre, for years an apologist for Moscow's most egregious abuses, sounded as though he had been personally betrayed; the invasion, he wrote in *L'Express,* was "a crime against humanity." Not since Stalin signed a nonaggression pact with Hitler in 1939 had the party sustained such a blow. One morning I drove out to the Renault automobile factory in Boulogne-Billancourt, a Paris suburb, where the Communist-controlled labor union, the Confédération Générale du Travail, spoke for nearly all the rank and file. The workers were on their break in the courtyard; one of them, a mechanic, told me over coffee, "I never thought I'd live to see the Red Army slaughtering ordinary guys like us."

Calculating that a display of unity would camouflage the discord, the party convened its annual congress in the grimy port of Le Havre, and I took the train there for the crucial event. The Communist municipal council had adorned the huge auditorium in the ugly concrete city hall with red pennants, hammer-and-sickle escutcheons, banners inscribed with slogans and icons of Marx, Engels, Lenin and the martyred Jean Jaurès. I could judge from their attire—ill-fitting jackets, sweaters, caps and berets—that the seven or eight hundred delegates were predominantly workers. Transported to town in special railway carriages, they were being sheltered and fed in school dormitories, and shuttled back and forth in chartered buses under the gaze of cadres. Also present was the general secretary, Maurice Thorez, a brawny former coal miner with the battered face of a pugilist. He had deserted the French Army on the eve of World War II and spent five years in Moscow—an embarrassment that the party lamely sought to cloak by mythologizing him as "*le premier résistant.*" Out of gratitude to the Communists for their role in the maquis, de Gaulle had designated him a minister of state in the provisional government after the Liberation, which puffed up Thorez's ego.

Emulating Stalin's personality cult, he encouraged his flacks to idolize him. His perquisites included a chauffeured limousine and three mansions, among them one on the Côte d'Azur. At his behest, his shrewish wife, Jeannette Vermeersch, was elevated to the Politbureau. His acolytes celebrated his fiftieth birthday in 1950 with seminars, dances, concerts and a play recapitulating his life. A commemorative plaque was affixed to his boyhood home. He was showered with gifts of precious sculptures, porcelains and tapestries; a Communist philosopher equated him with Montaigne, Descartes and Voltaire; and the party's literary weekly, *Les Lettres Françaises,* editorialized: "We rejoice in our adoration of *nôtre cher* Maurice Thorez, our beacon. He stands with the deities of the Enlightenment."

A few months earlier Nikita Khrushchev had revealed Stalin's atrocities, but the atmosphere at the congress was palpably Stalinist. Goons had forbidden the "Anglo-Saxon" correspondents from mingling with the delegates, and we felt stumped until an English colleague, Boris Kidel, devised a clever ploy. A Russian by origin, he posed as a visiting Soviet apparatchik and strolled around freely, picking up nuggets that he generously shared with us. One delegate's remark to him punctured the veneer of harmony: "Budapest has been a catastrophe for us."

Unless he muffled the dissidence, Thorez realized, it would enfeeble the party. He had recently suffered a stroke and, propped up on the podium by aides, laid down the line in a trembling voice: "We encourage differences, but once the party has chosen the correct course, dissension only plays into the hands of our foes." The conclave concluded with a contrived note of solidarity as the cheering delegates rose to their feet, dutifully clenched their fists and chorused the "*Marseillaise*" and the "*Internationale.*"

The Socialists, located adjacent to the Communists in the legislature, held about one hundred and twenty seats. Founded by Jaurès at the turn of the century as a branch of the world proletariat movement, the party subscribed to the Marxist principle of global revolution—an aspiration mirrored in its official name, Section Française de l'Internationale Ouvrière. But, eclipsed by the Communists following World War II, its clientele consisted chiefly of minor civil servants and schoolteachers, whose only common denominator was a nostalgia for their past crusades against clericalism, militarism and unbridled capitalism. Conspicuously missing from its ranks were prestigious intellectuals—a disgrace for a party that had once prided itself as the vehicle for France's brainiest elite.

The Socialists attained their peak during the 1930s under Léon Blum, a uniquely scrupulous figure. The son of a prosperous Alsatian Jewish clothier, he was reared in comfort and rivaled André Gide for the Greek and Latin awards at their lycée. He graduated from the École Normale Supérieure and studied law at the Sorbonne, becoming at the age of twenty-three the youngest magistrate on the Conseil d'État, the supreme tribunal. As a sideline he contributed articles on horse racing to a Paris daily, wrote book and drama reviews for highbrow journals, and won recognition for his penetrating critiques of Goethe, Stendhal and Ibsen. Soon he was hobnobbing with Anatole France, Verlaine, Zola, Proust and Gide in the fashionable literary salons of the Faubourg Saint-Honoré. Labeling themselves "intellectual anarchists," they deplored injustice and inequality. But they were just dilettantish parlor pinks until the 1890s, when the Dreyfus affair awakened in the intelligentsia the importance of engaging in politics.

Joining the Socialist Party, Blum volunteered his legal skills to Zola's campaign to vindicate Dreyfus and, in 1919, was elected to the Chambre des Députés, the precursor of the National Assembly. His potential was tested the next year at the party's congress in Tours. The Bolsheviks, now in power in Moscow, insisted on complete fidelity from the Socialists. Blum and others refused, and the pro-Moscow leftists stormed out to form the Communist Party, taking with them the treasury and three quarters of the Socialists' membership. But, with a segment of workers behind him, Blum single-handedly resurrected his moribund movement. By 1936, demoralized by the Depression and financial scandals, citizens were clamoring for change. With the country in turmoil, Blum created the Front Populaire and became France's first Socialist premier. Backed by the Communists, he introduced a gamut of innovations, such as the forty-hour workweek and paid vacations. He was vilified by disgruntled employers while monarchists and fascists went on a rampage, screaming, "Rather Hitler than the Jew Blum." The French, however, were fascinated by this peculiar bird with a droopy mustache and pince-nez glasses, who delivered didactic lectures better suited to an audience of students.

During the Occupation, the Germans deported Blum to Buchenwald, where he was treated better than most of the other inmates. Later, back in politics in Paris, he formed a purely Socialist cabinet that, though it lasted less than a month, began to restore a degree of normality to the country. He probably could have been elected president of the republic, but recoiled from exchanging his Olympian status for the symbolic job, and, by a wide margin, the dubious distinction was bestowed on Vincent Auriol, a seasoned Socialist from

Toulouse. A tubby former baker with a poached-egg eye and a lilting southern inflection, he resembled an overdressed duck in his black swallowtail coat, striped trousers and top hat, his ample girth swathed in a tricolor sash. His humble origins notwithstanding, he rapidly adapted to the grind of inaugurating hospitals, pinning ribbons on prize pigs and waddling between rows of braided Gardes Républicains to greet kings and queens. Once I watched him at his annual shoot for the diplomatic corps at the presidential château in the forest of Rambouillet. Squinting through spectacles as thick as milk-bottle bottoms, he bagged eight pheasants and thirteen rabbits. He did more than conduct ceremonies, however. The parties valued his ability as a mediator and regularly solicited his advice. He was supplanted in 1953 by René Coty, a good-natured mediocrity from Normandy who, five years later, called in de Gaulle to dismantle the Fourth Republic.

Managed by Socialists, the early postwar governments included Communists—until, in 1947, a convulsion shattered the honeymoon. More than three million workers, infuriated by soaring inflation and their stagnant salaries, unleashed a wave of wildcat strikes and boycotts that quickly engulfed the country. They crippled factories, mines, buses, and public utilities, depriving the population of gas, electricity and water. Garbage littered streets, mail piled up in post offices, newspapers ceased publication. Shops closed, as peasants, taking advantage of the turbulence to ventilate their own grievances, blocked shipments of food and wine to the cities. The Communists were caught in a dilemma: how to respond to walkouts they had not sanctioned. Initially they excoriated the agitators as "Trotskyist" provocateurs and even mustered scabs to attack them. But, alarmed that their grip on the laboring classes was slipping, they abruptly reversed gears and claimed responsibility for the strikes. The only option for the Socialists was to expel them from the cabinet. The Communists shifted to the opposition, which they would have done anyway on Moscow's instructions. With the Cold War then escalating, France was staunchly in the American camp, and the Russians could not tolerate the idea of a satellite party connected to its number one enemy.

Stymied by the chaos, the Socialists relinquished the premiership to Robert Schuman of the Mouvement Républicain Populaire—the MRP—a centrist Catholic movement. But the irascible Jules Moch, a Socialist, remained in the government as minister of interior. Alleging that the Communists had instigated the violence as a prelude to seizing power, he mobilized eighty thousand troops and police, equipped them with tanks and armored cars, and crushed the strikers, especially in the industrial north. For his own purposes Moch undoubtedly exaggerated their intentions, but henceforth the Communists were to be less a danger than a nuisance. As the Swiss commentator Herbert Leuthy later put it: "The sword of Damocles suspended over the Fourth Republic had fallen—and broke."

Many Socialists never forgave Moch for his brutality, which stained the party's reputation in the eyes of the working class. They were also dismayed by the revelation that their labor union, Force Ouvrière, had been receiving CIA stipends surreptitiously channeled through the American Federation of Labor. Frail and melancholy before his death in March 1950, at the age of seventy-seven, Blum confided to a visitor to his cottage in Jouy-en-Josas, a village near Paris, that his greatest regret was that the Socialists had been unable to bridge the chasm between the working and middle classes, as the British Labour Party had. He could not understand that French workers were too hostile toward the bourgeoisie for such a reconciliation.

The Socialists' image was further tarnished under Guy Mollet, a former schoolteacher from Normandy. The son of an impoverished textile worker and a housemaid, he had been an intransigent leftist and an ardent pacifist. But, out of expediency, he swerved to the right as he crawled up the political ladder. After ascending to the premiership in 1956, he intensified the war in Algeria and, the same year, strained the Atlantic Alliance by cooperating with Britain and Israel in an expedition against Egypt for expropriating the Suez Canal. "The Socialists have a beautiful future behind them," insiders quipped. As shrewd parliamentary jugglers, however, they guaranteed their continued participation.

Their neighbors in the chamber, the Union Démocratique et Socialiste de la Résistance—the UDSR—had been organized by de Gaulle's postwar finance minister, René Pleven. Its twenty-four members had abandoned the Socialists to found a more pragmatic party. Spoofed as "generals without soldiers," they were unknown outside their own districts—though, as a pivotal faction, they exercised leverage that far surpassed their size. Pleven served twice as premier and as minister in several cabinets while François Mitterrand, also of the UDSR, held portfolios in nearly every government.

Straddling the center of the assembly were the MRP's eighty or ninety deputies, headed by Robert Schuman, Pierre Pflimlin and Georges Bidault. The movement was conceived early in the Occupation by a nucleus of liberal Catholics. Defying the upper echelons of the Church hierarchy, which had openly backed the Vichy regime, they hid Jews, ran secret radios, edited clandestine papers and fought as guerrillas. They viewed themselves as the scions of the priests and laymen who during the nineteenth century had contested the premise that Christianity and democracy were incompatible, and that only the abolition of the republic would make the Church secure. While the reactionaries dreamt of regaining the prerogatives enjoyed by the entrenched clergy before the Revolution, the progressives declared that it was an ethical imperative for Catholics to struggle for a more equitable society on earth rather than preach salvation in heaven—even if it required colluding with the devil. The

Dreyfus case aggravated the schism as the two sides quarreled over his innocence or guilt. On one issue, however, they agreed: the need for the state to underwrite religious education.

Following the Liberation, the MRP scored a resounding success at the polls, largely because the prewar Catholic parties had been discredited by their collaboration with Vichy. Many French, despite their anticlerical bias, also hoped that the emergence of a vigorous Christian Democratic group might help to end the dispute over *laïcité* that had long scourged the country. Paramount for several of the movement's leaders was the unification of Western Europe. Schuman, a gaunt Lorrainer with the mournful look of a minor apostle, toiled with Jean Monnet to cement a economic union aimed at bringing about a rapprochement between France and Germany. He was seconded by Pflimlin, a somber Alsatian destined to be the Fourth Republic's last premier. But they were not always in tune with Bidault, a native of Auvergne in his late forties. Educated by Jesuits, he taught history at a Lyon lycée and, like his colleagues, had catapulted from the Resistance into politics. A dwarfish man given to egotistical tantrums, he drank heavily, and I would often spot him staggering into the chamber from a boozy lunch and lurching down the aisle to his bench. Nevertheless, he served as premier in 1946 and again in 1949, and held the foreign affairs portfolios in a string of governments. Under his tutelage, France sank deeper and deeper into the quagmires of Indochina and North Africa—until the MRP, its strength waning and its spirit fading, degenerated into another tired horse on the parliamentary merry-go-round.

From 1956, when they were thrust into the limelight by incensed taxpayers, until the demise of the Fourth Republic, the fifty-two Poujadistes occupied the far right flank of the assembly. Engineered from a distance by Pierre Poujade, who had abstained from running for office, they were crude and rambunctious, and were usually brushed off as lunatics. But, by combining with other diehards, they carved out a niche for themselves in the kaleidoscopic legislature.

Professing to be heirs to the Revolution, most French perceived themselves to be *hommes de gauche.* Accordingly, the Gaullists wildly objected to being relegated to the right fringe of the chamber—though where precisely they belonged was unclear. The movement, launched by de Gaulle in 1947 as the Rassemblement du Peuple Français—the RPF—was supposed to be, instead of simply another party, an association open to every citizen but the Communists, whom he dismissed as "*séparatistes.*" He vowed to dissolve the legislature and, echoing his stirring plea in 1940 to the French to take up arms against the Germans, exhorted the country to confer on him the task of reviving "*la gloire de la France.*" Magnetized by his legend rather than by his ambiguous platform, a spectrum of voters, from Resistance veterans to Vichyites seeking redemption, elected nearly one hundred and twenty of his candidates. Once in parliament, however, the RPF was riddled with internecine bickering. By the end of 1952, about fifty members had split off to hatch a new group. The loyalists, headed by Jacques Soustelle, a young ultranationalist, altered their name to the Centre des Républicains Sociaux and, shunted to the sidelines, waited for de Gaulle to make a comeback.

The conservative Centre National des Indépendants et Paysans could have been rock-ribbed American Republicans. Catering to the business community and the landed gentry, its one hundred deputies opposed state interference in the economy, high taxes and government expenditures except for religious education and the military establishment—while advocating subsidies to industry and, to shield themselves from competition, stiff tariffs against imported agricultural and manufactured products. The party's oracle had been Paul Reynaud, the last premier of the Third Republic, until he was superseded by Antoine Pinay, who became premier in March 1952. The mayor of Saint-Chamond, a town near Lyon, where he owned a tannery, Pinay epitomized the petit bourgeois. A slight figure with a hint of mustache, he seldom traveled abroad and spoke no foreign language; the little he knew about the world outside France came from the papers or the radio. Satirists lampooned him as a rube, but he was a wily politician with an acute sense of public relations. Trailed by reporters and photographers, he roamed the provinces on weekends, buttering up ward heelers, bussing old ladies and cuddling babies. One Saturday afternoon I observed him in Dijon. Wearing his signature porkpie hat, he poked into bakeries, groceries, butcher shops and cafés, shaking hands with their proprietors and customers. "*Comme vous, je ne suis qu'un français moyen,*" he would announce, then ask them for their complaints. Their reply was unanimous: "High prices."

Averse though he was to meddling in the free market, Pinay leaned on wholesalers and retailers to slash prices, and, for the first time since the war, inflation began to ebb. He also generated revenues by floating a tax-exempt bond that was snapped up by investors. Even his severest critics gave him high marks, and he remained in office for a year—a lifetime by Fourth Republic standards.

In the middle of the muddle sat the Radical Socialists. Neither radical nor socialist, as the platitude went, they eluded simple definition. Comprising only forty or fifty thousand members, most of them concentrated in central and southwestern France, they were a diverse collection of local Babbitts—lawyers, doctors, merchants, affluent peasants—mainly linked by a faith in science, an animosity toward the clergy and a pious if vague reverence for the tenets of Jacobinism. Their patriarch, Édouard Herriot, articulated their doctrine in one of those nebulous aphorisms so dear to the French: "Radical socialism is the political expression of rationalism." When I asked a party stalwart to clarify the epigram, he was just as amorphous. "*Le radicalisme,*" he said, "*est un état d'esprit.*"

Formally called the Parti Républicain Radical et Radical Socialiste, the movement was founded in June 1901 by several conscientious bourgeois elements fearful that the army and its confederates, after inculpating Dreyfus, would go on to subvert the legacy of the Revolution. In contrast to the Socialists, they rebuffed Marxism on the grounds that the concept of class conflict was outmoded, but promoted such daring notions for the period as the eight-hour day and an income tax. Their star, Georges Clemenceau, taught school in Connecticut and was married briefly to an American before returning home to plunge into politics. The party's liberal social agenda, he contended, should not preclude the use of force to defend the state against disorder; and as minister of interior in 1906, boasting that he was *"le premier flic de France,"* he sent troops to smash a coal miners' strike in the Pas-de-Calais. Their opponents derided the Radicals as hypocrites. "They are like radishes, red on the outside and white on the inside," went one barb; another ran, "Their hearts are on the left, and their pocketbooks on the right." With the same tenacity, however, Clemenceau guided France to victory in World War I, earning the sobriquet *"Le Tigre"* and, after he died in 1929, a place in the nation's pantheon of immortals.

His successor, Herriot, was a towering intellect whose treatises included studies of Diderot, Chateaubriand, Beethoven and Madame Récamier. Also propelled into politics by the Dreyfus affair, he was elected mayor of Lyon in 1905, a job he held until his death a half century later at the age of eighty-three. He doubled as premier, but, by the 1930s, the Socialists and Communists overshadowed the Radicals. After World War II, the party was regarded by voters as a tainted relic of the Third Republic and won only about seventy-five seats in the assembly—though its leaders, agile parliamentary navigators like André Marie, Edgar Faure and René Mayer, surfaced again and again as ministers. Another of them, Henri Queuille, a sleepy-eyed physician from a destitute region of central France, incarnated the Fourth Republic. His prescription for governing, he said, was "to do the least harm possible," labeling the approach *immobilisme*—inertia. He served as premier three times, once for thirteen months—a record for longevity.

Fervent gourmets, the Radicals punctuated their annual congresses with stupendous feasts, which I covered as often as I could. One year I had a phenomenal bouillabaisse in Marseille and the next, in Strasbourg, a fabulous *choucroute garnie*. But nothing matched the banquet in Lyon in October 1956 to honor Herriot, who was then on the verge of death. The ambience was redolent of the belle époque. Nearly all of the fifteen delegates at my table at Chez la Mère Brazier were corpulent notables in black suits, some of them with walrus mustaches. Napkins tucked under their chins, they plowed through such *spécialités* as *pâté de foie gras aux truffes, quenelles au gratin, rognons de veau en croûte* and *crêpes aux pistaches flambées*, paralleled by innumerable bottles of Sancerre, Côtes de Brouilly and Veuve Clicquot. Over coffee, cognac and cigars they listened with moist eyes as Herriot, his husky voice quivering, lifted his *coupe de champagne* in tribute to "*la bonhomie charmante du parti radical*" and "*les beautés gastronomiques de Lyon.*" One delegate said to me, "Only we Radicals still appreciate the art of *savoir-vivre.*"

Across the smoky room I discerned Pierre Mendès-France, the maverick Radical, a squat, swarthy figure of forty-seven with a broken nose, whose morose look seemed to convey his disdain for the revelry. As premier two years before, he had raised hopes that the ossified system could be rejuvenated. But his experiment faltered, leaving the Fourth Republic to stumble toward self-destruction.

The son of a Jewish tailor, Mendès grew up in an apartment above his father's modest shop in the medieval neighborhood near the Place de la République. His ancestors, fleeing the Inquisition in Portugal, immigrated to Bordeaux as early as 1300. Originally called Mendez or Mendozo, they attached France to the name either out of deference to their adopted land or because of marriage to a Franco. But even though he traced his lineage in France back six centuries, Mendès *père* still seemed to be sensitive to charges by anti-Semites that the family was not truly French. "*Croyez-moi, monsieur,*" he bristled when I interviewed him in his shop, "we have been patriots for generations. My great-grandfather fought with Napoleon, my grandfather in the conquest of North Africa, my father in the Prussian war and I myself was at Verdun."

A precocious child, Mendès obtained the *baccalauréat* at the age of fifteen, then enrolled at the École des Sciences Politiques and the Faculté de Droit. He was aloof, solemn and bookish—what French kids mock as "*un fort en thème.*" While other students caroused, he would sit up at night with his chums at La Source, a café on the boulevard Saint-Michel, wrangling over such recondite subjects as the devaluation of the franc and the nationalization of banks. He started a left-wing discussion group, the Ligue d'Action Républicaine et Socialiste Universitaire, which made him prey for the Camelots du Roi, monarchist bullies who prowled the Latin Quarter. Once, in a scuffle, they attempted to throw him out of a third-floor window, but he got away with only a broken nose. He finished his law course at nineteen, at the top of his class of nine hundred, and became France's youngest attorney. His voluminous dissertation, an assault on Premier Raymond Poincaré's monetary policy, provoked an indignant letter from Poincaré himself. A publisher turned the thesis into a book, using the letter as a blurb.

Mendès was barely out of his adolescence when, slated to address a Radical meeting, he lost his notes and winged it. Herriot, who was present, embraced him: "You are one of the most brilliant minds for your age I have ever met." Thus anointed, Mendès toured the circuit of Radical clubs—one of which, in the Norman town of Louviers, persuaded him to move there and run from there for the Chambre des Députés. In 1932, he edged out the conservative incumbent and, at twenty-five, became France's youngest deputy. He was four months above the legal age for a member and, to appear older, sprouted a mustache. A year later he married Lily Cicurel, a stunning Egyptian whose Jewish family owned a chain of department stores in Cairo. The witnesses at his wedding, Édouard Daladier and Georges

Bonnet, were cabinet ministers. Plainly, Mendès was being groomed for bigger things.

In 1938, when Blum brought the Radicals into his second Popular Front coalition, he appointed Mendès undersecretary of state for the treasury, making him the youngest government official of the Third Republic. Like many national politicians who retained a foothold in the provinces, Mendès acted as mayor of Louviers, a nonpaying job he cherished. Years later he mused to a handful of journalists, myself included, "Here in Paris it takes so long to get results, but in a small town you can really exert influence."

He enlisted in the air force at the outbreak of World War II but, now thirty-three, was too old to qualify as a pilot and became an aerial observer. Shortly after France capitulated to Germany, he fled to Morocco, where he was convicted by a Vichyite court-martial of desertion and transferred to a prison at Clermont-Ferrand. Hardly had he arrived than he started to plot his escape, and the episode illustrated his audacity and diligence.

One day, spying a six-foot length of notched lightning rod lying in the courtyard, Mendès considered that it might make a ladder. But he was physically flabby, and for weeks did push-ups in his cell. He saved the pocket money doled out to inmates, traded cigarettes for ration coupons, somehow dug up a train schedule and was ready to go—only to find that the rod had disappeared. Beginning again, he stole a rusty saw from a workshop, found a rubber stamp and forged an identity card. Then, by luck, the prison doctor decided that he had a liver ailment. Confined to the infirmary, he invoked his right, as an officer, to a private room, and before long was briskly hacking away at the bars on the windows. Finally, on a warm June evening, he packed a small valise and shinnied down a rope made of bedsheets to a roof. He was braced to descend when he heard murmurs coming from a couple nestled under a tree. The boy had a proposition, the girl hesitated. Waiting anxiously, Mendès worried that the local cinema would empty and spill people into the streets. After a while the girl acquiesced, and the pair drifted off. "Never did it seem more urgent for me to see a woman lose her virtue," Mendès subsequently wrote, adding a paragraph directed at the anonymous girl: "The day that we account for our behavior before the Creator, I will take on myself, if you wish, the fault you committed that evening. For I wished it, I swear, even more passionately and more impatiently than did your young lover."

Mendès reached Grenoble and spent eight months in the Resistance before making his way to England. There he was welcomed into the Free French air force, trained as a navigator and flew twelve bombing missions over Europe. In 1943 de Gaulle summoned him to the French headquarters in Algiers to draft plans for France's postwar reconstruction, and later named him minister of economy in the provisional government. To avert inflation, Mendès emphasized, it was essential for the French to tighten their belts. But, with de Gaulle's assent, the cabinet protested that, after the ordeal of the Occupation, fresh rigors could not be imposed on the people. Rather than compromise, Mendès quit and, for the next decade, shunned ministerial posts.

If he championed austerity, it was largely because he himself was austere. He neither drank nor smoked, and ate sparingly. During a sojourn in the United States he became enamored of drugstores, where he could grab a sandwich and a glass of milk—but he had a particular weakness for cherry pie à la mode, a dish alien to France. Later he embarked on his famous drive to curb the French appetite for alcohol, which triggered a torrent of controversy. He rarely attended fancy receptions and opening nights with *le tout Paris*, choosing instead to spend his evenings in earnest conversation with a few friends. As one hostess told me, "He can be charming, though fundamentally he is a lonely man."

Banishment to the political wilderness did not silence Mendès. On the contrary, he became a Cassandra, stressing that its illusions of grandeur threatened to doom France. "*Il faut choisir,*" he reiterated.

"It is absurd to pretend that we are still a world power. We must limit our ambitions and, however painful it may be, live within our means." Castigating French capitalists for their narrow, Paleolithic attitudes, he asserted that they could stimulate the economy by infusing it with "incentives, investments and efficiency." Inspired by FDR, he referred to himself as PMF but, unable to invent a Gallic equivalent of Roosevelt's reforms, came up with an awkward Franglais analogue for his own program—"*le New Deal.*" His dynamism soon attracted a coterie of young, urbane disciples, many of them wealthy matrons and pretty girls who lent a touch of chic to his entourage. One of his whiz kids, Jean-Jacques Servan-Schreiber, the son of a prominent publishing family, provided a pulpit for his sermons by founding *L'Express,* a weekly modeled on *Time.* Mendès's heretical candor at first surprised, then enthused the French electorate, which had grown weary of pompous, duplicitous politicians. He even elated skeptical Paris reporters; infected by the mood, we at *Time* unabashedly exalted him in our dispatches.

Among his other arguments, Mendès had repeated that the colonies were an unaffordable burden and should be granted autonomy—or else, he predicted, they would drain France's resources. His warnings proved to be prescient. By 1954, the war in Indochina had dragged on for eight years, costing France one third of its annual budget, eighty percent of its American aid. Nearly one hundred thousand French soldiers and auxiliaries, including its finest officers, had been killed or wounded. Disgusted, the public overwhelmingly favored withdrawal. Though most of the deputies agreed, they lacked the courage to speak out until May 7, when they were shocked by the news that Ho Chi Minh's tattered battalions had overrun the besieged French garrison at Dienbienphu. It was France's worst catastrophe since the surrender to Germany. After nurturing the fantasy that the debacle might be avoided, Premier Joseph Laniel's cabinet disintegrated, and Mendès stepped in. Confronting the assembly, he pledged to fly immediately to Geneva, where an international conference was striving to reduce tensions in the Far East, and promised to resign unless he returned within four weeks with a truce. With Communist and other support, he sailed into office but subtracted the Communist votes from his total; it would be indecent, he explained, to constitute a government backed by a party that "had sullied men who died for their country." I happened to be in the chamber that night, and it was bedlam. Furious at being snubbed, the Communists banged their desks while their whip, Jacques Duclos, stomped through the foyer outside, muttering, "*Sale youpin*"—dirty kike.

Mendès's bold gamble paid off. In Geneva he covertly negotiated with the Chinese and Soviet foreign ministers, Chou En-lai and Vyacheslav Molotov, who circumvented their Vietnamese comrades and handed him the peace he wanted by his deadline. Later he evolved a blueprint for Tunisian independence and finessed the thorny question of rearming Germany by proposing its admission into the North Atlantic Treaty Organization. But on February 13, 1955, after seven and half months, his time had elapsed, and, in a frenzied session that climaxed at five in the morning, Mendès was toppled by a composition of odd bedfellows—Communists, the MRP, the Gaullists, assorted right-wingers and, most decisively, twenty Radical colleagues resentful of his concessions on Tunisia. Rather than yield quietly, as deposed premiers customarily did, he climbed up to the rostrum and, scowling, excoriated the legislature: "I hope that tomorrow, under more congenial circumstances, we may transcend those hatreds that have made us such a pathetic sight in the eyes of the world. *Vive la France!*" Deluged by cheers and boos, Mendès and his experiment passed into history.

Most of the French, especially young voters, bemoaned his ouster. He was succeeded by five premiers, each more feckless than the last—until, late in 1958, the Fourth Republic crumbled under the weight of its own contradictions to become a surrealistic memory.

20

The Maghreb

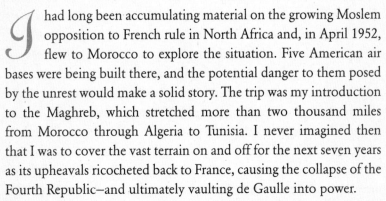

I had long been accumulating material on the growing Moslem opposition to French rule in North Africa and, in April 1952, flew to Morocco to explore the situation. Five American air bases were being built there, and the potential danger to them posed by the unrest would make a solid story. The trip was my introduction to the Maghreb, which stretched more than two thousand miles from Morocco through Algeria to Tunisia. I never imagined then that I was to cover the vast terrain on and off for the next seven years as its upheavals ricocheted back to France, causing the collapse of the Fourth Republic—and ultimately vaulting de Gaulle into power.

Once the westernmost frontier of Rome's African empire, Morocco was overrun by the Arabs in the late seventh century. They converted its indigenous Berbers to Islam before sweeping north to occupy Spain for seven hundred years. Pushed back to Morocco, their successors largely unified the *bled el mahkzen,* the urban centers, but failed to dominate the *bled el siba,* the remote deserts and mountains, whose roving tribes continually menaced the Crown. Yet their line endured, so that the current sultan, Sidi Mohammed ben

Youssef, could credibly advertise himself as the scion of one of the world's oldest dynasties.

At the turn of the twentieth century, in their scramble for colonies, the French acquired Morocco except for a slim Spanish zone in the north. They labeled their new possession a "protectorate"—a façade that recognized the sultan as a Descendant of the Prophet and supreme *imam,* or Commander of the Faithful, but vested real authority in a viceroy euphemistically titled *résident général.* The position was initially entrusted to General Louis Hubert Gonzalve Lyautey, a seasoned colonial officer. His top priority—benignly termed "pacification"—was to subdue the fractious chieftains. He deployed contingents of French regulars, Foreign Legionnaires and Senegalese troops bulwarked by Moroccan and Algerian auxiliaries called *goumiers,* and the offensive was to drag on for fifteen years. One of Lyautey's strategies was to fuel the age-old animosities of the rural Berbers for the citified Arabs. He depended on Thami el-Mezouari el-Glaoui, the cunning and ruthless pasha of Marrakech. A former brigand, el-Glaoui was always available to put his intrepid Berber cavalry at the disposal of the French, in exchange for which they permitted him to amass an enormous fortune by squeezing local notables for "gifts" and pocketing a portion of the tax revenues.

An implacable monarchist with a paternalistic streak, Lyautey sought to preserve Morocco's traditions. He barred infidels from mosques and required that Christians and Moslems dwell in separate districts. Concerned that they would blemish the country's pristine character, he also tried in vain to keep out the flotsam and jetsam of southern Europe—poor Spaniards, Italians, Greeks, Maltese and especially Corsicans. Dubbed *pieds-noirs*—an allusion to their black shoes—they were accorded French citizenship, with all its advantages, became fierce jingoists and constantly opposed concessions to the Moslems. They reminded me of Mississippi rednecks dedicated to thwarting the advancement of Negroes.

In 1927 the French chose ben Youssef over his elder brothers and designated him sultan. Then seventeen, the youth seemed to be a perfect stooge. Fond of sleek cars and pretty women, he was bequeathed a generous stipend and encouraged to pursue his harmless hobbies. But in his late twenties he began to read English constitutional history and tales of Morocco's bygone grandeur, and contemplated the notion of independence. Morocco, he knew, had signed a pact with the infant American republic as early as 1789; perhaps a royal version of the United States could be a model.

When Franklin D. Roosevelt visited Morocco in 1944 to confer with Winston Churchill, he tendered a dinner for ben Youssef. The president talked amorphously about the need to emancipate colonies following the war, and word circulated that America favored Moroccan autonomy. The Istiqlal, or Independence, Party, which a group of Moslem elites had organized not long before, issued a manifesto quoting a phrase in the Atlantic Charter supporting self-determination for oppressed peoples. The French reacted by rounding up scores of militants. The sultan was distressed, but prudently remained silent. Then, in 1947, he declared that the moment had come for Morocco to be granted its "full rights."

The weak Socialist government in Paris, under pressure from the North African lobby to appear tough, appointed General Alphonse Juin, a diehard, the new *résident* in Morocco. A *pied-noir* born in Algeria, where his father had been a gendarme, Juin prohibited Moslem political gatherings and tightened censorship. A torrent of protests erupted, and, in 1951, Juin insisted that the sultan disavow the Istiqlal or he would depose him. When ben Youssef declined, Juin notified el-Glaoui, and shortly thousands of Berber horsemen descended from the mountains into Rabat, the capital. French medals decorated their djellabahs, and bits of tricolor fluttered from their lances and muzzle-loading muskets. Fearing bloodshed, the sultan acquiesced, and Juin pledged, "From now on, Morocco will be tranquil." His optimism was an illusion, as I sensed when I got there the next year.

Casablanca bore not the faintest resemblance to the Bogart classic. A sprawling metropolis laid out by the French on what had once been a tiny port, it was a contrast of wealth and poverty. Luxury apartment and office buildings soared above broad boulevards located near *bidonvilles,* slums slapped together from wooden crates and oil drums. Clustered in the suburb of Anfa were handsome pastel villas designed in a hybrid of French and Moorish styles known as Mauresque, their gardens lush with bougainvillea and frangipani. The tenderloin was packed with whorehouses whose tattooed Berber girls lay half naked in cribs. I noticed that numbers of Europeans performed routine jobs as traffic cops, restaurant cashiers and postal employees, as though the town were situated in France.

One afternoon I met with Philippe Boniface, *chef de la région,* a sinewy man with a gray crew cut. A Parisian by birth, he had lived in Morocco since 1912 and had adopted a singsong North African accent. "When I came here," he said, "these people were languishing in feudalism. We gave them schools, roads, harbors, dams, electricity—and now a few mischief makers want to throw us out. *Quelle ingratitude!* If we departed, it would be sheer chaos. I know my Moroccans; *croyez-moi, monsieur,* they are incapable of governing themselves."

An Istiqlal activist, Mehdi ben Barka, steered me to a bistro in the *medina,* the native quarter, where we sipped mint tea and dined on chicken couscous and *bisteeya,* a flaky pastry confected from pigeon, dates and almonds. Slight and wiry, with bushy black eyebrows, he was mild and articulate, contrary to French portrayals of the nationalists as fanatics. I liked him immediately, and we were to become friends. "We owe a debt to the French," he said, "but they developed the economy for their own profit, not ours. Only five percent of Moroccan children attend school, fewer than ten percent of senior administrators are Moroccan. We're persecuted by the police and denied elementary justice. The principles of *liberté, égalité et fraternité* are irrelevant here."

The next day I hired a taxi and cruised south across an arid landscape to Marrakech. Along the route I passed families, the father astride a donkey, his wife and children dutifully walking beside him. I spotted camels turning waterwheels in sunbaked villages, peasants tilling fields behind yoked oxen and, in the distance, boys lazily tending flocks of sheep. At twilight the snow-crested summits of the High Atlas loomed into sight against the hazy horizon, and soon I pulled into Marrakech. Once the terminus for caravans trekking in from the Sahara, it was a labyrinth of sienna houses, their inner courtyards embellished with flowers and fountains. I checked into the sumptuous Mamounia hotel and strolled over to the Djemaa el-Fna. Illuminated by flickering kerosene lamps, the square was a carnival of actors, minstrels, acrobats, snake charmers, peddlers, beggars, astrologers and medicine men. The aromas of spices and herbs pervaded the air— cayenne, cinnamon, coriander, cumin, saffron, sesame, tumeric. In the *souk,* the market, vegetable and fruit stands bulged with olives, onions, peppers, quinces, oranges, pomegranates and dates of every variety. I paused at its stalls to sample a *kebab* or a *kefta* of grilled lamb or mutton. Not far off were brothels that featured girls, boys and kinky diversions.

In the morning, on the chance that el-Glaoui might receive me, I made my way to his palace. At the iron gate a gigantic Berber guard in brown robes took my card, and presently a functionary ushered me down a dim corridor into a tiled patio shaded by palms. There, attired in a simple beige cotton djellabah, lounged el-Glaoui, his leathery face furrowed by wrinkles. A bony figure nearing eighty, he clasped my hand, and a servant offered me a ritual glass of mint tea. We talked about the disturbances. "Only a handful of agitators are to blame," he said. "They have no idea what France has done for us. The sultan ought to teach them the truth rather than stir up their hatred."

Pressed for time, I raced north across the Middle Atlas to Fez. Dating back to the eighth century, the city began to flourish five hundred years afterward, when the Moors, evicted from Spain, constructed Karaouyin University and its superb mosque, the largest in Africa. They transformed the town into a vibrant hub of literature, theology, philosophy, astronomy and mathematics that attracted both Moslem and Christian scholars. Its winding lanes were now a hive of goldsmiths, weavers, dyers, tanners and artisans skilled at engraving brass and copper. One evening, in a smoky café, I listened to mournful chants like flamencos, nostalgically evoking the glories of Andalusia at the height of the Moorish era.

I hurtled down the coast from Fez to Rabat, where my request for an audience with the sultan had been approved—on condition that a French official monitor the session. At the palace, the Frenchman showed me the zoo, the gymnasium, the tennis courts and a garage filled with spiffy automobiles. He also nodded toward the harem, saying, "That, you will appreciate, is strictly off limits." We were conducted into the throne room, which could have been an upper-crust Paris salon. Ben Youssef was perched on a dais, clad in a fine white silk caftan, a matching cowl and yellow *babouches,* or slippers. His skin was pearly, and his eyes seemed to be lost behind blue-tinted glasses. Obeying protocol, I bowed twice, and he motioned me to a plush velvet armchair. Then, speaking flawless French, he emphasized his desire to foster education. When I asked how he intended to cope with the rising hostility toward France, he replied elliptically, "*Un monarch, c'est comme un père de famille.* His obligation is to tell his subjects what to do, but he must allow them to think as they wish."

Returning to Rabat in August 1953, I hoped to meet him again. Instead, I was amazed to see his palace encircled by Berber horsemen and French tanks. The following day he was hustled off to Corsica along with his two wives, children, concubines and ten tons of luggage, and would subsequently be banished to Madagascar. He was superseded by Sidi Mohammed Ouled ben Moulay Arafa, an elderly, indolent aristocrat chosen by el-Glaoui. The maneuver was engineered by Juin's replacement, General Augustin Guillaume, on instructions from Georges Bidault, the slippery French foreign minister, and Juin, who by then had been transferred to Paris. The cities remained calm but, within a month, Arab gangs brandishing knives and pikes were assaulting small towns and butchering French men, women and children while, with the connivance of the police, bands of French vigilantes assassinated Moslem nationalist leaders.

A year later, as tensions escalated, I went back with my boss, Frank White, and Tom McAvoy, a *Life* photographer. Searching for action, we tooled around the countryside until, on a scorching afternoon in Port Lyautey, we encountered a detachment of Foreign Legionnaires preparing to scour the *medina*—a procedure known as *un ratissage,* literally "a raking-in." Their aim was to retaliate for the slaughter the week before of fifteen French, including a mother and daughter who had been disemboweled. We joined them and, soaked in sweat, kept pace as they filed through the maze of narrow, lattice-covered alleys. Moving slowly from house to house, they smashed in doors, tossed in grenades and tear gas canisters and routed out every male Arab as women shrieked in horror. They shot at natives darting across rooftops, and soon the air reeked with the pungent smell of cordite. By dusk they had herded some eight thousand Arabs into a dusty sheep market, their hands above their heads. "Now for the fun," announced Colonel Jean Husson with a smirk and, setting the example, kneed a middle-aged man in the groin. A dozen gendarmes formed a gauntlet and, as we watched, beat other captives with clubs, rifle butts, barrel staves, even their fists. Periodically exhausted by the work, they urged civilian bystanders to participate. At the end of the day, about five thousand natives were shoved into trucks and trundled off to stockades. The town's French lined the streets to applaud the Legionnaires, then retired to their cafés. A terse communiqué from the *résidence* in Rabat mentioned that twenty-five Moroccans had died in the course of a *ratissage* in Port Lyautey.

But the turmoil continued unabated, alarming Premier Edgar Faure. By 1955 the Algerian war had begun to gain momentum, and he decided to reinstall ben Youssef rather than risk similar turbulence in Morocco. Now styled Mohammed V, the sultan came home in November, and el-Glaoui, accommodating to reality, begged his forgiveness. I caught up with the former exile shortly afterward in Fez, where he had gone to pray at his mother's tomb. Also addressing an assembly of fifty thousand, he recited, "Praise be to Allah, who has rescued us from our tribulations." To my surprise, he was gentle toward the French. "Independence," he said, "does not mean that we should rupture our ties to France."

Over the ensuing years, serious problems confronted Morocco—including dissidence in the Rif mountains of the north. There, during the 1920s, Abd el-Krim had stubbornly held out against the French, prompting Sigmund Romberg to romanticize his valor in *The Desert Song*, an operetta that resonated around the world. Finally crushed and imprisoned, he escaped to Cairo and assailed France for decades thereafter. By 1957, still bitter at the age of seventy-four, he spent his time denouncing Mohammed V as an accomplice of the French. His latter-day disciples, aroused by his diatribes, formed the Rif Liberation and Liquidation Movement to complain that they were suffering from police persecution and other abuses, and hinted that they might stage an insurrection. I was in Rabat when I received an anonymous telephone call inviting me to their territory. Naturally I agreed, and a covert intermediary appeared at a café near my hotel to provide me with a letter authorizing my entry into Riffi territory. Amelia Aragon, a Spanish friend who had been born in Morocco and was fluent in Arabic, volunteered to serve as my interpreter.

We motored to Chechaouen, a quaint town of whitewashed houses and cobbled streets nestled in a hillside, and waited in an inn until a guide fetched us. The night was cold and foggy as we set forth on muleback into the barren mountains. Sentries equipped with everything from spears and pitchforks to bazookas and machine guns repeatedly emerged from behind boulders and bushes to examine our papers. I began to feel giddy as we threaded our way along the edge of steep cliffs and dipped precipitously into ravines. After an hour or two we reached a camp, where a bearded tribesman in a tattered djellabah greeted us. I guessed that he was about thirty. Identifying himself as Mohammed Salem Mezzian, he led us into his shack, which contained a folding cot, two battery radios, a portable typewriter and stacks of mildewed documents and books. He handed us the inevitable glasses of mint tea and, while chain-smoking Chesterfields, launched into a monologue. Claiming to be Abd el-Krim's nephew, he had taught math in Tangier before concluding that the plight of the Riffis was more important. They had forwarded ben Youssef a list of eighteen demands, prime among them the rehabilitation of Abd el-Krim and a role for him in the Moroccan regime. "Our goal is not to overthrow the sultan," Mezzian said, "only to persuade him to reform. But if necessary, we will apply force."

At dawn he toured us around the compound. Old folks, unveiled women, and kids stared at us in curiosity. Armed lookouts squatted on craggy ridges above the bastion while, on a nearby pasture, raw recruits drilled using canes and umbrellas for rifles. Mezzian told us that the movement collected money from both fat-cat contributors and ordinary people, and bought its modern weapons from such fraternal Moslem nations as Egypt, Iraq, Syria and Libya. Its communications system consisted of an intricate network of flares, semaphore signals, secret mail drops, and couriers capable of carrying messages across the country at lightning speed. By noon we were back in his hut, where, crouched on a frayed carpet, we plowed through a colossal lunch of broiled chicken, skewered goat, roast lamb, mutton couscous swimming in a *tajine* of squash, carrots and artichokes flavored with lemon, melon, nut and honey cakes—and the ubiquitous mint tea. Groggy following the feast, we slept fitfully until dark, then zigzagged by mule down to Chechaouen.

A French magazine reprinted my *Time* piece, infuriating the Moroccan minister of information, Moulay Achmed Alaoui, who instantly expelled Amelia. We knew each other well from our student days in Paris, and, storming into his office, I howled, "I wrote the story, why don't you kick me out?" He smiled and answered, "I'd never do that to a *vieux copain*. Besides, I have an even worse fate in store for you. You're condemned to come back here."

I often journeyed to Tunisia, which was less volatile than the rest of North Africa. It was a popular venue for the French, British and American correspondents who roamed the area. Dubbing ourselves the "Maghreb Circus," we mingled in the bar of the tacky Tunisia Palace Hotel or at the lovely seaside town of Sidi Bou Said, where we lolled on the beach, ate at the open-air fish restaurants, flirted with girls and traded rumors. I concluded, at least then, that I preferred the Mediterranean to any other corner of the earth.

The eastern panel of the Maghreb triptych, Tunisia had been a rich Roman province before its conquest by the Arabs and, during the sixteenth century, was absorbed into the Ottoman Empire. After their takeover in 1881, the French established a protectorate as they had in Morocco, and governed through the puppet bey of Tunis. In 1920 several French-educated Tunisians created the Constitutional Party—the Destour—to clamor for autonomy. They were deported by the French, and by the 1930s, a new faction had surfaced. Labeled the Néo-Destour, it was directed by Habib Bourguiba, whose name would become synonymous with Tunisian nationalism.

I first observed Bourguiba up close in Tunis early in 1954. A bantamweight with tawny skin, ivory-white teeth and deep blue eyes, he had just been released from one of his many spells in jail and was haranguing a congregation of comrades. A charismatic rabble-rouser, he strutted back and forth across the platform, gesticulating, bellowing, laughing, weeping. Later, over syrupy Turkish coffee, he reminisced to me about his life.

Born in 1901, the youngest of eight children of a clerk in the French administration, he was reared by an older brother. He enrolled in a Tunis lycée, but tuberculosis interrupted his studies for three years. Still, he graduated and went on to earn a law degree at the University of Paris and a diploma at the École des Sciences Politiques. While in Paris he married a Frenchwoman, who bore him his only son, Habib Junior—nicknamed "Bibi." Then, going back to Tunis, he discarded the law and plunged into politics, for which he seemed to have an instinct. "I confess that I'm a political animal," he boasted, "and I am proud of it."

Initially he heckled French orators at public meetings. Then, in 1930, though he was not religious, he whipped up a demonstration against a Catholic conclave in the ancient city of Carthage on the grounds that it insulted Islam. He and a brother also started a French-language paper, *La Voix du Tunisien*, and, unhappy with the remnant Destour leadership, he stitched together the Destour. In 1938 he was sentenced to death without trial for "plotting against the security of the state," but a last-minute pardon by the French *résident* saved him from a firing squad. He remained locked up until France's defeat at the outset of World War II. Freed by the Germans, he traveled to Rome, where Mussolini vaguely promised him assistance. Soon afterward, however, the Allies liberated Tunisia and arrested him for treason. He was spared again, this time through the intervention of the American consul in Tunis, who reckoned that he might prove useful to the United States. It was a wise gesture. In the years ahead, Bourguiba was to rank among the Moslem world's most pro-American figures.

By July 1954 Premier Pierre Mendès-France had achieved peace in Indochina and was resolved to settle the Tunisian problem. In a shrewd gambit devised to mute his right-wing adversaries, he induced Juin to endorse an arrangement with Bourguiba that accorded Tunisia "internal autonomy" as a prelude to independence. The following spring Bourguiba returned triumphantly to Tunis, and I accompanied him.

We sailed from Marseille aboard the French liner *Ville d'Alger,* and my colleagues and I sat up into the wee hours, guzzling Scotch with Bibi and his cronies. In the morning Bourguiba was out on deck in a charcoal business suit and a tasseled red tarboosh. As the ship steamed into the Gulf of Tunis, he clung to the rail and sobbed nervously. Suddenly, their whistles screeching, a flotilla of fishing smacks, excursion boats, sloops, ferries, dhows and other craft approached us. They were draped with multicolored balloons, bunting, Tunisia's star-and-crescent flag, and banners proclaiming, "Hail to Our Hero." At the wharf porters and stevedores shouted, "*Ya hia Bourguiba!*"–"Long live Bourguiba." Stumbling down the gangplank, Bourguiba clambered onto a shed and, in an emotional outburst, said, "On this sacred day we have retrieved our land."

A decrepit Chevrolet convertible carried him to the outskirts of Tunis. There he was hoisted onto a white stallion and rode into the city in a cavalcade flanked by spahis in plumed helmets and tribesmen on camels adorned with silver ornaments. They proceeded amid the thunder of drums, the blare of cornets and the shrill of native pipers. The population went berserk with joy. Citizens hanging from their windows showered the cortege with confetti. Barefoot peasant kids ran alongside the marchers, and youngsters on bicycles and motor scooters weaved in and out of the parade while women in burnooses trilled *youyouyouyou,* a piercing cry of adulation. At one juncture, hysterical throngs surged through a cordon of police in an effort to touch Bourguiba. It was nearly four in the afternoon when, weary though exhilarated, he dismounted at the Place des Muttons, the main square. Sixty or seventy thousand people cheered him for fifteen minutes before he spoke in a cracked voice. "All men, Moslems, Christians and Jews, are brothers. We must tolerate each other, and thus make ourselves worthy of our sovereignty."

Conspicuously absent from the celebration were members of intractable *colon* associations like La Main Rouge and La Présence Française, which had cursed Bourguiba as a "lackey" of the Communists and the Americans. Subsequently I discovered that the French Sûreté had shunted them off to an oasis in the desert for the duration of the festivities.

I happened to be in Algiers on November 1, 1954, staying at the elegant Hôtel Saint-Georges, when I read in the papers that *fellaghin,* or bandits, had unleashed a wave of terror throughout Algeria the previous night—Halloween. From the Oranais in the west to the Constantinois in the east, they burned French farms, besieged French army barracks, attacked French police garrisons and murdered pro-French Moslems—a species derided by Algerians as *béni-oui-ouis,* or yes-men. They ambushed a patrol of gendarmes in the Kabylie, where they also destroyed a power generator. Near Kebouch, a town in the Aurès mountains, a French schoolteacher was slain and his wife raped. By morning, fifteen French and Moslems were dead and some thirty others wounded. Premier Mendès-France, shocked, dispatched two battalions of paratroopers as well as fighter planes to stiffen the French force already in Algeria. As the incidents multiplied, it became clear that they were being carefully orchestrated. "All this," wrote *Le Monde,* "seems to be the work of some invisible hand."

Before long the hand revealed itself to be the Front de Libération Nationale—the FLN. In broadcasts from Cairo, its propagandists asserted that the movement's objective was nothing less than independence. The only alternative for the French, they added, was whether to leave with a suitcase or in a coffin—"*une valise ou un cercueil.*" Algeria soon became the principal North African arena as France sank into a full-scale conflict costing more than two million dollars a day, tying up four hundred thousand soldiers, and claiming their lives at the rate of nearly one thousand a month. The venture further split French opinion. One side, pointing to the atrocities being committed by French troops, maintained that the involvement was immoral. Others argued that since Algeria comprised three *départements,* it was part of France, and that to withdraw would be illegal. Whatever the case, the struggle was essentially a civil war.

Algeria, like Tunisia, had been a Turkish dominion. Its interior was sparsely populated by nomads, its coast by pirates who marauded Mediterranean shipping. In 1827, during a quarrel over a financial deal, the bey of Algiers called the French consul a "wicked idolator" and swatted him with his peacock-feather fly whisk. After brooding over this outrage for three years, the French sent an expedition to Algeria, but not until 1845 did they control the country. Resorting to a tactic known as *la razzia,* they devastated entire villages, wantonly killing men, women and children. In one instance they set fire to a cavern in which five hundred natives had taken refuge, and suffocated them all. As a French officer confided to his diary, "The carnage was appalling and, I am ashamed to say, we are barbarians."

When France ceded Alsace-Lorraine to Germany in 1871, thousands of Alsatians immigrated to Algeria rather than become Germans. A trickle of other Europeans followed and, by the 1950s, they represented one tenth of the population of ten million. The stereotype of them as prosperous landowners and entrepreneurs was deceptive. They worked mostly at humdrum jobs but, like the *colons* elsewhere in North Africa, benefited from belonging to a privileged caste, while disease and destitution afflicted the majority of Moslems. French statutes further penalized Moslems, who could not become French citizens unless they abandoned polygamy and renounced Koranic law.

One of the vintage paladins of Algerian nationalism, Messali Hadj, founded L'Étoile Nord-Africaine in Paris in 1926. A dynamic, brilliant orator in French and Arabic, he exhorted Algerian laborers in France to subscribe to his scheme to foment a revolution in Algeria. He affiliated himself with the Communists, then switched to the fascist Croix de Feu, fulminated against Jews and was confined by the French to an island off Brittany. His star faded, but he inspired a generation of younger Algerians, among them Ferhat Abbas, who was to become the FLN leader.

I had learned that the FLN hierarchy was collegial, and that Abbas had been selected primarily for his eloquence, personal charm and ability to arbitrate disputes. In February 1957 I flew to Cairo, where he had his headquarters. A short man with hazel eyes, he looked like a doctor or a professor in his tweed sports jacket and twill slacks. He welcomed me into his neat apartment and, over glasses of orange juice, chatted as though we had known each other for years. "I am a reluctant rebel," he started, explaining that his dream as far back as adolescence was to be considered an authentic Frenchman. His father, an affluent landlord and magistrate, had been elevated to the Légion d'Honneur for collaborating with France. The four children attended French schools and conversed in French among themselves. After completing his lycée, Abbas did a stint as a sergeant in the French Army's medical corps, then moved to Algiers to study chemistry. He was awed by the city's French ambience, devoured Montaigne, Voltaire, Michelet, Hugo and Zola, and favored equality rather than independence. But, to his chagrin, he quickly understood that as a Moslem he could not be entirely assimilated. "So," he remarked with a Gallic shrug, "I was propelled by frustration into nationalism."

Abbas married an Algerian-born Frenchwoman and opened a pharmacy in the town of Sétif, but he principally focused on the

Algerian cause. Intermittently he got to Paris, where North Africans discussed their plans and dilemmas in Left Bank cafés. At the outbreak of World War II, he enlisted as a medic in a Senegalese regiment, leaving a maudlin farewell note: "If I should die, someone else will continue my task. *Vive la France! Vive l'Algérie!*" Once home, however, he altered his tune. The Nazi victory had shattered France's reputation in its colonies, and the American landings in North Africa raised hopes that imperialism would be buried. Abbas now promoted a new theme: "Henceforth, an Algerian Moslem will ask only to be an Algerian Moslem."

He became even more radicalized after the war, when French gendarmes attempted to block a Moslem demonstration in Sétif. Irate Moslems spilled into the streets, wildly slashing at Europeans with axes and cudgels while tribesmen poured down from the nearby hills to pillage the vicinity. Adopting a strategy called "collective responsibility," the French were pitiless. Cruisers shelled coastal villages, and air force bombers annihilated forty native settlements inland. In vengeance for one hundred European casualties, the French killed or crippled twenty thousand Moslems. "I deplored violence," Abbas told me, "but I saw that we had no other choice."

Young nationalists delved into the history of unconventional warfare, in particular accounts of the French maquis, Mao Tse-tung's guerrillas, Ho Chi Minh's partisans and Tito's commandos. They concealed caches of weapons and rosters of members, and trained in clandestine hideouts. Though frequently busted by the cops, they persevered, saying "We are mosquitoes battling an elephant." The FLN was later to rely heavily on Algerian veterans of the French Army; indeed, its minister of defense, Belkacem Krim, had been an infantry corporal.

A furtive figure, Krim dodged strangers, but one day in March 1957 I spotted him at the Tunis airport, bound for a pan-Arab conference in Cairo. I hastily purchased a ticket, jumped onto the Egyptian Mizrair Viking, and eased into the vacant seat beside him.

Slender, swarthy and balding, he eyed me warily until I convinced him that I was an American journalist, not a French intelligence agent. Then he began talking so passionately that he neglected his omelet lunch.

A Kabyle by birth, he breached custom by defying his father, a patriarch who wanted him to devote himself to the clan. Instead, Krim ran off to Algiers and, ignoring Islamic culture, became proficient in French. He first experienced discrimination in the army. "We Moslems were treated differently from the French," he recalled. "For example, they had red forms for us and blue forms for them. Trivial, *n'est-ce pas*? Not for me." Discharged in 1945, he drifted for a couple of years until the police accused him of shooting a man in a squabble. Rather than contest the allegation, he fled into the mountains, where other Algerian fugitives were hiding. "The idea of rebellion appealed to us," he went on, "but it would be a gamble. The French were formidable, and we had only a few outmoded guns. We forged ahead anyway."

They organized three-man cells, raided French arsenals for weapons and contacted disaffected Algerians throughout the country. On more than one occasion, Krim eluded capture by disguising himself as a veiled Moslem woman. Early in September 1954 delegates from nine combat zones known as *willayas* convened in a rented house outside Geneva to plan the forays that eventually ballooned into the insurrection. "The French could have stopped us at the beginning," Krim said. "Now we are invincible."

He was exaggerating—though not by much. As the war dragged on into the spring of 1956, it was evident that the French, despite their overwhelming superiority, faced an indomitable enemy. This was plain to me as I tagged along with their units on such operations as shielding both *colons* and natives harvesting their crops of wheat, barley and oats. Riding in an armored car, I visited an area in the Oranais in which eighty of the three hundred French farms had been set ablaze and eighteen Europeans killed within a month. "I've spent my life cultivating this soil," said one survivor. "My son and his son will spend theirs repairing the destruction—if they are still here." Near the town of Ain Alem, a French winegrower told me, sadly, that he was giving up. "I need protection, and there aren't enough troops to do the job," he explained. As our convoy inched down a dirt road, it drew fire from a hilltop. The soldiers leaped out, rifles cocked, but all they could see was four or five Moslems serenely scything their grain. The commander, a captain, muttered, "Compared to *cette merde*, Indochina was a picnic."

As new disclosures of cruelty unfolded, the protagonists in the drama seemed to be emulating one another. One week the corpses of French troops mutilated by the FLN would be dug up, the next the bodies of real or purported insurgents tortured by the French. In April 1956 a letter postmarked Algiers reached the mother of Serge Villemaux, a dead French conscript. Stamped with the FLN seal, it read: "Madame, we share your grief. Dry your tears. Join other mothers and wives, and implore your rulers to end this filthy war."

Paris salons became battlefields as the French debated the war. The usual array of conservatives and chauvinists championed the engagement on the theory that France's honor was at stake. But the reports of French brutality appalled numbers of prominent citizens, among them such prestigious intellectuals as Sartre, Mauriac and Malraux. The Catholic cardinals and archbishops published a statement warning that it was incumbent on all conscientious Christians "to respect human dignity and to avoid excesses that violate the laws of nature and the laws of God." A left-wing Catholic author, Pierre-Henri Simon, stirred Parisians with a book, *Contre la Torture,* in which he detailed examples of French soldiers and gendarmes interrogating Arabs by suspending them nude from ceiling beams and attaching electrodes to their ears, fingers and testicles. "We fought against Hitler's racist monstrosities," he charged, "and today we ourselves employ his grisly methods." Another scathing indictment came from Jean-Jacques Servan-Schreiber, the perceptive editor of *L'Express,* who had served for six months as a lieutenant in Algeria and won the Croix Militaire. In a series of articles, he related case after case of his fellow officers promiscuously killing innocent Moslems. Underlining the futility of the mission, he quoted a Major Marcus: "This is blind repression. For each false *fellagha* we wipe out, ten genuine ones fill the gap. We must either exterminate everybody—or quit."

But the French public's increasing revulsion against the conflict did little to deter René Lacoste, the *résident* in Algiers. A Socialist, he was being prodded by the *colons* to counteract the FLN's mounting terror and ordered General Jacques Massu to rid the city of *fellaghin*. Massu, a rugged paratrooper, was unswayed by such abstractions as human rights and, in the spring and summer of 1956, embarked on his own campaign of terror. His men combed the teeming casbah around the clock for nine months, pulling out Arabs regardless of age or gender and submitting them to gruesome tortures. Disgusted, General Jacques de Bollardière applied for a posting back in Paris, where de Gaulle congratulated him for "upholding the integrity of the army." The outcry indicated that many French, their reverence for *l'état* not withstanding, had the capacity to vent their indignation against their government's unethical behavior.

The solution to the war lay in the French legislature, but Guy Mollet, the premier since early 1956, presided over a coalition cabinet that lacked a consensus on Algeria. So he juggled and waffled—talking ambiguously about cementing the bonds between the French and the Moslems while sending in reinforcements. Having heard the tedious litany before, I was getting bored. Then, in 1957, I was awarded a Nieman Fellowship at Harvard, and sailed for America.

J was grappling with the complexities of economics under the tutelage of John Kenneth Galbraith and Barbara Ward when, on May 13, 1958, Algiers exploded. A coterie of intransigent French army officers and *colons*, suspecting that Mollet was surreptitiously seeking to negotiate a compromise with the FLN, ousted the French governor and his staff. Swarms of Europeans rampaged through the streets, de-molishing shops and public buildings and shrieking "*Algérie française! Algérie française!*" It was a rebellion within a rebellion—and a cata-clysmic story I could not afford to miss. Dropping everything, I left Cambridge before the end of the semester and scurried back to North Africa as fast as I could.

Thrilled to be out of academia and reporting again, I was desper-ate to get to Algiers. But the airport was closed and I rushed to Rome, where I chartered a private plane. I landed at Blida, a suburb of Al-giers, and took a taxi to the Hôtel Saint-Georges. Over lunch on the terrace restaurant overlooking the Mediterranean, a group of my col-leagues were boisterously celebrating the birthday of Annette An-drew, the beautiful, saucy cultural attaché at the American consulate. During the melee, infuriated *colons* had roughed her up and ran-sacked her center, and, with nothing much to do, she hobnobbed with the correspondents who had flocked into the city for the events. She and I clicked—and became, in the lingo of gossip columnists, "an item."

On May 24, in a bid to project their influence toward metropoli-tan France, the mutineers in Algiers sent a brigade of paratroopers to Corsica. Anticipating a possible clash, I eagerly went along. The episode was pure opéra bouffe. Our two planes set down at an air-field outside Ajaccio, the island's capital. We sped by truck into town, only to find it in its habitually festive mood. Instead of resist-ing the invaders, the Corsicans were out in the cafés, gaily gabbing over their apéritifs. The prefect and gendarmerie surrendered, and a seditious colonel, whom the Algiers junta had named military gov-ernor, solemnly decreed that Corsica had seceded from France. By now, with the Fourth Republic unraveling, word was spreading that even Paris might be threatened, and the police began to erect barri-cades on the Champs-Élysées.

Only one man could master the crisis—de Gaulle. The parliament confirmed him as premier on June 1, and he arrived in Algiers shortly afterward. He realized that the putsch could disrupt France unless he reassured the town's jittery French that it was his intention to defend their interests. Thousands of them were crammed into the square in front of the administration building, where he was scheduled to speak. Wearing a uniform to symbolize his military credentials, he stepped out onto the balcony, squinted in the glaring sunshine, and, in a cryptic phrase that meant everything and nothing, intoned, *"Je vous ai compris."* The crowd responded with a roar of relief and delight, never expecting that four years later he would concede to independence for Algeria.

Annette was soon shifted to the American embassy in Paris, and we moved into a picturesque houseboat moored on the quai Anatole France, across the Seine from the Place de la Concorde. Now and again, we would revisit North Africa together. After an indecent interval I proposed matrimony, and, on the morning of April 21, 1959, we flew from Tangier to Gibraltar, a nine-minute flight with a headwind. Frank White came down from Paris to give the bride away; and the shadowy Gibraltar stringer, who had arranged for a local justice of the peace appropriately called Amor to perform the ceremony, officiated as our witness. By coincidence it was the queen's birthday, and Union Jacks festooned the Rock—a portent of good luck. A month later, I was reassigned by *Time* to Hong Kong as chief correspondent for Asia. Nearly a decade of wandering around the Maghreb had prepared me for its daunting challenges.

21

Toujours Paris

———

I n May 1968, after an absence of ten years, I returned to Paris
and, out of nostalgia, dropped into the Crillon Bar for a drink
before lunch, as I had done every day in times past. Nothing
had changed. A few of my old colleagues were still there. So was
Louis, the bartender, his pomaded hair as slick as ever. Without bat-
ting an eye, he extended a limp hand and mumbled, *"Bonjour,*
M'sieur Karnow. Back from vacation?"

Index

ABOUT THE AUTHOR

STANLEY KARNOW has covered Europe, Africa and Asia as a correspondent and author for forty-five years. Theodore H. White called
him the "foreign affairs experts' expert on foreign affairs."

He graduated from Harvard in 1947, went to Paris, where he studied at the Sorbonne and the École des Sciences Politiques, and began
his career in 1950 as a reporter for *Time* and *Life*. In 1959 he was assigned to Asia, where he remained for eleven years, successively representing *Time, Life, The Saturday Evening Post, The Observer, The
Washington Post* and NBC News. He has contributed to *The New York
Times Magazine, Foreign Affairs, Foreign Policy, Esquire* and *The Smith-
sonian*.

His previous books include *In Our Image: America's Empire in the
Philippines,* for which he won a Pulitzer Prize; the best-selling *Vietnam:
A History; Mao and China: From Revolution to Revolution,* which was
nominated for a National Book Award; and *Southeast Asia*. Karnow
has received two Overseas Press Club awards and won six Emmys for
his role as chief correspondent for the PBS series *Vietnam: A Television
History*. He was a Nieman Fellow at Harvard, and a fellow at Harvard's

John F. Kennedy School of Government and the East Asia Research Center. He belongs to the Council on Foreign Relations, the American Society of Historians and the Century Association.

During World War II, Karnow served with the U.S. Army Air Corps in the China-Burma-India theater of operations.

Karnow resides in Potomac, Maryland, with his wife, Annette, a painter and former foreign service officer.